PENG

TEXTBO

CW00523416

Yogeswar, earlier known as T.R worked with *The Hindu* for nearly thirty-five years. While in his early forties, because of a persistent cold, he tried yoga and Naturopathy and was amazed at the results. He started studying the theory of yoga and, in about fifteen years, became an authority on it. He established the Yoga Centre at Chennai and some of his pupils later became yoga teachers.

Among Yogeswar's books, *Textbook of Yoga* was prescribed as a standard textbook for the Degree/Diploma courses in fourteen Indian universities. Despite requests from some foreign countries to establish yoga centres there, he preferred to develop them in India. He trained many doctors and was a consultant in many hospitals. The ESI Hospital, Chennai, opened a yoga wing due to his efforts and he was a yoga instructor at Bharathiya Vidya Bhavan, Chennai, for a long time. He passed away when he was eighty-three.

Textbook of Yoga

YOGESWAR

PENGUIN BOOKS

Penguin Books India (P) Ltd., 11 Community Centre, Panchsheel Park, New Delhi 110 017, India
Penguin Books Ltd., 80 Strand, London WC2R 0RL, UK
Penguin Group Inc., 375 Hudson Street, New York, NY 10014, USA
Penguin Books Australia Ltd., 250 Camberwell Road, Camberwell, Victoria 3124, Australia
Penguin Books Canada Ltd., 10 Alcorn Avenue, Suite 300, Toronto, Ontario, M4V 3B2, Canada
Penguin Books (NZ) Ltd., Cnr Rosedale & Airborne Roads, Albany, Auckland, New Zealand
Penguin Books (South Africa) (Pty) Ltd., 24 Sturdee Avenue, Rosebank 2196, South Africa

First published by Yoga Centre 1986
Published by Penguin Books India 2004
Copyright © S. Balasarojini
Illustrations copyright © Penguin Books India 2004

Illustrations by George M.

Typeset in Sabon by S.R. Enterprises, New Delhi.

Printed at Chaman Offset Printers, New Delhi

Contents

PRANAYAMA **348**

Introduction

Yoga, developed by the sages in India, has been practised down the ages as a composite system of physical, mental and spiritual discipline.

This Do-It-Yourself manual describes in detail thirty-six Asanas, four Mudras, three Bandhas, three Kriyas and Pranayama which are simple and easy to learn. A useful selection can be made from this varied fare by people from different walks of life. They can derive immense benefit by following the guidelines and precise instructions outlined in this book.

The method of practising each exercise is explained in detail. The progress from each intermediate step to more advanced levels is presented lucidly with apt illustrations. This step-by-step approach helps the aspirant move on comfortably from one stage to the next and reach the final position easily. By systematically practising the exercises at a fixed time every day, these can be mastered in a few months.

Your daily scheme of yoga practice should be well-balanced and should exercise every part and organ of your body including the spine and abdomen.

Stretching the spine is effected in various different directions:

- the upward or vertical stretch (Talasana);
- the sideways or lateral stretch to the right and left (Chakrasana);

- the backward or posterior stretch (Ushtrasana);
- the forward or anterior stretch (Pada Hastasana);
- the rotation to the left and the right (Ardha Matsyendrasana).

By making the foregoing simple movements, the entire spine is stretched in all directions and becomes more flexible.

By doing Uddiyana and Nauli, the organs of the abdomen get toned up.

Surya Namaskar, designed by the sages on a scientific basis, exercises every part of the body and brings about a harmonious development of the body and mind. This invaluable exercise is explained in great detail with appropriate illustrations.

Savasana, the most effective way to relieve stress and mental tension by means of deep relaxation, is discussed comprehensively.

The asanas of yoga are recommended for women to remain fit and to pass smoothly through the critical pre-natal and post-natal stages. Yogic remedies are also suggested for some common female disorders.

The chapter on food stresses the importance of taking the right kind of food at the right time. The various benefits of periodical fasting are also emphasized.

In the section on Yoga Hygiene, topics such as sleep, bath, cleanliness, regular habits and shunning vice are dealt with in detail.

As a teacher and practitioner of yoga for several decades and as a consultant to hospitals, I have carefully recorded my experiences in the chapters on yoga therapy. Yogic remedies, based on clinical studies, for some common ailments are also recommended.

The book is complete in itself as it contains the essential features of yoga aimed at physical fitness and mental poise.

I dedicate this handy, updated volume to students and teachers of yoga all over the world.

Madras   YOGESWAR
June 1986

How to Use This Book

- If a qualified teacher is not available and you have the confidence to practise at home, you may ask someone to read out from a reasonable distance in a slow, even tone of voice, the exercises mentioned in this book and you may practise them precisely according to the instructions given.

- While practising the exercises, the person who reads out should check up and correct whenever you go wrong. He must not add any comments of his own, but must strictly follow the instructions given in the book.

- Later, you may change places and read out the instructions to your partner and, as you watch him perform, you will learn a great deal.

- As soon as you have mastered the techniques, you may dispense with the reader.

- Even after mastering the exercises by following the instructions given in this book, you will benefit by reading the full text of each exercise which will aid your memory and enable you to perform better. You can also avoid mistakes as you advance in the practice.

- The details given are of great importance. If they are not followed, full benefit cannot be derived from the exercises.

Acknowledgements

I am indebted to Smt. Lakshmi Ramanathan, Managing Trustee, and other Trustees of Sri Ramanath Charities (Madras-31) and M/s. Sundaram Charities, Madras, for their ready response to my request for help to fund initial expenses.

My special thanks are due to Mr. P.A. Seshan, Deputy Editor, *The Hindu,* Madras, for advice and guidance in producing this book and keeping my spirits high.

I am thankful to Dr. C.S. Mohan Dass, Dr. M.L. Ramadurai, Dr. V.R. Sadayappan and Dr. V. Venugopal who encouraged me with valuable suggestions while preparing the section on Therapy.

YOGESWAR

1

Benefits of Yoga

वपु: कृशत्वं वदने प्रसन्नता नादस्फुटत्वं नयने सुनिर्मले।
अरोगता बिन्दूजयो ग्रिदीपनं नाडीविशुद्धिर्हठसिद्धिलक्षणम्।।

Slimness of body, lustre on the face, clarity of voice,
brightness of eyes, freedom from disease, control over sex,
stimulation of gastric fire, and purification of the Nadis
are the characteristics of success in Hatha Yoga.
—*Hathapradipika* 11–78

आसनं विजितं येन जितं तेन जगत्त्रयम्।

He who masters the asanas conquers the world.
—*Trisikhibrahmanopanishad (Mantrabhaga)* 52

'Yoga' means 'union' in Sanskrit. It is both a discipline leading to, and the experience of, reunion of the embodied Individual Self (Jiva) with the Universal Self (Brahman) of which it is a partial expression. This is the goal of human life and endeavour.

One can attain this goal by adopting a spiritual way of life, characterized by moral restraint, ethical discipline and hygienic living. These, when combined, help a person to keep his physical force in balance and to develop his mental and spiritual powers. With a progressive control of the body, senses and mind and the development of the latent powers of body and mind, a change occurs in the lifestyle of the yoga practitioner, leading to physiological harmony, mental poise and a positive outlook. Yoga is the science which teaches the methods to attain this.

The physical basis of yoga comprises Asanas, Mudras, Bandhas, Kriyas, Pranayama and moral restraints and observances. These practices condition the body and the mind for spiritual advancement. A concerted practice of yoga leads to concentration of the mind and self-realization which is the spiritual basis of a yoga teacher. The guidance of a spiritual person (guru) and constant individual effort are needed to practise the spiritual aspect of yoga.

Rightly performed, yogic practices help to keep your body in proper shape and balance and refine your mental faculties, thus making you fit for spiritual advancement. The benefits are thus both physical and spiritual.

A. PHYSICAL BENEFITS

Yoga exercises have been practised down the ages and have stood the test of time. They are best suited to the human system.

Yoga practices keep your body fit and supple and ensure that your faculties remain intact. To keep diseases at bay and prolong life, yogic exercises are unequalled by any other system and are the finest that human genius has ever designed.

Yoga exercises promote harmony and balance in all functions of the body by providing proper exercise and tone to every part of the body. They also enable you to develop a complete control over your bodily functions and mental activity so that you can retain good health throughout your lifespan.

Even old people taking to yoga can remain youthful as the decay of tissues is arrested and the ravages of age are removed quickly. Poor vision, grey hair, loss of teeth, thinning muscles, wrinkled skin, a bent back, stiffness of the joints, reduced mobility, hardening of the arteries and other degenerative symptoms of old age are arrested as yoga practices slow down ageing and prolong youth by the generation and assimilation of life energy. Many ailments of old age are also prevented.

If practised faithfully, with due concentration and awareness, yoga practises begin to show results within a few weeks. Regular practise will tone up the nervous, lymphatic and muscular systems and keep them in good condition. The respiratory muscles become strong and the respiratory passage gets cleared of all impurities. The blood circulation improves and it can be diverted to any gland or organ needing it urgently without undue strain on the heart. Food will be assimilated better and the waste products more promptly eliminated. The abdominal organs are held in place and will work at optimum efficiency. The endocrine glands will function at their peak and in proper balance. The spinal column is reshaped and becomes more flexible. The reproductive system will function better. The vital organs retain their youthful vigour and efficiency. The body becomes light and resilient with better neuro-muscular coordination and metabolic efficiency. With increased suppleness of body and mind, the senses also work better.

The other physical benefits of yoga practice are:

1. Regular practice will develop the body and its limbs to their normal proportions and establish natural harmony and functional balance between the various organs, leading to better health and a feeling of well-being.

2. All parts of the body are adequately exercised with minimum effort in a minimum time without causing strain, fatigue, excessive heat or perspiration.

3. Yogic exercises strengthen the weak parts of the body without any panting and puffing which accompany athletic training. They are particularly effective in preventing the weakness of the abdominal muscles.

4. Stiff muscles regain their elasticity and tone by their contraction and extension. The mobility of the joints also improves and is maintained even at an advanced age.

5. The involuntary muscles can be developed and controlled by the application of concentrated pressure upon them.

6. The activity of the heart gets regulated and cardio-vascular fitness improves.

7. A conscious control over most of the autonomic functions of the body can be attained which is not possible through any other system of physical culture.

8. Minor structural and functional defects can be rectified and a uniform development of the entire body achieved by the consistent practice of the

asanas. A sagging abdomen, stooping back, bulging hips, flabby thighs, drooping shoulders and a hollow chest may be rectified and their form regained. The spine is kept supple and straight. The limbs of the body thus become symmetrical, leading to an improvement in the posture.

9. Yoga postures help to cure obesity by removing excess fat and redistributing it over the body in the correct proportion. Loss of weight achieved through yoga stays that way.

10. Asanas help to regulate weight. If you are underweight, you gain weight; if you are overweight, you lose the extra weight.

11. Correct breathing habits are developed.

12. Blood pressure gets normalized and more blood reaches more tissues.

13. You will sleep better.

14. Eyes become brighter and the voice deeper. Your complexion and posture improve. A slim waistline can also be developed.

15. Bowel movement will become regular and accumulated toxins in the body will get easily eliminated without drugs.

16. The need for tranquillizers and stimulants with their negative side-effects can be avoided.

17. By correcting the cause, many common complaints and psychosomatic disorders can be alleviated without doctors and drugs.

18. A high degree of physical endurance and resistance to disease is developed by the correct functioning and invigoration of the internal organs and the re-establishment of the body's self-adjusting mechanism.

19. Even after prolonged illness, yoga practices accelerate the recovery phase as they generate and conserve energy and increase vitality.
20. The ability to bear heat and cold and to endure pain and strain is increased.
21. Yoga teaches the art of relaxation. Fatigue, both muscular and nervous, is removed and deep relaxation and increased vitality are brought about.
22. All tensions—physical, mental and emotional—get gradually eliminated and the body, mind and emotions work in harmony until late in life.

B. SPIRITUAL GAINS

1. Yoga practices bring you a lifetime of rewards such as better awareness, mental poise and unruffled serenity.
2. Continued practice enables you to get a better control over your emotions as your mind is gradually freed from the sway of the senses.
3. Yoga practices help you to arrest your wandering mind and increase your power of concentration.
4. The practical discipline of yoga helps you to look within, resulting in an integration of personality and the awakening of a new consciousness. When the mind is turned inward and stilled and the senses are under control, animal passions are restrained, desires and the craving to satisfy them die out, the blandishments of the world cease to allure and inner peace is achieved. Hallucinations disappear and all your thoughts, words and deeds become meaningful.

2

Yoga for all

युवा व द्धो तिव द्धो वा व्याधितो दुर्बलो पि वा।
अभ्यासात् सिद्धिमाप्नोति सर्वयोगेष्वतन्द्रितः।।

He who untiringly practises Yoga in all its aspects attains
success whether he is young, old, decrepit, diseased or
weak.

—Hathapradipika 1–64

1. Every person with a sound body from any walk of
   life can start practising yoga after eighteen years and
   can continue to do so throughout his lifespan.
2. It is never too late to start yoga exercises. However,
   if the muscles are exercised regularly from youth, they
   continue to be supple and the internal organs remain
   strong so that good health can be maintained till late
   in life and a multitude of ailments avoided.
3. It is always best to start young as such persons can
   master yoga easily. Those past the prime of life may
   practise yogic breathing and postures moderately

according to the condition of their muscle, internal organs and general health.

4.   The easy course of yoga may be learnt slowly but not practised regularly from the age of twelve up to sixteen. The full course may be started after reaching the age of eighteen. Difficult postures may be attempted by students at about the age of twenty, but these exercises should be omitted in late middle age and beyond if any strain is felt during their practise. Persons who have crossed the fifties should have a medical check-up once a year and practise only such postures as are simple, non-strenuous and which do not take much time because of the slackening of metabolism which occurs as age advances.

5.   Children under eight years should never attempt yoga asanas, whether static or dynamic. As their spines are too weak and their bones and muscles are still growing, forcing them to do asanas may cause deformity of the spine and other disorders. Also, they may lack concentration and their attention may waver. Children between eight and twelve years of age need and like outdoor play and games which are more conducive to their growth than systematic yogic exercise. They may watch and practise a few simple yoga postures so that they may develop an aptitude for practising the more difficult ones later in life. They should, however, avoid such asanas which overtax their ability and affect their growing bones. Children of this age-group may practise Surya Namaskar.

Boys and girls while in their pre-puberty stage may learn a few simple yogic postures which promote their growth, including Surya Namaskar. They should not do such exercises which involve great strength, putting or exerting pressure as they are not physically mature and do not have the muscle control of adults. Besides, their vital organs, glands and nervous system are not sufficiently developed and the endocrine balance is not mature enough. They should avoid the upside-down positions which may affect the thyroid gland. They should practise more advanced postures, synchronized with breathing, only after they attain full maturity.

6. Persons who are mere 'skin-and-bones' and fat persons with a protruding belly can practise asanas to the best of their ability provided they have no disease affecting their organs. They will look fit after a few months of regular practice.

7. Persons with any defect in their organs or functional disorder but who are supple enough to do the asanas easily should take the advice of a doctor who knows yoga and who can recommend postures suitable to each person individually. Those with physical deformities and those who have suffered any serious dislocation of the limbs need not give up yoga practise but take the advice of a yoga therapist and perform the recommended postures.

3

Preparation for Yoga

आमकुम्भ इवाम्भस्थो जीर्यमाणः सदा घटः।
योगानलेन संदह्य घटशुद्धिं समाचरेत्।।

The body invariably wears away like an unbaked earthen
pot immersed in water. Therefore, the body should be
conditioned by tempering it with the fire of yoga.

—Gheranda Samhita: 1–8

1. Medical Check-up. 2. Learn From a Teacher. 3. Follow
Traditional Method. 4. Condition Your Mind. 5. Confidence.
6. Patience and Perseverence. 7. Regularity. 8. Time. 9. Place.
10. Seat. 11. Dress. 12. Silence.

1. MEDICAL CHECK-UP

1. Have a medical check-up before starting yoga. Start
    only if the doctor gives you the go-ahead.
2. Persons who have a history of serious illness should
    check with their doctor and perform only such
    postures which they can safely undertake.

3. Persons who are in poor health should undergo a medical test and should be guided by an expert in yoga. They must do a preliminary course of simple postures for at least three months and then draw up their own scheme of practice. Only after they have gained sufficient strength and are able to move their limbs freely, should they go in for an advanced course.

4. Persons suffering from any acute illness should get cured before starting yoga practice.

5. Persons with high or low blood pressure or any disease of the organs or functional disorder should practise Savasana or only selected asanas suited to their physical condition and under the guidance of a doctor and a competent teacher. They can do regular yoga practice only when they become physically fit either by practising such asanas as may cure their ailments or by medical treatment.

6. Persons with high blood pressure should avoid altogether the topsy-turvy postures which cause blood to rush to the brain. They should avoid the exercises in which the head is put down and the legs are raised.

7. Persons with heart trouble should always consult their doctor and should not do anything which is strenuous.

8. Persons with a sinus or nasal infection must avoid all inverted yoga postures.

2. LEARN FROM A TEACHER

1. Practise yoga only after learning its techniques from a qualified teacher (guru) in whom you have confidence and who has been trained on traditional lines.

2. Practise yoga at home only after gaining sufficient experience during the training period. If you start without proper training, it becomes difficult to correct mistakes as you will not realize the errors in your practice. If yoga is not practised properly, the mind gets affected and a feeling of uneasiness results. It is, therefore, all the more necessary to learn yoga under the strict eye of an able preceptor until you master the technique.

3. Practising asanas and Pranayama based on theoretical knowledge acquired from a textbook or from a correspondence course is risky as the techniques are difficult to describe correctly. A misreading or misunderstanding of an instruction may cause damage or injury. One may have difficulty in memorizing the correct sequence. It is also not possible to know whether you are practising correctly or making any progress.

4. Do not practise asanas merely by looking at pictures and diagrams since they leave much unexplained.

5. Observing the masters while they are practising the yoga exercises will be helpful in correcting mistakes but make sure they are experts in the field of yoga.

3. FOLLOW TRADITIONAL METHOD

1. Learn the traditional method of doing the asanas and Pranayama since it is always the best.

2. Having learnt the classical yoga exercises by the traditional method and if they suit you well, do not go on changing the technique by adopting other systems which may result in fatigue and ill health.

3. While doing yoga exercise, avoid following other systems of physical culture as they are quite unnecessary

and may also cause fatigue. Do not combine them as the technique and physiological effects of yogic practices are entirely different from those of other systems of physical culture.

4. CONDITION YOUR MIND

1. Always begin yoga practice in a sitting posture like Padmasana, Siddhasana or Sukhasana. Stay in that posture comfortably for a few minutes and condition your mind for doing the exercise in a serene state of mind.

2. Practising yoga while in good spirits drives away laziness and mental tension, and generates enthusiasm. Hence, begin with any comfortable sitting posture and keep as still as possible for a minute or two and gradually prolong the period up to five minutes so as to calm the mind and turn it inward.

3. Stay composed and try to keep your mind away from all distractions of the outside world. Keep clear also of all diverting thoughts racing through your mind. Try to pass over them gently and allow your mind to become quiet.

4. While in the sitting posture, condition your mind for doing the exercises just as you prepare yourself for having dinner or before starting on a job. A positive attitude is essential since yoga exercises should be practised calmly and slowly without haste or emotional tension.

5. The practitioner should cultivate patience, concentration and a capacity for endurance so as to achieve optimum results. Exercising reluctantly will not result in much benefit.

5. CONFIDENCE

1. Take your body into confidence before starting the exercises and practise with confidence in the results. By doing so, the benefits will be greatly enhanced.
2. Every day, make up your mind to better the performance of the previous day.

6. PATIENCE AND PERSEVERENCE

1. Despite starting yoga practice enthusiastically, do not expect too much too soon. If no perceptible benefit has accrued from your initial efforts, do not lose confidence and discontinue the routine. Once you get going, practise continuously for a minimum period of six months since the more you practise, the more you gain. Having started the practice and known the benefits, you should continue it for the rest of your life.
2. Though you will begin to notice the benefits to your body and mind within a few weeks of regular practice, the body needs at least six months of daily practice to condition itself to doing the exercises. During this period, the stiffness of the muscles unused to exercise disappears, the functions of the organs and glands get normalized and the body begins to acquire a proper shape and weight. A corresponding change will occur in the lifestyle and outlook of the practitioner.

7. REGULARITY

1. Only persistent practice, fashioned according to one's capacity, will bring positive results. Hence, establish

a daily routine of yoga practice after the training period and make it a lifelong habit.

2. Make the practice of yoga part of your daily life; doing asanas and Pranayama must become a regular habit like eating and sleeping.

3. Regularity and punctuality in doing the asanas are as essential as the intensity with which you do them or the time you devote to them. Practising at irregular intervals, instead of at a particular time, will bring about only a marginal benefit.

4. Set aside a minimum time daily and gradually increase the period up to a maximum of one hour. Practise at the same time every day with patience and without haste.

5. Once you start, resolve not to let a single day go by except for reasons beyond your control. Even when you are in a great hurry and racing against time, never omit the practice entirely. If, however, you miss the daily regimen for some reason, do not feel unduly concerned but perform the exercises the next day with more vigour.

6. Omission of the practice for a day or two will not matter much, but try to avoid irregularity or long interruptions.

8. TIME

1. Set aside a fixed time each day for yoga practice. Choose the time which suits you the best, provided your stomach is empty. Do not practise when the sun is too hot or it is too late in the day.

2. The exact timing of the exercises should be fixed by you according to your convenience, the time available and the nature of your work.

3. Generally, 5 a.m. to 7 a.m. will be the best time for most people, though the actual duration of the practice need not exceed an hour.

4. It is good to start half an hour before sunrise and finish the asanas just as the sun rises. As the sun rises, start with Surya Namaskar and Pranayama and finish off within half an hour after sunrise and before the sun gets hot. One will be interrupted less during this time.

5. The confluence of night and day, namely twilight or the start of dawn when the stars are still visible, is the ideal time for starting yoga practice for various reasons: (a) At this time of the day, the surroundings are peaceful. (b) The air is fresh and cool. (c) Both body and mind are relaxed after a comfortable night's rest. (d) The stomach will be empty and the waste matter in the colon can be readily evacuated. (e) Regularity can be maintained. (f) After finishing the practice, you will be ready for the new day with ample time to cope with the day's work. (g) After the practice, you will be physically fit and mentally alert throughout the day and will be able to face the world and overcome the challenges without strain. Thus, the advantages of starting the day with yoga are both physical and mental.

6. If you find your muscles and joints stiff in the morning, doing a few Surya Namaskars and some easy asanas first will loosen them.

7. One can also practise asanas in the evening after 5 p.m. till the time of dusk but this time should be considered as second best since most persons will be too tired from the day's toil and the stomach may not be completely empty.

8. It is not necessary to practise the same asanas both in the morning and in the evening.

9. PLACE

1. For practising yoga, select a quiet place, away from the bustle of daily life, where you are exposed to nature. An open airy space is best such as a garden, terrace, veranda, lawn, field or the bank of a river (about hundred feet away from water). Since you are disturbed minimally by the external world in these places, you can concentrate on what you are doing.

2. The place selected must be free from moisture, draught, dust, smoke, insects, mosquitoes, foul odours and visual distractions.

3. Avoid exposure to cold winds if you are practising outdoors.

4. Do not practise when the weather is excessively hot or cold or when the wind blows hard and buffets your face.

5. Do not exercise in an air-conditioned room or very near the seashore.

6. Do not do asanas in a place where the sun's rays fall directly on your body.

7. Do not practise where the air is polluted.

8. The surface of the floor where you practise must be firm and flat so as to provide a stable base while you execute the movements.

9. Since your face, chin, nose and the top of your head come in contact with the seat while doing some of the asanas, the seat must be firm and comfortable. Do not practise on rocky ground.

10. The ground where you practise must not be uneven or sloping in one direction. It must not be slippery or wet.

11. If you are practising in the privacy of your room for reasons of personal convenience or to avoid the vagaries of weather, the room must have good ventilation and plenty of natural light. Always practise at normal room temperature before an open window through which the sky is clearly visible. If the room is stuffy, you can use an electric fan but its breeze must be gentle and the fan should work silently. Keep only a minimum of furniture and at a distance from you since it may impede bodily movements. A clock with an easily readable second's hand may be kept nearby so that you can see it at all times.

12. A raised platform or a large table may be used if you are practising in a room.

13. The room where you are practising must be free from any unpleasant association.

14. Try to practise in the same place, at the same time, every day for the same length of time so that a regular habit may be formed.

15. Doing yoga while facing the East is the traditional practice which may be followed wherever possible.

10. SEAT

1. To practise yoga, you need no apparatus. All that is necessary is a mat, rug or blanket covered by a cotton cloth. A thick cotton cloth, folded over two or four times, may be used.

2. You may use a full-sized woollen carpet with a smooth upper surface and a floor-hugging under-surface to prevent crinkling. It may be covered by a clean cotton cloth which should be washed or exposed to sunshine after use. The carpet must not collect dust.

3. The carpet or mat should be thick enough for comfort yet thin enough to prevent the hands and feet from slipping, specially during the balancing postures.
4. The size of the rug or carpet should be such as to accommodate your whole body in lying-down position.
5. Spread the carpet or rug on the floor and cover it with a clean cloth or bedsheet. Never use the carpet or bedsheet used by another person and keep yours exclusively for yoga.
6. Do not practise on a soft sofa or in bed since your body will tend to sink in and you will be unable to balance properly. Do not practise on sand or grass.
7. Do not do asanas on the bare floor since you may catch a chill. A mat or carpet will ward off the dampness.

11. DRESS

1. For practising yoga, your dress should be sparing and suited to the climate and the season. Wear only minimum clothes which allow free movement.
2. Your dress should be clean, simple and comfortable. It must be loose-fitting so as to allow full and free movement of the limbs in any direction, with no constrictions around the neck, chest, abdomen, waist or wrists. A brief or a pair of drawers is enough for men, while women may wear a swimming costume or anything comfortable. Any clothing that might hamper circulation or inhibit movement should be loosened or removed.
3. The clothing should not be made of artificial fibres. Cotton clothing is recommended.
4. The dress must be airy and light and of porous weave. Avoid a dress which does not absorb perspiration.

5. When the climate is good, the body must be exposed as much as possible during the practice so as to give free play to all the muscles and limbs. In the case of men, it is desirable to keep the body bare above the waist, exposing it to fresh air.

6. When the air outside is chilly and damp or when cold winds are blowing, you may wear a pair of slacks, a cotton shirt, or a vest if necessary and none of these should be tight-fitting. The pockets should be empty.

7. Do not do yoga exercises while your body is cold.

8. Remove your shoes as asanas must always be performed barefooted.

9. Take off your tie, belt, watch, spectacles and loose ornaments, if you are wearing any. They may get damaged and may also cause discomfort.

12. SILENCE

1. Once you have learnt the yoga exercises, practise them alone in silence and in privacy as far as possible so that you can relax completely and concentrate on what you are doing.

2. Avoid chit-chatting or discussion with friends as you should not be distracted while doing the asanas.

4

Precautions for Beginners

अत्याहारः प्रयासश्च प्रजल्पो नियमाग्रहः ।
जनसंगश्च लौल्यं च षड्भिर्योगो विनश्यति ।।

Yoga gets futile by overeating, exertion, talkativeness, severe austerity, public contact, and unsteadiness.
—Hatha Pradipika I–15.

1. Keep Stomach Empty. 2. No Warming Up. 3. Measure of Time. 4. Avoid Strain. 5. Avoid Fatigue. 6. Pain. 7. Sneezing and Cough. 8. Illness.

1. KEEP STOMACH EMPTY

1. Asanas should always be practised on an empty stomach. However, a cup of milk may be allowed about an hour before a practice session to those who need it.

2. Asanas should not be performed immediately after the main meal of the day. They should be practised at least four hours after a large lunch, two hours after

a light snack, and one hour after a glass of juice, milk or any other liquid.

3. Students and those who practise in the evening should not take any light refreshments just before the practice.

4. Food may be taken in moderate quantity an hour after the practice. Heavy tiffin may be taken an hour later.

5. Taking a cup of milk or fruit juice with some honey dissolved in it half an hour after completing the practice will refresh you.

6. Asanas should not be practised when you are hungry or thirsty since hunger and thirst disturb the mind.

2. NO WARMING UP

1. No warming up or limbering up is necessary before an asana session. Though there may be some stiffness of the muscles and joints, it will ease off while the asanas are being practised. Doing the simple asanas first will also limber up muscles and joints.

2. Performing a few Surya Namaskars before starting the asanas will be helpful in loosening up the stiff muscles and joints. It also helps to get the blood flowing to your muscles and to dilate the arteries around the heart.

3. Persons who find their limbs too stiff in the morning may take a brisk walk for about ten minutes before the practice.

3. MEASURE OF TIME

1. For a person of average health, an hour a day is quite enough for doing asanas, Mudras, Bandhas, Kriyas and Pranayama. Start with half an hour of exercise and work up gradually to an hour.

2. Do not exercise for more than half an hour in the initial stages and increase the duration gradually. Even when you become more adept, do not do the exercises for more than an hour including frequent rest periods in Savasana.

3. You may increase the time for the exercises by about fifteen minutes daily in the winter months if your system allows it. Practise moderately in the hot summer days.

4. If you exercise less, you will not get its full benefit and if you exercise in excess, the results will not be positive. Therefore, exercise in adequate measure for which you are the best judge.

5. Do not tire yourself by trying to do all the asanas at once. Going beyond your stipulated limit will result in pulled muscles, torn tendons, strained joints and slipped discs.

6. The asanas which are chosen, the period earmarked for each, the number of repetitions and the total time of workout must suit the build and physical condition of the student. No common fixed procedure can be laid down as the capacity for physical exercise varies from person to person and everybody is not built in the same manner. Hence, do the asanas bearing in mind your own capacity and limitations and the precaution to be taken.

7. The quantum of exercise to be done and the total time to be devoted to it should be worked out by you according to your age, motivation and lifestyle. The condition of your body on each day at the time of practice should be taken into account as it may be stiff on some days and may not respond as well as the years slip by. You may feel better on some days

and wish to do the more difficult postures. On other days, you may not feel so good and wish to do only the simple asanas.

8. Since you know best your own exercise requirements, it is for you to decide whether you should do one, two or more repetitions of each asana and the total duration of the exercises. But a pattern of practice once fixed also needs to be changed as you gain more experience and advance in age.

9. It is not possible or necessary to do all the multitude of asanas and their infinite variations mentioned in the textbooks to achieve and maintain an all-round fitness. All the asanas you know need not be practised at one go and even the whole routine need not be gone through daily. Select about ten basic asanas, one Mudra, one Bandha and Pranayama for the daily practice which is all that is necessary to keep you healthy and youthful even in old age. A few extra postures may be worked up gradually. They should suit your time and specific needs.

10. A few asanas done with vigour and confidence is much better than going through mechanically a long list of asanas which will only strain the muscles and result in fatigue.

11. Important asanas in the basic group must not be omitted from your daily schedule of practice under normal circumstances. If you miss some important postures in this group in one session, include them in the next. Skipping a few non-basic asanas or optionals will not matter much.

12. You may, if you wish, include a variation from time to time in your daily practice to break the monotony

of routine. It may be noted, however, that these 'variations' are only rhythmic exercises adapted from the original asanas and differ from them only on minor points. Some of these variations are a combination of movements of the basic asanas while most of the others are merely unnatural contortions of the body. As many of these variations are merely modifications and simplifications of the classic asanas and since only a small benefit accrues by practising them, they may be done occasionally, and if you have the time and taste for them. Youngsters, however, may find the practice of asanas interspersed with such variations interesting.

13. Practise the variations of the postures after the principal ones when time permits. The variations should not replace the principal ones.

4. AVOID STRAIN

1. The performance of asanas correctly will not cause pain anywhere in the body as there is nothing to be lifted, pushed, pulled, carried, drawn or pressed; nor is there any question of competing with anyone or trying to break records.

2. Perform the exercise with pleasure and enjoy every movement. Do no violence of any kind to the body or strain yourself as it might sprain a muscle or tear a tendon. There must not be any distortion of the features or flushing in the face which indicate that you are straining.

3. Do not attempt any asana which is beyond your level of attainment or which will strain any weak organ, joint or muscle. Do not attempt a posture too many times.

4. While stretching a muscle or limb, do not use force. Do not pull against the tension of a stiff muscle; pull only when it is relaxed, in which case it will not cause any strain. The abdomen should always be kept relaxed during the practice.

5. While doing an asana, feel your way gradually, knowing and accepting your limitations, and do not exceed them. See how far you can go without getting tired and go a little further every time you practise. When you feel stiff, go easy and do not persist with it to the point of exhaustion. As soon as the going becomes hard or strenuous, discontinue the movement at once, as the emphasis should be on strength, not on strain.

6. Overworking your muscle in your anxiety to get quick results is asking for trouble. If you perform under strain, concentrating the mind on the movements will become difficult and serious disorders may result.

5. AVOID FATIGUE

1. You should not feel fatigued either at the end of each exercise or at the end of the practice session.

2. During the first few days after starting yoga practice, you experience some fatigue after completing the exercises. After a few days of regular practice, you will feel fine and tiredness will disappear.

3. A slow and controlled performance of asanas done in moderation and with economy of effort will never cause fatigue; on the contrary, it will leave you feeling refreshed and relaxed. You will have a feeling of well-being, both physical and mental, after the practice.

4. If asanas are performed properly, you will feel refreshed

at the end of each posture and after completing all the postures, you will feel as good as you do when you wake up from a sound sleep.

5. If you do not feel fine after doing an asana, something is wrong in the technique adopted or you have strained yourself too much.

6. You need not perform every day all the asanas you have learnt and thus get fatigued. Learn them first from a competent teacher and practise the basic asanas daily according to your schedule. If time permits, devote a minute or two for each of the optionals and a maximum of ten minutes to complete all the optionals for the day. You will then not get fatigued after completing the practice scheduled for the day.

7. Increase the time for holding the final position and the number of repetitions of each asana very gradually so that you do not feel below par after the exercise.

8. If fatigue accumulates during the execution of the postures, you must realize that you have had enough for the day. Stop for the day and relax in Savasana.

9. To remove your fatigue, you may drink a large glass of milk fifteen minutes after every yoga session.

6. PAIN

1. When you start practising yoga for the first time, you may find some muscles a little sore for a day or two. Take it easy.

2. You should put up with minor discomforts in the early stages of practice as they will gradually become easier to bear and pass off as your muscles and joints loosen up and elasticity is gained.

3. If your muscles are too stiff, you will experience slight

aches and pains during the first few days but with a few days of regular practice, these symptoms will disappear as your body adjusts itself to the regimen.

4. If yoga exercises are performed correctly, there will not be pain anywhere in the body either during the practice or after it. Pain indicates that you have either performed wrongly or attempted too much.

5. Pain is a contraindication but it should not be confused with the minor discomfort caused by the stretching of a muscle or a ligament which has not been used for a long time.

6. While assuming any particular posture, if pain is caused by tension in the muscles, do not continue. Retrace your steps and ease off for a few minutes in Savasana and start the practice again. If the pain persists, give it up for the day or for a few days until the pain has passed away.

7. If any particular asana is causing you pain, discontinue it temporarily until your body becomes conditioned to it.

8. Do not practise any asana which causes pain in any part of the body, particularly in the chest, abdomen or the back. If you feel a severe pain anywhere at any stage of the practice, stop at once and ascertain the cause from a doctor. You may resume the exercise when the pain has disappeared.

9. Whenever you strain a muscle or joint due to a violent or wrong practice, stop that particular exercise for some days and resume it cautiously later on. These conditions gradually right themselves.

7. SNEEZING AND COUGH

1. If you sneeze or cough while practising any asana,

return at once to the starting position and begin again.

2. If you start perspiring while performing asanas, wipe yourself with a dry towel.

3. Stretching the muscles slowly and gently does not lead to cramps but performing asanas strenuously or in a jerky manner does. Relaxation and skilled massage will bring significant relief by loosening the muscle fibres concerned.

4. When you perform asanas in which you invert your body, you should not swallow the saliva but keep it in the mouth. Swallow it when you revert to the upright position.

8. ILLNESS

1. Avoid asanas on those days in which you are out of condition and feel uneasy and unable to practise. You may do Savasana and Yoga Deep Breathing on those days.

2. Avoid all strenuous practices if you have a cold, cough, headache, vomiting, diarrhoea or other systemic upset. Do only Savasana until you are back to normal.

3. Do not practise asanas if you feel any discomfort or are running a temperature. Do only Savasana until you feel better.

4. If you have had a surgical operation, you should do the exercises only after the advice of a doctor who knows yoga.

5. Asanas should not be practised during or immediately after a serious illness when your body is weak.

6. After a serious illness, start the practice only after recouping sufficient strength and resistance. Do only

Pranayama and special corrective and curative exercises until the doctor has said all is well. After your system reverts to normal, start the exercises moderately and gather momentum slowly, increasing the exercising time a little daily.

7. If there has been a long delay of a few months or years in practising yoga due to illness or any other reason, resume the exercises gradually with not more than fifteen minutes to start with.

5

How to Practise Asanas

उत्साहात् साहसाद्धैर्यात्तत्त्वज्ञानाच्च निश्चयात् ।
जनसंगपरित्यागात् षड्‌भिर्योगः प्रसिध्यति ।।

Yoga is successfully performed by the following six methods: effort, perseverence, courage, discriminative knowledge, determination, and abandoning public contact.
—*Hatha Pradipika* I–16

1. Beginners. 2. Relaxation. 3. Poise and Balance. 4. Proceed Gradually. 5. Perform Slowly. 6. Avoid Haste. 7. Concentration. 8. Understand the Principle. 9. Sequence. 10. Select Your Asanas. 11. Simple Postures. 12. Difficult Postures. 13. Reaching the Final Position. 14. Holding the Final Position. 15. Returning to Starting Position. 16. Repetitions. 17. Breathing. 18. Closing the Eyes. 19. Don'ts.

1. BEGINNERS

1. 'Asana' means 'posture' in Sanskrit. Asanas are practised while standing, sitting, kneeling, lying,

balancing or in inverted positions. Their performance consists mostly in stretching, twisting, contracting and relaxing muscles, ligaments and tendons aimed at securing a steady posture for a given period of time. During the performance of the asanas, the body bends forward, backward and sideways and the trunk is twisted to the right and left.

2. Yogic exercises will be rather irksome for beginners during the first few days, but will become easy with practise and once mastered, no longer create tension in the muscles.

3. If you are practising asanas for the first time, you will not have an easy time for the first few days as your muscles, tendons and joints are likely to be stiff due to lack of regular exercise. You will not be able to execute the final position, and even if you do, you will find it difficult to maintain it. But once you have familiarized yourself with the techniques and manage to do it, the movements become easy.

4. Do not aim at perfection in the very beginning since to attain perfection takes time, patience and perseverance. Do not imagine that all yoga exercises must be carried out perfectly if they are to be beneficial. Benefit accrues even if you practise small movements every day. The flexibility of the muscles and joints already achieved in the intermediate positions will not be lost and your body will gradually get attuned to the final posture. Do not worry about small mistakes; they get corrected as you proceed.

5. Even if you are not able to attain the exact posture, the stretching involved brings good results and

improves your ability to accomplish the final posture. It is the attempt that counts.

2. RELAXATION

1. Do not start practising yoga when you suffer from tension either of the mind or of the body. Start only when you feel fresh and in a calm and pleasant frame of mind. If you are mentally upset or physically fatigued, do Savasana and calm down completely before starting the practice. If you are extremely tired, do only Savasana since what you need is rest.

2. Do not begin yoga practice if you are tired or are perspiring. If you are feeling tired after a hard physical labour or sports, practise asanas only after half an hour's rest.

3. Relaxation is as important as the postures as it revitalizes the exhausted parts and helps recoup spent energy.

4. While practising the asanas, the body is bent, twisted and stretched, causing some strain to the muscles. The spine is also moved in all directions, forward, backward, sideways and twisted. To relieve the strain, take up Savasana in which every cell, limb and nerve fibre gets rest and the body recoups quickly. If there are any aches and pains in your muscles or joints or in any other part of your body, with Savasana they will disappear.

5. Before starting yoga practice, thoroughly relax the limbs and muscles in Savasana for a few minutes. Practising Savasana for a brief period before starting other asanas will enable you to perform better besides creating the right mental condition.

6. Do not rush from one posture to another without proper relaxation at intervals since every contraction of a muscle should be followed by its relaxation.

7. Relax all muscles thoroughly for at least a few seconds before starting another asana. After relaxation, you will be able to stretch your muscles better since during relaxation, blood flows in great quantity to the muscles which have been commissioned for use. Also, relax all muscles after completing each asana to give the body time to readjust.

8. After completing one posture and before starting the next, pause for a few seconds and relax the body completely until the heart rate and arterial pressure return to normal. A minute's rest between the asanas and a few relaxing breaths between the turns of each asana will generally suffice to help your heart to slow down to its normal beat.

9. When your breath becomes short or you feel exhausted after a particular asana, do not repeat it but relax in Savasana so that your pulse rate may drop to normal and you feel fresh again before you restart.

10. Whenever you do an asana which begins with lying down flat on the back, always relax in Savasana for a few minutes at the start and at the end of the movements. You can also relax in Makarasana after practising the lying-down posture since it gives quick relief from strain.

11. Always rest in Savasana after taking any inverted posture.

12. It is not, however, necessary to rest for a prolonged time in Savasana after each and every asana except in the case of the difficult ones. You may relax for

two to three minutes between a group of three and four asanas or whenever your breathing is laboured.

13. Learn to relax in Savasana as quickly and as thoroughly as possible before and after each set of yoga practice by quickly running over your body in your mind and relaxing as many muscles as possible.

14. Total relaxation in Savasana for ten to fifteen minutes after completing the practice for the day removes fatigue, if any, and enables the blood circulation to readjust itself. The temperature of the body reverts to normal and perspiration, if any, will dry. The mind also gets relaxed.

3. POISE AND BALANCE

1. Perform asanas in slow motion, maintaining poise and balance, which will have a calming effect on the body and mind.

2. The movements should be smooth, slow, steady, rhythmic and graceful.

3. Be fully aware of the starting position and go through the exercises step by step with good coordination of the movements and timing.

4. While assuming a yoga posture, try to obtain a complete control at every stage.

5. The body must not shake; it should be as firm as a rock during the practice.

4. PROCEED GRADUALLY

1. Do not hesitate to start yoga practice under the impression that your body is not pliable and that you will not be able to practice even one asana correctly. Select a few which are easy to learn and simple to do

and perform them as well as you can and gradually improve your performance as you gain greater proficiency and muscular strength.

2. Each time you perform, try to advance a little from the previous position, and when you graduate to the final position, hold it for a few more seconds than the previous day. A gentle progression to extend your limits is the best way to attain the final position and hold it for the maximum retention period.

3. Note the physical and mental changes you experience as you advance in the practice.

5. PERFORM SLOWLY

1. Practise the exercises slowly and in a relaxed manner and in tune with your breathing to get the maximum benefit.

2. Make progress slowly but steadily, paying proper attention to the details as every movement counts. The temptation to speed up progress should be resisted, although you may feel capable of doing so.

3. The stretching, contraction and relaxation of the muscles should be effected slowly, progressively and naturally which alone will give you worthwhile results. If you try too hard, you will just tire yourself out.

4. There are three main stages involved in a posture: (a) getting into it, (b) staying in it, and (c) getting back to the original position. Master each stage before going to the next posture.

5. The slow and correct performance of the preliminary stages by which the final posture is attained is as important as the posture itself and thoroughness is

more important than speed. Do not try to do too much too soon by jumping over the intermediate stages.

6.   Do not try to reach quickly the final stage of an asana as shown in the illustrations as they are only models of what you might achieve after long practice.

7.   Do not pull or push yourself too far while practising an asana in order to attain the highest standard. Avoid jerky movements as they will be injurious and ineffective and prevent muscular relaxation.

8.   Avoid all artificial props or apparatus to help you to attain a posture quickly.

6. AVOID HASTE

1.   Avoid practising asanas in a hurry in order to finish them as soon as possible.

2.   If those who get up late, wake up an hour earlier than usual, they will get ample time to practise and reap the full benefit of doing the asanas. This will require going to bed an hour earlier.

3.   If you feel that you cannot go through all the asanas in your practice schedule on any particular day due to fatigue or want of time, do not try to rush through all of them at whirlwind speed which will only make you more tense. If time is a problem, reduce the number of asanas but do them in a relaxed manner and without quickening the pace. You may also reduce the number of repetitions of each asana but not their holding period.

4.   If you devote more time for a few selected asanas to derive full benefit out of them, you may cut short the time for the additional asanas and the optionals which may be done only if time permits.

5. If you omit any asana which works best for you either for want of time or due to oversight, do not feel concerned as you can perform it later when time permits.

7. CONCENTRATION

1. Yoga exercises, though they look simple, are very potent and should not be practised haphazardly which will do more harm than good. If they are practised mechanically, they will not bring any worthwhile results. Hence, always practise with awareness, concentrating on what you are doing and on the sensations you experience.

2. The effectiveness of an asana depends as much on the concentration you bestow on its practice as on the correct following of its technique.

3. After starting an asana, your mind must follow the movements and the breath.

4. Do not allow your mind to wander. Turn your attention inwards so that the mind controls the movements at every stage. Focus your attention on the technique and the parts of the body being moved in their minutest detail and the different stages involved in it. Experience the 'feel' of the stretching until the final position is reached so that you perform slowly and correctly and derive full benefit from the posture.

5. Concentration on the anatomical regions involved in the exercise will aid in getting at and holding the final position with ease besides cultivating your skill in performance.

8. UNDERSTAND THE PRINCIPLE

1. Before starting an asana, understand the principle behind it and the benefits you derive from practising

it. Mere mechanical performance will bring only minor physiological benefits.

2. If an asana is performed while adhering to its principle, one can derive its full benefit even if some little detail is missed and even if it is not performed perfectly.

3. Try to follow the exact technique of each asana while practising it and you will be able to master and practise it correctly in the course of time.

9. SEQUENCE

1. After undergoing a course of training from a competent yoga teacher, do not peform haphazardly at home on the spur of the moment. Proceed systematically, following a definite order. Each practice should be followed step-by-step as recommended by your teacher.

2. Group the postures you have learnt according to their physical benefits and ease of performance. Select the sequence of the postures and fix the duration of each posture by experience and stick to the select sequence tenaciously.

3. In the general scheme of practice, the following order has been found to be the best: a. Surya Namaskars b. Asanas c. Mudras d. Bandhas e. Kapala Bhati f. Savasana and g. Pranayama.

4. The following order may be followed in the case of asanas: a. Standing postures; b. Sitting postures; c. Lying down postures and, d. Inverted postures. The meditative (cross-legged) postures should precede the physical postures.

5. Try to do one set of exercises at one sitting and relax in Savasana before doing another set.

6. Do each asana separately and as a whole. Do not combine the asanas as specific benefits are gained from the final position of each asana and the effect of one may be neutralized by the other if performed together. The combinations and variations are also endless. Do not break single asanas into small independent movements to facilitate learning.

7. Asanas which are performed on both sides of the body, such as Trikonasana, should not be performed on one side only as there will be unequal development of the body. They should be performed on both sides for an equal number of time. This will ensure that all the muscles are exercised and that both sides of the body are equally exercised and evenly developed.

8. Generally, there is a counter-posture for each posture. This means, bending in one direction should be followed by bending in the opposite direction, as in Supta Vajrasana and Yoga Mudra, when practised one after the other. The counter-postures should be done alternately to balance the pressure and to secure the maximum amount of benefit.

10. SELECT YOUR ASANAS

1. Select those asanas which appeal to you the most, taking into consideration your age, gender, size, weight, build, suppleness, physical condition, capacity and adaptability and practise each one of them correctly and in the proper sequence. Perfect the performance of the asanas you select.

2. Your daily exercise programme should be well balanced: it should work out all parts and organs of your body including the abdomen and spine.

3. Spinal stretching and bending is of primary importance and should consist of: (a) its upward or vertical stretch, (b) sideway or lateral stretch to the right and left, (c) backward or posterior stretch, (d) forward or anterior stretch, and (e) rotating to the left and the right.

4. Bhujangasana which stretches and relaxes the vertebrae one by one is a must. Sarvangasana, Halasana and Paschimotanasana, done one after the other, form an excellent trio. The Abdominal Lift, Savasana and Pranayama must also not be omitted from your daily practice schedule.

5. Young persons will benefit a lot by doing the standing postures since they develop the skeletal muscles, loosen the joints, and improve the overall blood circulation and breathing.

6. It is better to perform a few asanas correctly than to try several whose benefits are in doubt and to feel fatigued. One can gain some benefit by performing even one asana correctly.

7. Those postures in which you feel the most at ease and can remain the longest without strain are the best for you, and not those which demand more of your strength, suppleness, control and balance.

8. If you like any particular asana better than the others and if it proves to be exceptionally good for you, you may practise it for as long as possible without tiring yourself. Do not, however, neglect the other important asanas.

9. While preparing your asana programme, do not forget those postures which strengthen the weak parts of your body.

10. Persons who want relief from a specific ailment should choose the asanas which are particularly beneficial to their condition.

11. SIMPLE POSTURES

1. Since it takes time to train your stiff muscles and joints to move to their full range, start off with the simplest and easiest asanas in the order worked out for you by your teacher. You can tackle the complex and relatively more difficult ones gradually as you increase your strength and improve the flexibility of your joints and muscles.

2. At first, always practise those asanas which come to you easily and are pleasant to perform. Get on with them and master them one by one by patient and persistent practice until you become adept in all of them. As your fitness improves, add a daily ten-minute practice of a few of those postures which are difficult and gradually master all of them.

3. Some asanas appear to be simple but prove to be difficult when attempted. You should not give them up as impossible. Perform them as best as you can, slowly and without strain. They will soon begin to get easier with each repetition as your joints and muscles start loosening up.

4. Some postures will be easy for some, but difficult for the others. If you are not able to practise any particular asana which others do easily, do not feel dismayed by your apparent lack of progress. You may feel your way into it in course of time as your joints, muscles and ligaments loosen up by regular practice. Even if it proves to be a challenge and not suited to

your bodily proportions, do not get concerned as there are other asanas which may suit you better.

12. DIFFICULT POSTURES

1. Only persons who have undergone a training in simple postures and acquired enough suppleness of body should attempt the postures which are difficult to accomplish. Otherwise, physical disorders may crop up.

2. If you find the performance of the basic asanas too demanding at first, go over them slowly and cautiously as best as you can without strain and improve you performance day by day. Do not discard them. The optionals, however, may be taken up after your muscles and joints become more flexible and you feel free to do them.

3. At the beginning, try to hold the difficult positions for only a few seconds and repeat them three to five times. Increase the holding time gradually as the strain decreases and reduce the number of repetitions.

4. Keep trying to do the basic asanas, though in the initial stages they may strike you as being too difficult. As you make headway and your body becomes sufficiently supple, all movements to attain the final position and holding on to it will become easy enough.

5. When the difficult postures become less tough through repeated practise and are accomplished with relative ease, do not lose interest in them or give them up on account of their simplicity as you may lose what you have gained.

6. After learning the more demanding postures, do not discount the value of the simpler ones learnt earlier. They are still most effective: keep in mind that practising

them in the wrong manner or holding them beyond your capacity will lead to serious disorders.

7. Complicated and extremely difficult postures, which require great physical strength and endurance and long periods of devoted practice, may be learnt, if you like, through the personal instructions of an expert. Many of these postures, however, are difficult to attain and hold if you are not in top condition. These spectacular positions are not necessarily the best and they are neither desirable nor necessary for the average person whose body is generally stiff and who has little time for daily practice. Furthermore, many of these acrobatic postures do not have the slightest resemblance to traditional yoga.

13. REACHING THE FINAL POSITION

1. Do not try to get into the final stage of a posture right away as you may need to practise a great deal at first to get it right. All intermediate stages must be mastered and gone through properly before the final stage is attempted. While going through the intermediate stages, hold the last position already attained for increasing periods of time and proceed slowly day by day, gradually increasing the resistance. As you inch your way little by little, the muscles get trained and their tension is gradually removed by the slow and methodical stretching and relaxing.

2. In the beginning, practise the asanas only by stages and the final stage will be reached gradually with daily practise. After mastering the movements, give up going by stages since every asana is a complete whole and there are no stages.

3. Even after long practise, you should not rush to the final position haphazardly, but attain it by slow and continuous progression with complete control over the movements involved and without any strain. The final position can be reached and maintained only if you are in prime condition.

4. The final position of an asana can be attained only by prolonged practise, day after day, with patience and perseverence. Make only a minimum effort to attain it and do not take risks or use tricks. It should be attained very slowly by increasing the tension on the muscles concerned gradually. Continuous practise until you attain the final position will improve your ability.

14. HOLDING THE FINAL POSITION

1. Once the final position of an asana is attained, make some last adjustments if necessary and hold it for as long as you can which will extend as your body becomes more supple.

2. Try to increase the holding period gradually day by day to the required count. The time of retention can be measured by mentally counting numbers.

3. It is better to gradually increase the holding period of each asana rather than trying to practise a large number of asanas with a very short holding period.

4. Lengthen the holding period of the posture you are attempting as the strain decreases with regular practise and becomes easier to manage, but do not go beyond your capacity to maintain long timings.

5. Once the final position has been attained, hold it motionless like a statue for the prescribed period of

time which requires perfect control of your body and mind. Do not lose control and let go.

6. Hold the final position in a poised and relaxed manner and in complete stillness. Your body then will not be rigid and you can hold the posture more easily.

7. After you attain the final position, be comfortable in it and hold it as long as possible with the greatest economy of effort. The measure of success of a posture is the ease and comfort you feel in it and in which you can keep still for the specified time.

8. After attaining the final stage of an asana, remain immobile and relaxed in it. If done correctly, a sense of well-being spreads over you after completing the practice. If you feel restless and fidgety during the holding period, come off the posture immediately in the reverse order.

9. While holding a posture, there will be a feeling of lightness of the body. This is a healthy sign and indicates that you have performed the asana correctly.

10. Concentrate on the benefits, not the difficulty, while holding the posture.

11. When the final position is reached, forget it and arrest all distracting thoughts. Relax your body and keep your mind calm. This will increase the effectiveness of the practice.

12. While remaining in the posture, keep your mind still so that the consciousness of your body and of the outside world is effaced for the time being. However, this can be achieved only by advanced students after years of patient and persevering practise.

15. RETURNING TO STARTING POSITION

1. After holding the final position of an asana for the required length of time, take as much care in coming back to the starting position as you did in going into it.
2. Come out of the posture slowly with grace and control, avoiding hasty and jerky movements.

16. REPETITIONS

1. Mere mechanical repetitions of an asana will not bring the desired results.
2. If you are able to practise an asana correctly and hold the final position comfortably for the maximum retention time, you may reduce the number of repetitions.

17. BREATHING

1. Since the movements involved in the asanas can be performed with ease when synchronized with breathing, follow the breathing regulations for achieving the maximum effectiveness.
2. Movement and breath foster a soothing rhythm in your body's functions.
3. Rhythmical and synchronized breathing help you to concentrate on the movements and augment their efficacy.
4. Synchronized breathing indicates to the practitioner whether the physical limit of an exercise is reached when breathing becomes difficult.
5. After some practise, breathing adjusts itself as a natural sequence of the movements of the limbs and the position assumed by the body, and you can know

yourself when the inhalation, retention and exhalation should occur in each exercise.

6. Breathe through the nostrils only, with the mouth closed.

7. Take a few normal breaths both before starting an asana and after completing it.

8. While performing asanas, breathing should always be smooth and never hurried or strained.

9. Avoid inhalation and exhalation in quick succession and do not gasp for breath at any time during the practice.

10. Stop the exercise whenever you suffer from palpitation or run out of breath and resume it when breathing returns to normal. Any asana practised with laboured or inadequate breathing will be harmful in the long run.

11. As a general rule, breathe out as you bend forward, breathe in as you bend backward or stretch, and breathe normally at other times.

12. Breathing in the final position of all static postures should be rhythmic and natural.

13. If a posture has to be maintained for a long time, breathe freely during the holding period.

14. Beginners may pause and take a fresh breath in between movements if they find it difficult to perform the whole action in a single breath as instructed.

15. You have to hold your breath while assuming some postures. Feel comfortable while holding your breath. Never hold it to the point of discomfort or a moment longer when strain is felt.

16. Beginners who cannot hold their breath for the required count may take another. After a little

practise, they will be able to retain their breath for longer periods.

17. CLOSING THE EYES

1. You may half close your eyes, if you like, while holding some of the static postures. Keep them open while practising the dynamic ones so that you may see whether you are practising correctly or not.
2. Closing the eyes partially while holding a posture will help concentration besides calming your mind and nerves. Closing the eyes fully may cause loss of awareness.

18. DON'TS

1. Do not perform asanas in a competitive or emulative spirit.
2. While doing asanas or Pranayama, do not stop in the middle to refer to any book.

6

Surya Namaskar

सूर्य आत्मा जगतः तस्थुषः च।।

Sun is the sustainer of the Universe, composed of movables
and immovables.

—Rig Veda 1— 115–1.

1. 'Surya' means 'Sun' and 'Namaskar' means 'bowing
    down' in Sanskrit. Surya Namaskar means offering
    prostrations to the Sun.
2. The age-old practice of Surya Namaskar was
    designed by sages on a scientific basis to bring about
    a harmonious development of the body and mind by
    exercising every part of the body and keeping the
    mind alert. It is the best system of physio-spiritual
    culture the world has ever known and no other
    system can surpass it.
3. Each Namaskar consists of a sequence of twelve
    simple postures grouped together as a harmonious
    blend of exercise and breathing. Each posture

counteracts the one before, stretching the body in a different direction. It is thus the best all-round exercise for the body.

4. Surya Namaskar can be performed by boys and girls above the age of eight. The twelve positions are of special benefit to the elderly and to those approaching middle age whose limbs have become stiff from having given up regular exercise and games. Even persons in poor health may practise them after a medical check-up, and they will become strong and feel revitalized.

5. Surya Namaskars can be performed at home and need no special equipment or facilities. They also involve very little time.

6. You may incorporate them in your daily routine of yoga exercise. If they are performed as a preliminary to the practise of asanas, it will limber up your whole body and make it easier for you to do the asanas. They may also be performed on their own.

7. If you are short of time on some days, Surya Namaskars may be practised as a substitute for asanas, each Namaskar taking only about half a minute. You will feel relaxed and refreshed after the practice as in the case of asanas.

8. Those who are unable to practise asanas for any reason may practise Surya Namaskars as a 'keep-fit' exercise.

POINTS FOR PRACTICE

1. Practise the Namaskars in the open air or in an airy room.

2. Practise them while facing the rising sun, if possible. They are done traditionally at sunrise. Do not perform them when the sun is hot or at night.

3. Surya Namaskar, performed early in the morning, removes stiffness in the body experienced in the mornings. It also removes laziness and invigorates the whole body.

4. Practise on an empty stomach after finishing the morning ablutions and bath. If one likes to have a bath after performing the Namaskars, allow the body to cool off after the exercise.

5. Wear only light and minimum clothing to allow the skin to breathe and to absorb the sun's energy.

6. The twelve positions follow one another with unbroken rhythm. Go through each position while concentrating your mind on the breathing and movements.

7. Each position should be held for about five seconds.

8. Avoid strain and jerks while practising the Namaskars.

9. Whenever you feel a pain in the back or any other part of the body while executing the movements, return slowly to the starting position, relax, and begin the Namaskars again the next day.

10. If you perspire after performing the Namaskars, rub your body with a wet towel. You may bathe after fifteen minutes.

11. After completing the Namaskars, relax the body completely in Savasana.

BREATHING

1. During each Namaskar of twelve positions, six complete inhalations and exhalations are made. There is no retention of the breath at any stage except in positions 2 and 11 for about five seconds each. Hold out your breath while maintaining position 6.

2. In this exercise, each movement is initiated by either an inhalation or an exhalation.

3. Beginners should do free breathing throughout as they will find regulated breathing difficult. They should coordinate movements and breath only after mastering the movements.

4. After mastering the mechanics of the practice, synchronize your breathing with the movement and be completely aware of your breath and movements.

5. After continuous practice, your breathing will adjust itself naturally.

MEASURE

1. Each Namaskar consists of a cycle of twelve connected positions, which are the progressive stages of the practice. Go through all of them consecutively, one leading to the next, which constitute a single Namaskar. Repeat as many Namaskars as possible, at an even pace, without getting tired.

2. It is best to perform the Namaskars slowly, pausing a little at the end of each position. Each position should be held for about five seconds before proceeding to the next. The Namaskars can also be performed more swiftly with very little pause between the different positions, but this should be attempted only after mastering all the twelve positions. Beginners should go slow during the early stages of the practice. Children may perform the Namaskars more quickly than adults.

3. It is enough if you practise Surya Namaskars for ten to fifteen minutes, resting in-between, if you are practising this alone. If you are practising the Namaskars along with other asanas, perform only

three cycles at a time in the beginning and gradually increase the number by three every week, according to your capacity, until you reach twelve.

4. It is better to practise a few Namaskars carefully and systematically with the appropriate breathing cycle rather than rush through a large number hurriedly and carelessly.

SEQUENCE

- As you start practising this exercise, learn the sequence of the movements.
- You may initially experience some difficulty in co-ordination, but once the movements synchronized with breathing are committed to memory, the practice will become easy.
- The breathing cycle will be easy to remember if you bear in mind that you should exhale as you bend forward and inhale as you bend back.
- You may paste an illustrated chart on a cardboard and hang it on a wall at eye level until you know the sequence by heart. The following table will help to memorize the positions and specify when to exhale or inhale in a Surya Namaskar cycle:

1. Stand upright and exhale completely.
2. Inhaling, stretch your arms above the head and hold your breath (breath No. 1).
3. Double over (exhale).
4. Take right leg back (inhale: breath No. 2).
5. Take left leg back (exhale).
6. Keep body flat on the floor (inhale, breath No. 3 and then exhale while lowering the body and hold out your breath while maintaining the position).

7. Head and trunk should be raised on arms (inhale: breath No. 4).
8. Inverted 'V' (exhale).
9. Right foot should be brought forward (inhale: breath No. 5).
10. Bring left foot forward and double over (exhale).
11. Inhaling, stretch arms above the head and hold your breath (breath No. 6).
12. Stand upright (exhale).

Positions 1 and 12, 2 and 11, 3 and 10 are the same.

THE 12 POSITIONS

Position 1

Spread a blanket, mat or carpet on a level floor. Stand erect on it facing the East. Keep the feet about ten inches apart and on a level with each other. Keep the arms straight down and close to the body. Knees should be held stiff. Heels, back, and the back of the head should be in a line. Keep the chest raised and the abdomen drawn in.

Fold the arms and bring the hands inward before the chest. Both palms should be joined together lightly with the fingers well stretched out and pointing upwards. Turn the palms up with the fingertips and thumbs touching each other and both thumbs touching the middle of the chest in a prayerful gesture. The forearms from elbow to

Fig. 1

elbow should be in alignment. Keep the mouth closed and look straight ahead. Stand well balanced. Exhale and take a few normal breaths. Relax the whole body. This is the starting position (Fig. 1).

Worship the rising sun, if possible. Keep your mind calm and assume a prayerful mood.

Position 2

Breathe out slowly and completely and inhale deeply and slowly (breath No. 1). While inhaling, open out your hands and, turning the palms outwards, raise your arms slowly forward and upward without bending the elbows and knees until they are straight above your head. While doing this, keep the arms stiff, with the inside of the upper arms touching the ears. Keep your arms parallel in a straight line with the trunk and keep the distance of the shoulders between the hands. Complete the inhalation. Look up between your

Fig. 2

fingertips. Stand erect with your feet firmly planted on the ground and hold your breath.

Without pausing, stretch up and pull your arms backward in one smooth movement, your eyes following the tips of your fingers. While pulling your arms back, bend your head and trunk slowly from the waist as far back as balancing permits without bending the elbows and knees and keeping the inside of the upper arms touching the ears. While arching back from the waist, push your pelvis forward and bend the spine, shoulders, neck and head together backwards as far as you can without overbalancing, keeping the chin up and arching the neck and back.

Knees and elbows should be kept straight and stiff. Hold your head steadily between the upper arms which should touch the ears. Push your chest a little forward and look back as far as possible between your fingertips. Having reached the limit of your capacity to bend backward, hold the position firmly without strain for about five seconds, holding your breath (Fig. 2).

BENEFITS

1. The chest expands and the capacity of the ribcage increases while assuming this position.
2. The arching of the back exercises the shoulders, spine, ribs and the back muscles. While the front of the neck is stretched, the back is compressed.
3. The lumbar and sacral regions of the spine become more supple.
4. By leaning backward, the abdominal muscles are gently pulled and strengthened.

Position 3

Exhale slowly and while exhaling, start moving your head and arms together forward and downward slowly, keeping the head steadily between the upper arms which should be touching the ears. Bending the trunk forward from the hips and drawing in the abdomen, bring down your hands steadily to the floor, keeping the arms stretched out and the legs straight.

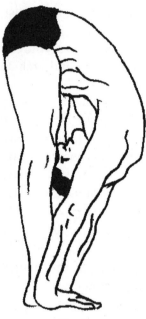

Fig. 3

Press the ground with the fingertips, first in the most comfortable position and then place your palms flat on the floor at shoulder width and about five inches in front of your toes. The palms should be parallel to each other, with fingers close together and pointing forward. Pushing back the pelvis, press down on the floor with your palms. The body will now be doubled at the hips, resembling a hairpin, supported on your hands and feet. After bending down and placing the palms flat on the floor, draw in your abdomen and pull your head in towards the knees and try to touch them and your forehead, avoiding strain at the back of the thigh. Bring the chin towards the chest and touch it if possible. Keep the knees straight and the heels pressing the ground. Look up towards your waist. Hold this position motionlessly until you complete the exhalation (Fig. 3).

POINTS

1. In the beginning, your hands will not reach much below your ankles, but go down as far as you can, curving your back in order to reach further down. As your fingers come closer and closer to the ground with persistent practise, first, allow the fingertips to come as near the floor as can be managed and,

finally, touch it without strain. After repeated practise, place your palms flat on the floor just opposite to, and as near as possible to, the respective toes with fingers close together and pointing forward and keeping your knees and elbows straight. In the initial stages, you may bend your knees slightly, but regular practise, extending over many weeks, will enable you to place your palms flat on the floor without bending your knees.

2. After placing the palms flat on the floor, adjust the distance between them and their distance from the toes according to the build of your body. As you continue the exercise, try to place the palms as near your big toes as possible and at shoulder width.

3. From now on, the palms should remain flat on the floor in the same position until Position 10 is completed.

4. The forehead should be as close to the knees as possible.

5. Increase the backward and forward stretches gradually.

6. The strain which is felt in the calves, the backs of the thighs, waist, hips and spine by beginners will fade away with regular practise.

7. This position is the counterpose of position 2 and resembles Padahastasana.

BENEFITS

1. In this position, the spine is stretched to the utmost. The muscles of the neck, the sides, the back of the thighs and calves are brought into play and strengthened. The hips and the waist are also well exercised. The muscles of the abdomen are tightly contracted by the extreme forward bending of the body. The hamstring muscles are also stretched.

2. By bending the head and pulling it towards the knees, the brain receives an extra blood supply and the facial tissues are nourished. The pituitary, pineal, thyroid and parathyroid glands also get a good supply of blood.

3. The sacral and lower lumbar regions of the spine become more supple by assuming this position. Pushing back the pelvis eases the fifth lumbar vertebra.

4. Surplus fat in the abdomen and hips is reduced.

Position 4

Keep the left foot and palms firmly planted on the floor. Inhale deeply (breath no. 2). While inhaling, slightly bend both legs at the knees and without bending the arms or shifting the position of the palms on the ground, press down hard on the hands. Lowering your posterior, stretch the entire length of your right leg straight back, sliding your right foot backwards along the floor as far as it goes and rest it firmly on the toes. While going down on your right knee, raise your trunk and head. Keep the right foot fixed perpendicularly on the floor. The thigh and foot of the extended right leg must be in line with the vertical right arm. Hold the extended right leg as straight as possible, keeping the knee a little above the floor.

While extending the right leg backwards, bend the left leg also at the knee, keeping the sole of the left foot and the left palm in the same position firmly on the floor. The left thigh should be kept very near the trunk and the left knee should be just a little ahead of the straightened left arm. The left side of the left thigh should touch the vertical left arm. Press the palms and left foot on the floor and maintain your balance. Keep the arms vertical and in the same position. Push forward the chest and stretch your head and neck as far back as possible, arching the spine to the maximum extent. Raise the chin as high as possible and look up. Support the weight of the body on both hands, the left foot and the toes of the right foot which should be bent to grip the floor. Hold this position firmly until you complete the inhalation (Fig. 4).

Fig. 4

POINT

Hold the extended right leg as straight as possible, keeping the knee a little above the floor. Beginners, however, may rest the knee on the floor for support.

BENEFITS

1. In this position, the spine and the neck are stretched in a direction opposite to Position 3.
2. The pelvis, arms and thighs are also exercised.

Position 5

Start exhaling slowly. Without bending the arms or changing the position of the palms and the right foot on the ground, stretch the entire length of your bent left leg straight back along the floor and rest it firmly on the toes. Keep your legs straight and the knees above the floor. Keep both your feet perpendicular to the floor. The thigh and foot of the extended left leg also must be in line with the vertical left arm. Press the palms and toes on the floor.

The whole body is now lifted from the floor and kept straight as an inclined plane from shoulders to heels and its entire weight is borne by the hands and toes. The head, trunk, thighs and legs should be in line, propped up on the vertical arms and feet and sloping from the shoulders to the heels. Look down at the floor. Maintain your balance and hold this position comfortably and motionlessly until you complete the exhalation (Fig. 5).

Fig. 5

POINT

Once the feet are placed correctly on the floor in this position, they should remain so until Position 8 is completed.

BENEFITS

This position provides good exercise to the wrists, arms, shoulders, back, legs, ankles, feet and toes and improves the posture. It is also beneficial to the abdominal muscles.

Position 6

Keep the hands and toes firmly on the ground in the same position and keep the whole body motionless. Inhale slowly and deeply (breath no. 3). After completing the inhalation, exhale slowly and while exhaling, lower your body very slowly to the ground and assume the prone position as follows.

Fig. 6

Bending the elbows and knees, bring down very slowly your knees, upper abdomen and forehead to the ground one after the other and the chest last. Place the forehead at the farthest point possible on the floor. Keep the lower abdomen and pelvis as high as possible from the floor. The palms should remain in the same position alongside the chest. The bent elbows should be raised high and the arms kept close to your sides. The feet should not be moved; they should be held perpendicularly, the toes only touching the ground and curled under. Complete the exhalation while drawing in the abdomen. Holding out your breath, maintain this position for a few seconds, allowing your muscles to slacken. You have now come half way in the practise of Surya Namaskar (Fig. 6).

POINTS

1. While assuming this position, apply pressure on the forearms and balance the body on the toes and palms which should not be moved from their position.
2. Hold the body rigid while lowering it slowly.
3. In this position, the body lies prostrate on the ground, with the abdomen drawn in and the hips raised off the floor. The lower abdomen must be kept slightly raised from the floor. The palms lie flat on the floor by the side of the chest.
4. In this position, eight parts of the body come in contact with the floor, namely, the two sets of toes, the two knees, the two palms, the chest and the forehead (Sashtanga Namaskar). The other parts of the body should not touch the ground.
5. Those who are fat may find holding this position difficult as their abdomen sags, but they may draw in the abdomen and try to keep their hips and lower abdomen as far above the floor as possible.

BENEFITS

The whole body is exercised while you assume this position. The muscles of the neck, shoulders, the upper arms, forearms, back and abdomen are brought into play. The wrist-joints as well as the joints of the legs and arms will be strengthened.

Position 7

Keep the toes, knees and palms firmly in the same position and lower the pelvis to the floor. Bend your head and neck backward, keeping your chest on the floor. Inhale slowly and deeply (breath no. 4). While inhaling, press the palms and toes down on the floor and raise first your head and then the upper and lower parts of your trunk from the waist smoothly and as high as possible, at the same time straightening the arms and legs fully.

The straightened and vertical arms will prop your trunk up from the floor. While stretching up the trunk and head, the position of the feet and palms should not be changed. Keeping your elbows stiff, push your chest forward and bend your head and neck backward to the fullest extent, arching the spine as much as possible. Only your palms and toes should touch the floor and support the body. Keep both feet perpendicular to the floor. The lower body from the waist to the feet must be parallel to the ground. Look up towards the sky or ceiling. Complete the inhalation and hold this position rigid. Concentrate your mind on the base of the spine (Fig. 7).

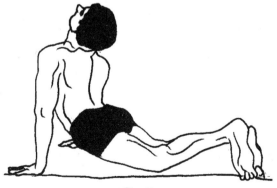

Fig. 7

BENEFITS

1. In this position, the spine is bent backwards to its fullest extent which makes the lumbar region more flexible. Minor deformities of the spine and slipped disc are also corrected.
2. The muscles in the front of the neck are stretched to their capacity while those in the nape are compressed.
3. In this position, the weight of the upper part of the body is borne mostly by the triceps muscle of the arms which become strong and supple. Flabby upper arms get corrected. The shoulders and wrists also become strong.
4. The pectoral muscles of the chest are expanded and developed.
5. A bulging belly gets reduced as the abdominal muscles are stretched.
6. It keeps the waist firm and supple.

NOTE

1. This position is the counterpose of Position 3.
2. It resembles Bhujangasana with the difference that here the elbows are kept straight and the knees, thighs and pelvis are raised slightly from the floor.

Position 8

Keep the palms and toes firmly on the floor in the same position. Start exhaling slowly. Pressing the hands and toes down on the floor and bending your head, raise your knees slowly and while raising them, lift your hips as high as possible without moving the toes and palms. While doing so, slant your arms backwards and straighten them. Pushing your hips further backwards and stretching the hamstrings, place your feet flat on the floor with both heels pressing the floor without strain. Arch your back and bring your head down between the upper arms in an effort to rest the chin on the chest. Keep the knees and elbows as rigid as possible. The abdomen must be drawn in. The legs and arms should be completely stretched and the body should be kept stiff from the palms to the feet. Look down at your navel. Complete the exhalation.

In this position, the whole body is raised and bent at the waist and a high backward arch is done. The legs, trunk and arms resemble an inverted 'V' and the whole body forms a triangle with the floor. The entire weight of the body is balanced on the hands and toes. Hold this position motionless for a few seconds, holding out your breath (Fig. 8).

Fig. 8

POINTS

1. Though various parts of the body are moved to attain this position, all the movements should be synchronized.

2. This position is the counterpose of Position 7 as the spine is bent in the opposite direction.
3. You will find that as the hips rise, the head goes down automatically.
4. Beginners may feel some strain in the arms, ankles, calves, thighs, the heel tendons (Achilles) and the muscles and ligaments behind the knees, but this will wear off with regular practise.
5. Your legs may tend to slide away at first, but this can be overcome after some practise.

BENEFITS

1. While assuming this position, the wrists, forearms, upper arms, shoulders, neck, back, abdomen, hips, hamstrings, calves, ankles and feet are limbered up.
2. The legs are stretched in different positions and their muscles, joints, tendons and ligaments are strengthened.
3. It relieves the pressure on the main veins in the legs and thus counteracts sciatica and varicose veins.
4. The sacral area of the spine becomes more supple.
5. This position stimulates the blood supply to the brain, scalp, face, heart and the internal organs.
6. It improves breathing as it opens and expands the chest.
7. It helps to relieve flatulence and digestive disorders.
8. It reduces tension in almost every part of the body.

Position 9

The return to the starting position begins with this position. Here, Position 4 is repeated backwards.

Inhale deeply (breath no. 5). Without bending the elbows or changing the position of the palms on the ground, bend the right leg slightly at the knee and sliding forward the right foot, place it flat on the floor about five inches behind the right arm which should be brought to a vertical position again along with the left arm. The right thigh should be kept very near the raised trunk and the right knee should be just a little ahead of the right arm. The right side of the right thigh should touch the vertical right arm.

Fig. 9

As the right foot is slided forward, your trunk and backside will lower themselves of their own accord. Bend your left knee and lowering your left leg, rest the toes firmly on the floor. Keep your left foot fixed perpendicularly on the floor. Hold the extended left leg as straight as possible, keeping the knee a little above the floor. The thigh and the foot of the extended left leg should be in line with the vertical left arm. Keep the palms and the right foot firmly on the floor. Raise your trunk and head up. Thrust forward your chest and stretch your head and neck as far back as possible, arching the spine to the maximum extent. Raise the chin as high as possible and look up. Support the weight of the body on both hands, the right foot and the toes of the left foot. Hold this position firmly until you complete the inhalation (Fig. 9).

Position 10

Return to Position 3 as follows: exhale slowly and while exhaling, fix the palms firmly on the floor. Bending the left knee, slide forward the left foot up to the right foot in line with it and place the sole flat on the floor about five inches behind the vertical left arm. While doing so, raise the hips high and pressing down the palms on the floor, bend forward from the waist and straighten up the legs without altering the position of the palms and the right foot on the floor.

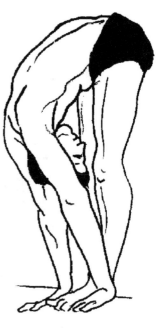

Fig. 10

Push back the pelvis and keep your palms and feet flat on the floor. Keep the arms vertical and the knees rigid. Bend down your head and keep it between the upper arms which should touch the ears. Draw in your abdomen and try to touch the knees with your forehead, avoiding any strain at the back of the thighs. Keep the legs straight and look up towards your waist. Hold this position motionless until you complete the exhalation (Fig. 10).

POINT

The feet and palms should be placed flat on the floor in the same places as in Position 3.

BENEFIT

The muscles at the front of the thighs are strengthened and the spine becomes flexible by assuming this position.

Position 11

Resume Position 2 as follows: inhale slowly and deeply (breath no. 6). While inhaling, bend the upper body backward slowly from the hips and come up to the standing position without bending the knees and elbows. While rising up, keep the inside of the upper arms touching the ears and bring the arms straight above the head. Turn the palms outwards with the fingers pointing upwards. Complete the inhalation and hold the breath. Without any pause, pull the arms backward and bend the body backward slowly from the waist without bending the elbows and knees, and pushing the abdomen and pelvis forward, make an anterior arch of the spine as before. Hold the head steadily between the upper arms and look back. Maintain this position firmly without strain for about five seconds, holding your breath (Fig. 11).

Fig. 11

Position 12

Finally, resume the first position as follows: exhale slowly and while exhaling, straighten the spine and lower the arms slowly. While the arms are being lowered, bring the hands to the middle of the chest and join the palms together in a prayerful gesture as you started. Complete the exhalation. Bring your arms down by your sides. Stand upright at ease and look straight ahead (Fig. 12).

This completes one round of Surya Namaskar. Relax for a few seconds and recover your breath before starting on the next round from the same position. Relax completely in Savasana after completing all the rounds.

Fig. 12

Advanced Students

Advanced students may keep their heels and toes together and place their palms flat on the floor on each side of the feet with fingertips in line with the toes. The rest of the practice is the same.

BENEFITS

The performance of Surya Namaskar brings several lifelong benefits. The following are a few:

1. Surya Namaskar is a general conditioning exercise. The entire body is exercised and revitalized by twelve simple and well-balanced movements.

2. It tones and limbers up the limbs and organs of the body in one complete set of movements. The limbs of the body become symmetrical by regular practise. The body also becomes light.

3. The muscles of the neck, shoulders, arms, legs, hips and abdomen become firm. Eye muscles also are brought into play.

4. Stiff joints get loosened. The wrists particularly benefit since the weight of the body falls mostly on them while the positions are changed from 3 to 10.

5. The movements stimulate the blood circulation and help to distribute the blood to all the organs of the body. They provide an excellent warm-up for the entire body.

6. All the nerve plexes benefit and so does the entire nervous system. The function of the brain also improves.

7. The performance of Namaskars harmonize the endocrine system.

8. The capacity of the lungs increases by the deep breathing. The action of the heart also improves without strain.

9. Surya Namaskar stretches the spine in several directions and makes it supple. It also relieves aches and pains in the spinal area.

10. Deviations of the spinal curve are corrected and a good posture ensured.

11. Surya Namaskar stretches and contracts the abdomen and relieves congestion of the abdominal viscera. The organs of the abdomen receive a good massage and function more efficiently.

12. It reduces excess fat in the abdomen, waist, thighs and other parts of the body. Blood cholesterol levels also decline.

13. Bowels function properly as the peristalsis is stimulated.

14. Several ailments and disorders such as indigestion and backache can be cured or prevented by the regular performance of Namaskars.

15. It removes psychosomatic tensions and calms the mind.

16. The performance of Namaskars increases the power of concentration and develops an attitude of reverence and devotion to the Supreme.

Note

1. Each Namaskar incorporates the principle of the following three Yoga postures within the sequence of the twelve movements: a) Talasana b) Pada Hastasana, and c) Bhujangasana.

2. There are several variations in the practise of this dynamic exercise. The one given here is based on yoga asanas combined with breathing.

3. Women should avoid this exercise during the menstrual period. Those in an advanced stage of pregnancy should also not do it until they get back to their normal state of health after delivery.

आरोग्य भास्करात् इच्छेत्

Sun is the bestower of health.

7

ASANAS

1. Padmasana
(The Lotus Posture)

ऊर्वोरुपरि वै धत्ते यदा पादतले उभे।
पद्मासनं भवेदेतत् सर्वव्याधिविषापहम् ।।

Set right foot on left thigh and left foot on right thigh.
This is Padmasana which removes all toxins and diseases.
—*Trisikhibrahmanopanishad (Mantrabhaga)* 39

'Padma' means 'lotus' in Sanskrit. 'Padmasana' means sitting in the 'Lotus Posture'. This posture is called Padmasana because the arrangement of the hands and feet resembles a lotus when seen from a distance. The two feet placed upon the opposite thighs resemble the leaves while the two hands placed one over the other resemble the lotus in full bloom.

- Set the right foot on the left thigh and the left foot on the right thigh. Knees should touch the ground. Rest palms one over the other on the upturned heels. Head, neck and spine should be held erect.

SEQUENCE

- Sit erect.
- Stretch out your legs in front of you and keep the heels together.
- Hold the right ankle with the right hand and the right big toe with the left hand. Bending the right knee outwards, pull round the right foot towards your left groin line. Set the foot firmly at the root of the left upper thigh. The heel should lightly press the left side of the lower abdomen. The foot must lie fully stretched over the left thigh with its sole turned upwards. Keep the right knee pressing the floor.
- Similarly, fold the left leg and place the foot firmly at the root of the right upper thigh. The foot must lie fully stretched over the right thigh with the sole turned upwards. Keep the left knee also pressing the floor.
- With both legs now interlocked, keep the spine, neck and head erect.
- Place one palm upon the other, both turned upward and cupped, and rest them on the upturned heels a little below the navel.
- Remain in this posture in perfect ease until you begin to be uncomfortable.
- Unlock the footlock. Stretch out your legs and return to the original sitting position.
- Practise alternating the legs.

TECHNIQUE

1. Sit on the carpet in Sukhasana, keeping the spine, neck and head erect. (Sukhasana is a comfortable sitting posture.)
2. Stretch out the legs loosely in front of you and keep the heels together. Keep the arms by the sides (Fig. 14).
3. Form a firm footlock as follows: fold the right leg slightly at the knee-joint. Holding the right ankle with the right hand and the right big toe with the left hand, lift the foot gently. Bending the right knee outwards towards the floor, bring the right foot up slowly over the left thigh near the fold of your left groin. Set the foot firmly high up on the left thigh in such a way that the side of the heel lightly presses the left side of the lower abdomen. The foot must lie fully stretched over the left thigh with the sole turned upwards. Keep the right knee pressing the floor without causing any strain.
4. When you feel comfortable, fold the left leg also slightly at the knee-joint in the same way without disturbing the position of the right foot. Holding the left ankle with the left hand and the left big toe with the right hand, slide the outer edge of the foot along the floor. Lifting the foot gently over the folded right leg, bring it up slowly over the right thigh near the fold of your right groin. Set the foot firmly high up on the right thigh at the right side of the lower abdomen. The foot of the left leg must lie fully stretched over the right thigh with the sole turned upwards. The left ankle will now cross over the right ankle in front of the genitals. Keep the left knee pressing the floor.

5. Adjust both heels in such a way that they are in a
    line and opposite each other and their ends almost
    meet in front of the pubic area slightly above the
    genitals. Each heel must press the adjacent portion
    of the abdomen on either side of the navel. The soles
    which are turned upwards must lie flat on the thighs
    horizontally. This completes the footlock; keep it
    tight.

6. With both legs now interlocked, press the knees down
    gently with the palms so that they touch the floor
    and remain there comfortably. Ensure that the back
    of the thighs touch the floor closely as long as the
    posture is maintained.

7. Stretch yourself up and keep the spine, neck and head
    erect. The abdomen should be relaxed and held in.

8. Place the right palm upon the left, both turned upward
    and cupped, and rest them on the upturned heels a
    little below the navel and a little above the place where
    the ankles cross each other. Fingers should be slightly
    bent and close together. The back of the right hand
    should rest on the palm of the left, and the back of the
    left hand should rest on the heels. The edges of the
    palms should touch the wall of the abdomen below
    the navel. Alternatively, the fingers may be interlaced
    and the locked hands may be placed centrally over
    the heels. This is the final position (Fig. 15).

9. Relax the body completely. Look straight at a
    particular spot at the eye level. Eyes may be closed if
    you like or they may be half-closed, focusing the gaze
    on the tip of the nose. Breathe normally.

10. Remain motionless and at perfect ease until you begin
    to feel uncomfortable.

11. **Release:** When your legs grow tired, unlock the foot-lock gently by holding your left ankle with both hands and lifting the foot off your right thigh. Stretch out your left leg fully on the floor as before and then your right leg. Return slowly to the original sitting position.

12. Practise alternating the legs which will develop them evenly.

BEGINNERS

1. Beginners may practise this asana along with other easier cross-legged postures which make the legs supple.

2. They should practise this asana daily several times at different times of the day, increasing the period for retaining it gradually until they are able to assume the posture easily.

3. Beginners will experience some pain in the knees, ankles, shins, thighs and hips and find it difficult to hold the final position, but as their legs adapt themselves to the posture after some practise, they will not feel any discomfort. In case of discomfort in the initial stages, they may stretch their legs for a while and start again. The legs can also be alternated in case of numbness or pain.

POINTS

1. Proceed with this asana slowly. In the initial stages, do not exert undue pressure on the legs or strain the muscles to attain the final position quickly.

2. Do not lean back while folding the legs.

3. After folding one leg and placing the foot on the opposite thigh, hold it firmly so that it does not move

from its position while the other leg is being folded. Do not lose your balance.

4. After folding one leg, bring the foot of the other leg towards the opposite thigh and take it further up near the opposite groin. The higher your feet are placed on the thighs, the easier it is for you to lower your knees to the floor.

5. The feet should be drawn so close that the heels press lightly against the portions of the lower abdomen where they touch.

6. Both legs should be symmetrically crossed and the footlock must be tight.

7. The upturned soles should maintain their position, like the petals of a full-blown lotus, as the name of the asana suggests.

8. Do not lift the knees from the floor while maintaining the posture.

9. Both knees should rest firmly on the floor so as to maintain stability. If they rise up in the air, press them down gently with the palms without causing strain and, in the course of time, they will touch the floor easily. Do not, however, force your knees further than they go.

10. In the beginning, only the knee of the bottom leg will touch the floor, but once it touches, both can be made to touch the floor easily by alternating the legs.

11. After taking the posture, increase the period for maintaining it gradually day by day until your joints tire. Regular practise will enable you to hold the posture comfortably for at least ten minutes at a time and even longer.

PADMASANA

Fig. 15—Final position with eyes closed.

ARDHA PADMASANA

Fig. 18—Right leg is on top.   Fig. 19—Left leg is on top.

BADDHA PADMASANA

Fig. 20—Front View.   Fig. 21—Back View.

12. You may keep your eyes fixed on any object in front of you. If this asana is practised for concentration and meditation, you may fix your gaze on the tip of the nose with your eyes half-closed (Fig. 16).

13. Jalandhara Bandha (chin-lock) is not necessary except for Pranayama with Kumbhaka in this posture.

CAUTION

1. Do not sit in this posture while eating food or immediately after taking it.

2. Persons having sciatica or varicose veins in the legs should attempt this posture cautiously.

BENEFITS

A. Physical

1. The important muscles, ligaments and tendons of the lower extremities are extended and flexed while sitting in Padmasana and relaxed when it is released.

2. This posture promotes a rich supply of blood to the organs in the pelvic and the abdomino-genital regions while the flow of blood to the lower extemities is limited. Since more blood is made to circulate in the lumbar region of the spine and the abdomen, the spine and the abdominal organs are toned up.

3. It firms up the coccygeal and sacral regions of the spine and the sciatic nerve. It also tones up the colon.

4. This posture strengthens the thighs and calves and provides elasticity to the hamstring muscles.

5. It limbers up stiff knees and ankles and improves the flexibility of the hip-joints. It relieves arthritic pain in these areas.

6. Minor spinal deformities are set right.

7. Padmasana develops the correct carriage of the body with perfect equilibrium since the spine has to be kept straight during the practise.

8. The erect spine prevents the compression of the abdominal viscera while sitting in this posture.

9. Sitting in Padmasana will help to reduce excess fat in the abdomen, buttocks and thighs.

B. Therapeutical

1. Padmasana helps to cure many heart and lung diseases and digestive disorders owing to the erect position of the body and improved respiration.

2. It helps to cure sciatica and rheumatism of the legs.

3. It prevents lumbago.

C. Spiritual

1. Padmasana is largely practised as a posture for meditation from ancient times.

2. It has a calming effect on the mind and helps to turn it inward.

3. Sitting in Padmasana will prevent laziness and drowsiness since the position of the crossed legs and the erect spine keeps the mind alert. It is easy to attain concentration and tranquillity of the mind.

4. During deep meditation, Padmasana and Siddhasana hold the body steady and prevent it from falling. Since the weight of the body is evenly distributed on the thighs and buttocks, the spine is kept erect and the shoulders do not sag forward. The body is balanced on a broad and fixed base and kept at rest.

5. In higher states of meditation, the practitioner will be able to sit firmly and comfortably in this posture

for a long time and the tendency to move the legs will be less. It will also help to free the mind from the consciousness of the body.

6. Padmasana is considered to be the most perfect posture for Pranayama. Since the lungs expand more fully, the breathing becomes rhythmical. The expansion and contraction of the abdominal and respiratory regions also become easier.

Note

1. Padmasana is one of the basic postures of yoga and is often used while practising several other asanas and their variations in which the legs are crossed.

2. A mastery of this classic asana makes the practise of other asanas easier.

3. This asana is difficult to perform by obese persons or those accustomed to sitting on chairs and may cause pain in the knees and ankle-joints. However, after taking the posture and practising it continuously, doing it will become easy and will result in several benefits irrespective of how long it is practised.

4. Practise sitting in this posture daily for three minutes or longer and increase the time up to ten minutes at a stretch or as long as it does not bring about cramps in the legs. It will take several months to attain perfection and sit at ease in this posture, but once mastered, it is the most comfortable and relaxing sitting position possible.

5. Apart from prayer, meditation and Pranayama, you may sit in the Full or Half Lotus Posture for short periods of time while reading, writing, doing office work or watching television. You can even make it a habit to sit in this posture whenever the opportunity

occurs. You may adopt this posture for any length of time without any harmful effect.

6. Advanced yoga students may practise Uddiyana, Mula and Jalandhara Bandhas all together while sitting in Padmasana.

Source

1. *Yogakundali Upanishad*: 1—5.
2. *Darsanopanishad*: III—5.
3. *Sandilyopanishad*: I—3.
4. *Hathapradipika*: I—45-49.
5. *Shiva Samhita*: III—88-91.
6. *Goraksha Samhita*: I—11.

2. Ardha Padmasana
(The Half-Lotus Posture)

एकं पादमथैकस्मिन् विन्यस्योरुणि संस्थितः ।
इतरस्मिंस्तथाचोरुं वीरासनमुदीरितम् ।।

Placing one foot on the other thigh and the other foot under the other thigh is known as Virasana.

—*Sandilyopanisad* Ch. I Sec. 3, Verse 4.

'Ardha' means 'half' and 'Padma' means 'lotus' in Sanskrit. Those who are unable to assume the full Padmasana posture using both legs as described above owing to the stiffness of their legs or bulky thighs may begin practising with one leg at a time alternately until they are able to develop the full posture. With the practise of this asana daily, they will be able to take that posture for a long time without discomfort and switch on to the full Padmasana posture after sufficient practise.

SEQUENCE

- Sit erect in Sukhasana.
- Stretch out the legs in front of you.

- Set the right foot firmly at the root of the left thigh with the sole turned upward.
- Set the left foot beneath the right thigh with the sole turned upward.
- Both knees must touch the ground.
- Rest the palms comfortably on the respective knees and sit erect.
- Practise alternating the legs.

TECHNIQUE

1. Sit erect on the carpet in Sukhasana.
2. Stretch out the legs fully in front of you and keep the heels a little apart (Fig.14).
3. Fold the right leg slightly at the knee-joint. Take hold of the right ankle with the right hand and the right big toe with the left hand. Bending the right knee towards the floor, bring the foot up slowly towards your body and set it firmly at the root of the left thigh with the sole turned upwards and without changing the position of the extended left leg. The heel should lightly press the left side of the lower abdomen and

Fig. 14.

Fig. 17.

the back portion of the foot should rest on the left thigh (Fig. 17).

4. Press down the bent right knee gently with your palm so that it remains touching the ground.

5. Fold the left leg slightly at the knee-joint. Take hold of the left ankle with the left hand and the left big toe with the right hand. Bending the left knee outwards towards the floor, slide the outer edge of the foot along the floor and draw it gently towards the right calf. Slightly raise the right thigh and place the left foot beneath the right thigh in a comfortable position with its sole turned upward. The back portion of the left foot should lie straight along the floor. The left knee should also touch the floor closely.

6. Place the right palm on the right knee and the left palm on the left knee with fingers close together.

7. Keep the head, neck and spine erect. Look straight ahead (Figs 18 and 19).

8. Remain motionless and relaxed in this position as long as you feel comfortable.

9. Stretch out your legs and return to the starting position of Sukhasana slowly and without any jerks. Stretch out your left leg first and then your right.

10. Repeat changing the position of the legs.

BENEFITS

The benefits of Padmasana also accrue from this posture, although to a limited extent.

Note

1. The technique of this asana is similar to Padmasana.

2. Performing the Ardha Padmasana makes it easier to do the more difficult Full Padmasana as it makes the hip-joints, knees and ankles more flexible.

3. Everyone can practise this asana. You may sit in this position as long as you wish and even make it a regular sitting posture. It is also suitable for meditation.

4. This asana is also known as 'Virasana' or the 'Hero' posture.

Source

1. *Gheranda Samhita*: II—17.
2. *Hatharatnavali*: III—53.

3. Baddha Padmasana
(Locked Lotus Posture)

पद्मासनं सुसंस्थाप्य तदङ.गुष्ठद्वयं पुनः ।
व्युत्क्रमेणैव हस्ताभ्यां बद्धपद्मासनं भवेत ।।

Having well established the Padmasana posture, one should hold the two big toes with two hands stretched crosswise. This is Baddha Padmasana.

—Trisikhibrahmanopanisad (Mantrabhaga) 39–40.

वामोरुपरि दक्षिणं च चरणं संस्थाप्य वामं तथा
दक्षोरुपरि, पश्चिमेन विधिना ध त्वा कराभ्यां द ढम् ।
अङ.गुष्ठौ, हृदये निधाय चिबुकं नासाग्रमालोकयेत्
एतद्व्याधिविनाशकारि यमिनां पद्मासनं प्रोच्यते ।

Fix the right foot on the left thigh and the left foot on the right thigh. Hold the big toes by both hands, one by one, crossing the arms behind the back. Fix the chin on the chest. Gaze at the tip of the nose. This is called (Baddha) Padmasana which destroys all diseases of yogis.

—Hatha Pradipika I—44.

'**B**addha' means 'bound' or 'locked-up' in Sanskrit. The limbs of the body (both arms and legs) are firmly 'locked-up' and immobilized in this posture so as to give it steadiness.

In this posture, the big toes are grasped by the fingers with arms crossed from behind.

TECHNIQUE

1. Assume the Padmasana posture, placing the feet high on the thighs, close towards the groin.

2. Extend you right arm behind your back and reach round until your right hand is near the left hip. Lean forward a little. Twisting the trunk to the right, catch hold of the right big toe resting on the left thigh firmly with the forefinger and the middle finger. Sit erect and hold the position for a few seconds.

3. Similarly, extend your left arm behind your back and crossing the right forearm, reach round until your left hand is near the right hip. Lean forward a little. Twisting the trunk to the left and bringing the shoulder blades together, catch hold of the left big toe resting on the right thigh firmly with the forefinger and the middle finger. Sit erect and hold the position for a few seconds. The arms and legs are now firmly locked-up.

4. Keep the spine, neck and head erect. Draw in the abdomen. Both knees must press the ground. Look straight ahead. Breathe normally. This is the final position (Figs. 20 & 21).

5. Maintain this posture motionless for about ten seconds or as long as you are comfortable.

6. Release the hands and unlock the footlock. Stretch out the legs again and assume the normal sitting position.

7. Practise the same, alternating the legs.

POINTS

1. Practise this asana only after mastering Padmasana as it demands a high degree of skill.
2. After assuming the Padmasana posture, catch first the big toe of the foot which is uppermost. When you try to catch the other one, push the shoulder blades towards each other slightly; lean the trunk forward. After catching it, resume the erect position. Once you succeed in catching the big toes, the practice will become easy.
3. Grasp the right big toe with the fingers of the right hand and the left with the fingers of the left hand.
4. Beginners who find it difficult to catch both the toes simultaneously, may catch only one toe and after releasing it, catch the other. By repeating thus several times each day, their shoulder-joints will become more flexible and they will be able to catch both toes easily at the same time.
5. Increase the period for maintaining the asana gradually up to ten seconds, or as long as it is comfortable.
6. You may do Jalandhara Bandha in this asana to enhance the benefit.

BENEFITS

1. The benefits of Padmasana also accrue from Baddha Padmasana and bring greater flexibility to the legs.
2. The stubborn joints of the shoulders, elbows, wrists, lower back, hips, knees, ankles and toes are well stretched and become more supple.

3. Crossing the arms behind the back and pulling the toes expands the ribcage and opens up the chest. The intercostal muscles are also exercised.
4. The asana increases the range of the shoulder movements.
5. Pain in the shoulders and back is alleviated.
6. This asana keeps the body fit and virile and prevents many diseases of the abdomen.
7. It improves the posture by rectifying any unnatural curvature of the spine.

Note

1. Persons with a bulging belly will find practising the Baddha Padmasana difficult, but with persistent effort, everybody can practise it, whether lean or fat, young or old.
2. Pregnant women must not practise this asana.
3. Advanced students may do Yoga Mudra in this asana.
4. The description of Baddha Padmasana is found under the name 'Padmasana' in many classical textbooks of yoga.

Source

1. *Darsanopanisad*: III—4–5.
2. *Gheranda Samhita*: II—8.
3. *Hatharatnavali*: III—33.
4. *Goraksha Samhita*: I—11.

4. Paschimotanasana
(The Posterior Stretch)

प्रसार्य पादौ भुवि दण्डरूपौ दोर्भ्यां पदाग्रद्वितयं ग हीत्वा ।
जानूपरिन्यस्तललाटदेशो वसेदिदं पश्चिमतानमाहुः ।।

Having stretched the legs on the ground, like sticks, and having grasped the toes of both feet with both the hands, when one sits with his forehead resting on the knees, it is called paschimotana.

—Hatha Pradipika I—28.

'Paschima' means 'behind', 'back' or 'posterior' and 'Uttana' means 'stretch out' in Sanskrit. 'Paschimotana' means 'stretching the posterior regions' of the body.

- Sit erect.
- Stretch our your legs. Keep knees straight throughout.
- Bend your trunk and head forward from the waist. Reach forward and grasp each big toe with the hooks of the fingers of each hand.
- Pulling the big toes, bend forward further and rest the elbows on the floor.
- Rest the forehead on the knees.

- Release.

SEQUENCE

- Sit upright in Sukhasana.
- Stretch your legs straight out and keep them together. Place the palms on the respective knees.
- Bend your trunk and head slowly forward and downward from the waist. While doing this, slide forward the hands along the shins and grasp the corresponding big toes with the index finger, middle finger and thumb of each hand without bending the knees.
- Keep the head between the upper arms and pull the big toes steadily. While doing so, bend further forward, curve the spine and aim your forehead towards the knees.
- Bend the arms and rest the elbows gradually on the floor. Using the elbows as levers, rest your forehead on the knees which should not be raised or bent.
- Stay in this posture for a few seconds or as long as you are comfortable.
- Return slowly in the reverse order to the starting position.

TECHNIQUE

1. Sit upright on the carpet in Sukhasana, keeping the head, neck and spine erect.
2. Stretch your legs straight out in front of you and keep them close together so that the back, neck and head are at right angles to the legs. Heels should be kept close together. Point your feet at the ceiling and turn the toes inward. Keep the knees straight. The back

of the legs and knees should touch the floor closely.
Keep the palms on the floor on the respective sides
(Fig.14).

3. Place the palms
on the respective
knees with fingers
close together and
pointing forward
(Fig. 22). Breathe
normally and
relax the body,
specially the neck
and back muscles,
completely.

Fig. 22.

4. Keep your legs
fixed firmly to
the floor and stiff
like sticks. Bend
your trunk and
head slowly
forward and
downward from
the waist over
the stretched

Fig. 23.

legs. At the same time, slide your hands down the
front of your legs towards the feet until the
outstretched fingers reach the respective toes slowly
by stages. Hook the index finger, middle finger and
thumb of each hand and grasp the corresponding big
toes in these hooks slowly without bending the knees
or lifting the legs from the floor (Fig. 23). The grip on
the big toes must be full and tight. Press your legs
down on the floor. Feel comfortable in this position
and relax the body completely again.

5. Keep the head between the upper arms and relax the
    back and abdominal muscles. Bending the trunk and
    head forward again slowly from the waist, pull the
    big toes steadily and while pulling them, stretch the
    muscles at the back of the legs without lifting them,
    and keep the knees straight. Pause for a few seconds.

6. Take a deep
    breath and
    exhale slowly.
    While exhaling,
    tighten the legs
    and pull your
    body forward
    and downward
    again slowly to
    stretch the spine.

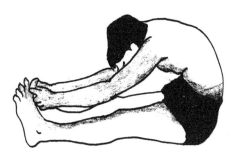

Fig. 24.

    Lower the head down as far as you can towards the
    knees, drawing in your abdominal muscles gently still
    grasping and pulling the big toes and keeping the
    knees straight. Avoid bouncing and jerks while
    bending down and curving the spine (Fig. 24).

7. Start inhaling and exhaling freely. During each
    exhalation, pull the toes lightly, and drawing in your
    abdomen, bend forward your head and the whole
    trunk from the hip-joints little by little without any
    strain or jerk; relax the back muscles at every stage
    of the bend and push the back of the knees firmly
    against the floor. While bending forward, bend the
    arms also gently at the elbows. Allow your elbows
    to bend outwards a little as they come down and
    rest them gradually on the floor, touching either side
    of the legs near the knee-joints.

8. Using the elbows as levers and relaxing the muscles of the waistline, stretch your spine to its fullest extent without straining it and bring down your abdomen and chest towards the thighs while arching your back slowly. Complete the stretch by lowering your head slowly and resting your forehead gently on the knees which should not be raised or bent. Hold the trunk as close as possible to the thighs, keeping the back arched and without the chest caving in. Keep the head steady between the upper arms and fix your gaze on the navel. Straighten the legs to their full extent and keep them flat on the floor. Keep the muscles of the neck, back and arms as relaxed as possible. The body will now be folded in two through the hip-joints and this completes the spinal curve. This is the final position in which the lower spine also is fully stretched (Fig. 25).

9. Exhale completely and holding out your breath, stay in this posture comfortably and motionlessly for about ten seconds. Do not allow the body to become tense. Concentrate your mind on the tip of the spinal cord.

10. **Return:** When you feel like inhaling, return slowly and smoothly in the reverse order to the starting position as follows: relax the pull of the fingers on the toes. Remove the hold on the toes and relax the trunk. Start inhaling and slowly bend back the trunk and head, at the same time straightening the elbows and sliding the hands backwards over the shins towards the knees. While doing this, allow your spine to curl back slowly in one continuous movement and complete the inhalation. Straighten up your spine,

neck and head and sit upright again with the legs still stretched forward and the palms resting on the knees. Freely exhale and inhale until your breathing returns to normal. Relax completely and take several breaths to recover before repeating the asana. After completing the turns, draw back the legs and resume the starting position of Sukhasana and finally relax the whole body in Savasana.

BREATHING

1. Breathe normally throughout this practice in the initial stages. Until you master the practice, take several extra breaths before reaching the final position, bending down during each exhalation or while holding out your breath, whichever is more comfortable. This will enable you to advance forward a little more every time you exhale. Inhale slowly while you raise yourself and resume the sitting position.

2. Since bending is easier during exhalations or while the breath is held out, make the most of every exhalation.

3. Advanced students who can maintain the posture comfortably for about half a minute, should breathe slowly, deeply and rhythmically during the period.

4. Breathing in this posture will be slightly deeper than normal owing to the bent position of the trunk and head, but do not force the pace of breathing.

5. Do not hold your breath during inhalation at any time.

6. After prolonged practise, your breathing will adjust itself naturally.

MEASURE

1. In the initial stages, you may take three turns, maintaining the posture for a minimum period of ten seconds. Increase the holding period gradually up to twenty seconds or as long as you can hold your breath comfortably.

2. In the advanced stage, take only one turn, holding the posture from fifteen to thirty seconds according to your capacity.

3. As your spine becomes fully elastic and you become relaxed in this posture, take only one turn with the total holding period ranging from fifteen seconds to half a minute according to the ease with which you can prolong the holding period, but do not exceed this limit. To avoid discomfort while maintaining the posture, lift your head a little, inhale slowly and exhaling, place your forehead on the knees again and breathe freely.

POINTS

A. General

1. Take your muscles into confidence by giving an auto-suggestion to them while performing this asana.

2. Before starting the asana, loosen up the body and perform it quickly three times, exhaling while taking the posture and inhaling while getting back to the starting position, then repeat it.

3. Practise this asana slowly and by stages, all the posterior muscles should be stretched. With regular practise, the spine will begin to show improved elasticity and the hamstring muscles (at the back of the knees) will be able to bear the strain better. With

PASCHIMOTANASANA

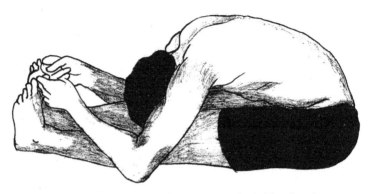

Fig. 25 (A)—Bending down the trunk and head and
curving the spine.

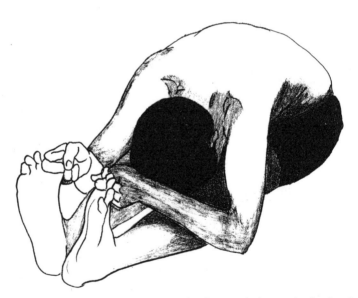

Fig. 25 (B)—Resting the elbows on the floor and placing the forehead
on the knees.

PASCHIMOTANASANA

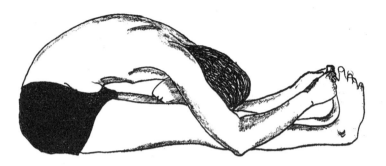

Fig. 25 (C)—Final Position (Side View).

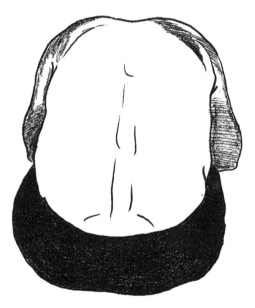

Fig. 25 (D)—Final Position (Back View).

continued practise, the muscles of the thighs, calves and the back will also get loosened and the stiff joints become more supple. With patience and perseverence, the elasticity of the muscles improves gradually, ultimately making the full posture not only possible but also comfortable and easy.

4. The muscles of the back must be kept relaxed throughout this asana.

5. All movements should be smooth and gentle: do this asana slowly and in a relaxed manner. Avoid jerky movements.

6. Do not bend forward with abrupt and repetitive movements since the back muscles will not remain passive and relaxed.

7. Put up with the little strain involved in the practice. It will do no harm and will condition the muscles in due course.

8. Initially, there may be a little pain in the back and the back portion of the knees and the thighs while maintaining the posture. The pain disappears after a week or two of regular practise and the relief you get from stretching the spine amply compensates for the pain. If the pain is excessive at times, relax in Savasana and try again the next day.

B. Getting into the posture

1. Catch hold of the big toes firmly and bend forward slowly. Catching the big toes with the hooks of the index finger and thumb is the traditional practice, but you may catch them with the thumb, index and middle fingers hooked together as this is more effective. To help catch the big toes, you may bend

the toes back towards you, at the same time pushing the heels away from you.

2. If beginners and pot-bellied persons experience difficulty in reaching their toes, they may grasp the portion of the legs just above the ankles and nearer the knees without bending the knees. If even this is too difficult owing to exceptional stiffness of the body, they may grasp the farthest part of their extended legs that is easiest to reach like their shins, knees or thighs. With practise, their spine will become more supple and the ligaments in the back of their thighs will stretch. After mastering the posture, they may grasp the big toes as stated earlier.

3. Heels must be extended and kept close together to facilitate bending.

4. The back of the knees should be close to the floor during the asana.

5. Knees should be kept stiff and straight and should not be raised or bent at any stage during the asana both by beginners and the advanced students though initially this may be difficult. This is crucial because straight knees are essential for securing and maintaining the full stretch of the lumbo-sacral region of the spine. Any error in this respect should be rectified gradually by tightening the muscles at the back of the thighs and pulling the trunk forward. Practising this asana while keeping the knees on the ground will also loosen the joints.

6. When you bend, keep the head between the upper arms and drop it downward gently with each exhalation. Do not hold it stiffly.

7. Relax all muscles completely while bending forward, particularly the muscles of the back, neck, shoulders and arms. This will make them flexible and enable you to bend further without strain.

8. Bend the trunk slowly and gently without straining any part. It will yield by itself in due course.

9. After catching hold of the big toes, allow the trunk to drop forward slowly, little by little and of its own accord. Let gravity do the work.

10. Do not be tense while bending. 'Let go' your trunk and head with each exhalation.

11. Do not allow the trunk and head to sway up and down and avoid any backward movement.

12. Do not tug at the toes or whichever part of the leg you are grasping. Do not struggle with your shoulders, hands or legs. Use your body's weight to help you bring the head closer to the knees, rather than tugging or forcing it.

13. While bending the trunk and head, straighten the legs as much as possible and keep them flat on the floor so that the spine is curved and stretched to its fullest extent.

14. Press the knees down and tighten the frontal thighs while bending forward.

15. Bending the elbows outward while pulling forward will enable you to pull more effectively, but do not widen the elbows too much. In the beginning, it will be difficult to get the elbows to the floor but in the long run, they will rest easily on the floor, touching either side of the legs.

16. Do not relax your hold on the toes during the asana but avoid pulling them too much which may cause soreness of the muscle.

17. The importance of this asana lies in the forward bending which stretches the back muscles, and not in getting the head on the knees.

18. Bring down the trunk forward over the legs in smooth movements; first the abdomen, then the chest, and finally the forehead. Bend right down from the sacral region of the spine, not from the middle or the shoulders, and work towards the cervical region. Do not round your shoulders while bending forward.

19. To get the forehead right down to the knees may present quite a problem in the beginning but the only answer to this is practise. Bend as low as you can, pulling yourself forward and downward a little farther each day without straining yourself. It may take several weeks or even months to reach the final position. All temptations to reach the final stage quickly should be avoided both by beginners and the advanced students. Forcing the pace to reach the final position may lead to spasm in the back muscles.

20. Bend forward only as far as flexibility admits. Hold on to the new position each time you inhale and gradually increase the period to maintain it at every stage. This will enable you to go a little way farther each time without strain.

21. Do not despair if you cannot get your forehead anywhere near your knees in the earlier stages. Go as far down as you can reach, a little more each day, aiming your forehead at the knees. You will be able to touch your knees with your forehead as your abdomen becomes more slender and your spine more supple.

22. In the advanced stage, you may bury your face in the hollow between the knees, stretching the back

and neck muscles and without bending the knees. Pulling the toes tightly, place the lower abdomen and chest on the thighs and the forehead on the shins up to three inches away from the knees.

C. Maintenance

1. In the final position, rest your forehead gently on the knees.
2. Keep your toes pointing up while maintaining the posture.
3. Eyes may be closed if it is comfortable.
4. Do not gulp down saliva during the period while maintaining the posture.
5. Be relaxed and comfortable in the final position and do not allow the body to become tense.

D. Return

1. Do not release the posture suddenly and get back to the starting position quickly. Unbend the spine slowly and gently while returning.
2. While returning, raise the body gradually until the upper part of the back is straight first, followed by the middle, and then the lower part. Raise the head first, then the chest and stomach, keeping the spine straight.

E. Caution

1. Perform Paschimotanasana on an empty stomach.
2. Persons who have back trouble or have undergone any abdominal operation should practise this asana only on the advice of a doctor who is knowledgeable about yoga.
3. Persons who have slipped disc or hernia and women who are pregnant must not practise this asana.

VARIATION

TECHNIQUE

1. Lie flat on your back at full length on the carpet.
    Stretch out your legs fully and keep them straight
    and together. Heels too should be kept close together.
    Toes should point upwards. Keep the arms on their
    respective sides with the palms turned down. Breathe
    normally and relax the body completely.

2. Slowly raise your outstretched arms straight over your
    head. Stretch them out on the floor behind and beyond
    your head as far as possible and keep them parallel to
    each other at shoulder width. The inside of the upper
    arms should touch the ears. Keep the palms upturned
    with fingers close together and the back of the palms
    resting on the floor. You now lie in a straight line from
    the fingertips to the heels (Fig. 26). Breathe normally.
    Relax the body completely.

3. Keep the heels, legs and thighs firmly on the floor
    and stiffen the upper part of your body.

Fig. 26.

4. Keeping the upper arms touching the ears and the
    arms firmly held above the head, raise the upper half
    of the body very slowly from the waist in one flowing
    movement until you assume a sitting position as
    follows: keep your arms, trunk and legs in line. Exhale

completely. Inhale slowly and deeply and hold your breath. Pressing down your heels and the posterior and contracting the muscles of the abdomen, raise your arms, shoulders, head and trunk very slowly all together from the waist, the upper arms touching the ears all along. While the arms move upwards in a continuous arc, keep them straight with the palms facing outwards and the knees rigid. Keep the legs steady and only the upper half of the body should move.

5. Still holding your breath, continue to bend forward slowly, keeping the inside of the upper arms touching the ears and the heels pressing the floor. When your upper back and head rise to an angle of about 45 degrees from the floor and you have come up to a half-sitting position, start exhaling slowly and lower your arms, head and trunk all together gradually towards your legs which should be kept straight and together. While you pass through the sitting position with your arms and head lowering towards the legs, balance on your posterior and legs and focus your eyes on the tips of your fingers.

6. Still exhaling slowly, continue to lower your arms, head and trunk gradually towards your legs, with a curling motion of the spine. While bending over the legs, draw in your abdomen and keep your oustretched legs straight and stiff with the heels pressing the floor. The knees should not be raised or bent. As soon as your fingers reach forward and touch the toes, focus your eyes on the big toes. Grasp the corresponding big toes with the hooks of the fingers, as stated above. Ensure that the whole length remains

as rounded as possible. You are now in a sitting position with the trunk and head bent forward. Inhale slowly and take a few normal breaths while in this sitting position.

The technique for the rest of the asana is the same as described above.

7. **Return:** Slowly return to the starting position in the reverse order, without bending the arms and legs, in one single movement and not in a rapid series of jerks. Relax the pressure on the toes by releasing the fingers. Inhale slowly and while inhaling, slowly bend back the head and trunk together, keeping the arms straight with the inside of the upper arms touching the ears. When the arms come perpendicular to the floor, (Fig. 27) start exhaling slowly. While exhaling, push down

hard with the heels and bend your head, trunk and arms all together further backwards very slowly and smoothly until the whole of your back rests on the floor first and then your head and arms. As you slowly lower your back to the floor, keep the movement under control. After lying flat on your back again, inhale slowly and breathe normally a few times. Bring back the arms to their respective sides and relax completely. This completes one turn. Take three turns.

Fig. 27.

POINTS FOR VARIATION

1. Perform the variation of this asana in slow motion without bouncing or stopping at any stage.
2. Use your abdominal muscles while pulling yourself up to the sitting position though initially a little swing of the arms will help to give the needed impetus.
3. Control your movements, particularly when you lower your trunk and head. Even as a beginner, lower yourself back very slowly and do not flop back.
4. Keep your arms and legs straight throughout the asana.
5. Breathe normally in the initial stages. After mastering the asana, breathe as stated earlier.
6. Do not bend the knees or allow your heels to leave the floor at any stage.
7. While returning, keep your heels together firmly on the floor to prevent you from rocking right back and thus returning too soon. Do not raise your legs from the floor.
8. While assuming the sitting position in the first stage of this practice, physically weak persons and beginners may stretch their arms on the sides and use their elbows as props until their abdominal muscles have gained sufficient strength.

Note

This variation of Paschimotanasana is a counterpose to Bhujangasana as it works on the spine in an opposite direction.

BENEFITS

A. Physical

1. Paschimotanasana is a fine stretching exercise for the back of the whole body, from the heels to the top of the spine. In one continuous movement, almost all the posterior muscles of the body, particularly the hamstring muscles at the back of the thighs and the muscles of the small of the back, are fully stretched and relaxed. The muscles of the neck, chest, shoulders, the spinal column, hips and the recti are also brought into play.

2. This asana stretches the spine to its maximum length, which makes it supple and flexible. The lumbo-sacral region, the seat of many disorders, is also kept in good shape.

3. Maintaining this posture for a fairly long time massages the heart and the abdominal organs.

4. This asana stretches the ribcage and its regular practise will expand the lungs more.

5. The nerves connected with the pelvic organs and those arising from the lumbo-sacral region of the spine are toned up.

6. On account of the extra stretching of the pelvic region, it gets more oxygenated blood.

7. The stomach, liver, kidneys, spleen, pancreas, bladder, the recti, the rectum and the prostate along with their nerves are supplied with abundant blood which tones them up. The uterus and the ovaries in women also benefit.

8. The adrenals and the gonad glands absorb the required nutrition from the blood and are reactivated.

9. The solar plexus is gently stimulated and freed from congestion.

10. By compressing the abdomen, the internal organs become firm.

11. The practise of this asana improves digestion and the peristaltic action of the bowels.

12. The joints of the arms, elbows, shoulders, legs, knees, ankles and hips become more elastic.

13. Regular practise of this asana will prevent the early ossification of the ribs.

14. This asana is good for reducing fatty deposits in the abdomen, hips, backside and thighs. Obese persons may repeat it as many times as possible to reduce their waist and protruding belly.

15. The loins and the waist get into good shape. The legs also become firm and develop evenly.

16. This asana rectifies minor postural defects and deformities in the curvature of the spine, and helps a person to attain his full stature.

B. Therapeutical

1. Paschimotanasana gives relief in cases of sciatica, muscular rheumatism of the back, backache, lumbago, slipped disc and asthmatic attacks.

2. It is a good remedy for constipation, dyspepsia, flatulence, belching, hiccoughs and digestive disturbances.

3. It can be recommended for the enlargement or sluggishness of the liver and spleen.

4. It will check the development of piles and prevent several functional disorders of the intestines.

5. Diabetic patients may practise this asana with advantage as it activates the pancreas.

6. Daily practise of this asana helps to cure impotency and seminal weakness, increases vitality, and enhances the power of sex control.

7. It will help to overcome several menstrual disorders.

Note

1. Paschimotanasana is a demanding posture, but all persons of normal health can practise it and women will find performing it easier then men.

2. Beginners may think that it is far beyond their capacity. Obese persons will find the movements very challenging and almost impossible at first, while lean persons with an elastic spine and posterior muscles will be able to do it with ease. Even fat persons will be able to do it if they practise slowly and steadily by stages, though in the beginning, they may not be able to touch their toes with their fingers. They should at first reduce the excess fat in their abdomen through restrictions in their diet and doing Bhujangasana, Shalabhasana and Dhanurasana and then practise this asana.

3. Those who find it difficult to do this asana because of an abnormally big abdomen or stiff joints may practise Janusirasana for some weeks which will make this asana easier for them.

4. If you discipline your body to practise this asana correctly, doing many other asanas will become easy.

5. Practise Ardha Matsyendrasana, Paschimotanasana and Ushtrasana one after the other to get the maximum benefit as the spine is stretched sideways, forward and backward in these three postures.

Source

1. *Gheranda Samhita*: II—26.
2. *Hatha Ratnavali*: III—65–6.

5. Trikonasana
(The Triangle Posture)

'Tri' means 'three', 'Kona' means 'angle', and 'Trikona' means 'triangle' in Sanskrit. The straight legs with the floor between the feet resemble the three sides of a triangle in this asana. Hence the name.

- Stand erect. Feet well apart.
- Stretch your arms out to the sides at shoulder level.
- Rotate trunk and head together to the side.
- Bend down and rest the fingertips of one hand on the opposite big toe. Stretch the other arm straight up perpendicularly.
- Look up at the raised fingertips and then at the toe and again at the raised fingertips.
- Release.

SEQUENCE

- Stand erect. Keep the feet sufficiently apart.
- Inhaling, raise and stretch out your arms sideways to shoulder level and parallel to the floor with palms

facing downward. Exhale slowly and breathe normally a few times.

- Take a deep breath. Exhaling slowly, rotate the trunk and head together from the waistline all the way around to the left without moving the feet or changing the position of the arms, and complete the exhalation. Hold this position for a few seconds while holding out your breath.

- Take a deep breath again. Exhaling slowly, extend your right arm downward towards the left big toe without bending the knees. While the right arm is moving downward, bend down your head and trunk slowly to the left from the waist. Rest the fingertips of the right hand on the left big toe. Raise and stretch your left arm straight up and bring it in line with your lowered right arm, keeping the left palm turned inwards.

- Holding out your breath, turn your head to the left and look up quickly at the fingertips of your left hand.

- Still holding out the breath, again turn your head downwards and look down quickly on the left big toe and look up at the fingertips of the raised hand a second time.

- Maintain this position as long as you can comfortably hold out your breath.

- Inhaling, release the right hand, twist the trunk and head back and rise up slowly to the erect standing position, lowering the left arm to the shoulder level and rotating the right arm sideways up to shoulder level in a wide circle. This is the starting position. Exhale slowly and take a few normal breaths.

- Repeat the whole exercise, twisting the trunk and head to the right.

TECHNIQUE

1. Stand erect. Keep the feet sufficiently apart with the toes slightly turned out. Adjust the distance between the feet according to your height and build (approximately one half the height of your body). Keep the arms at their respective sides, palms touching the sides of the thighs with fingers pointing downwards.

2. With the feet correctly positioned, inhale slowly and deeply. While inhaling, raise and stretch out your arms on the sides slowly to the shoulder level and parallel to the floor. Arms should be held in a straight line with fingers stretched out. Keep the elbows stiff and the palms facing downward. Keep the head erect and look straight ahead.

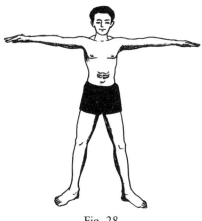

Fig. 28.

Exhale slowly and breathe normally a few times. This is the starting position (Fig. 28) and you have to return to this position after each turn while changing from right to left and left to right.

3. Hold your head in the same position. Keep the knees stiff and both feet firmly on the floor. Inhaling deeply, stretch your arms as far out as possible and keep the body upright.

4. Start exhaling slowly. While
    exhaling, slowly rotate
    your trunk, shoulders and
    head simultaneously from
    the waist to your left to the
    maximum extent without
    moving the feet or changing
    the position of the arms and
    complete the exhalation.
    The hips also will be twisted
    to the left. Move your arms
    as far around to the left as

Fig. 29.

you can without straining and hold them out in line
with your shoulders (Fig. 29). Maintain this position
motionless for a few seconds while holding out the
breath. Avoid any forward movement of the body
while assuming this position.

5. Keep the legs straight and feet
    firmly planted on the floor.
    Inhale deeply and then exhale
    slowly. While exhaling, extend
    your right arm downward
    towards the left big toe
    without bending the knees.
    While the right arm is moving
    downward, bend down your
    head and trunk slowly to the
    left from the waist, keeping the
    abdomen pulled in (Fig. 30).

Fig. 30.

Rest the fingertips of the right
hand on the left big toe. Raise and stretch your left
arm straight up perpendicular to the floor and in line

with the lowered right arm, keeping the left palm turned inwards. Both arms should be in line with the shoulders. Complete the exhalation.

6. Keep both arms fully stretched out with the palms turned in opposite directions to each other. Holding out your breath, turn your head gently to the left and look up quickly at the fingertips of your left hand, held high directly overhead with fingers opened out. Keep your left shoulders and elbow rigid and the knees straight.

7. Still holding out your breath, again turn the head downwards and look down quickly on the left big toe and look up at the fingertips of the raised hand a second time. Knees should be held straight while making these movements and the raised left arm must not be altered from its perpendicular position. This is the final position (Fig. 31A).

8. Maintain this final position motionlessly for about ten seconds or as long as you can comfortably hold out your breath, concentrating your mind on the spinal muscles. Keep the whole body stretched.

9. **Return:** Get back to an upright standing position very slowly as follows: keep your feet in the same position. Start inhaling slowly and deeply. While inhaling, release the right hand and twist the trunk and head back and rise up slowly to an erect standing position again, lowering the left arm to shoulder level and bringing the right arm sideways up to shoulder level in a wide circle. When the inhalation is complete, exhale slowly and take a deep breath followed by a few normal breaths. Keep the arms still stretched out sideways with the palms turned down, keeping the

same distance between the feet. Remain standing upright and relax for a few seconds (Fig. 28).

10. Go through the same movements, twisting the trunk and head to the right and following the same technique as follows: extend the left arm downward and rest the fingertips on the right big toe and raise the right arm up perpendicularly. Stay in the final position for the same length of time (Fig. 31B).

Fig. 31 (A)—
Final position. Trunk and head are twisted to the left. Left arm is raised up.

Fig. 31 (B)—
Final position. Trunk and head are twisted to the right. Right arm is raised up.

11. The two movements, one on the right and one on the left, should be considered as one turn. Take three turns on each side, alternating the sides. At the end of each turn, take several breaths to recover after bringing your arms back to a lateral position at shoulder level.

12. Following the final repetition, return to the basic starting position by lowering the arms gradually to the sides and bringing the feet together. Relax finally in Savasana.

BREATHING

Beginners should breathe normally. When you have made progress, inhale slowly and deeply while you stretch your arms sideways on a level with the shoulders. Exhale slowly and completely while twisting the trunk sideways. Hold out your breath while you touch the big toe, look up at the fingertips and look down again on the big toe. Inhale slowly and deeply while getting up to resume the starting position. Take several breaths to recover before making another attempt.

POINTS

1. Perform the movements of this asana gracefully and rhythmically, pausing for a while in each position. Perform very slowly and avoid abrupt movements and strain.

2. To find the optimum distance between the legs, stand with your feet together and see how long a stride forward you can take without lifting the heel of the rear foot from the floor. This distance will be optimal for most people.

3. After stretching your arms laterally, make sure that they make a straight line with your shoulders. They should be held out in a straight line with the shoulders in the final position also.

4. While twisting the trunk sideways, the arms and head must be held in position and they must not move or tilt.

5. The entire spine, starting from the low back, should be twisted gently.

6. While bending down and getting up, the arms and legs should be held stiff and straight. Knees should not be bent.

7. Do not twist the legs. Do not lift the feet from the floor or allow them to slip, keeping them pointing forward.

8. Beginners who cannot touch their toe may try touching their calf or ankle.

VARIATION

- Stand erect, feet apart.
- Raise one arm laterally above the head. While raising it, turn the palm upward from the shoulder level. Keep the upper arm touching the ear, and the knees stiff.
- Bend trunk and head sideways from the waist while sliding the palm of the opposite arm along the thigh and calf to reach the ankle-joint.

TECHNIQUE

1. Stand erect, keeping the feet well apart and on a level with each other, adjusting the distance between them according to your height and build. Keep the arms at their respective sides. Fingers should be close together and touching the sides of the thighs. Breathe normally. Look straight ahead.

2. Inhale slowly and deeply and while inhaling, tense and raise your right arm slowly and laterally until it is straight above your head, turning the palm upward while raising it from the shoulder level. Keep the inside of the upper arm touching the ear. Look straight ahead. Maintain this position until you have completed the inhalation.

3. Keep the feet fixed firmly on the floor. Exhale slowly and while exhaling, raise the right shoulder and bend the trunk and head together from your waist along with the raised right arm laterally over the left leg very slowly, keeping the hips still and the knees stiff. While the trunk and head are thus being bent laterally, the right arm must be held straight without bending the elbow and the inside of the upper arm must press the ear (Fig. 32).

Keep on bending the trunk and head laterally to the left, pressing the upper arm against the ear so as to be able to stretch the side muscles to the maximum. While bending thus, keep the left arm straight and slide the left palm slowly along the side of your left

Fig. 32.

thigh and calf as far down as possible and try to touch the left ankle-joint with the tips of the fingers which should point downwards. The legs should remain stretched to maintain balance and both feet should remain flat on the floor. The knees should be kept rigid and straight and the body must not sway forward or backward at the

T R I K O N A S A N A (Variation)

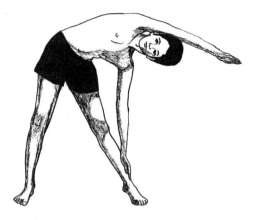

Fig. 33—Final position. Trunk and head bent laterally to the right
and the right hand is touching the right ankle.

Fig. 34—Final position. Trunk and head bent laterally to the left
and the left hand is touching the left ankle.

waist. When the bending is complete, ensure that the stretched right arm alongside the head is held straight and in line with the trunk and remains parallel to the floor on your left side. The upper arm must be held straight and touch the ear with the palm turned inward.

The right leg, the side of the trunk and the lowered right arm should form a curve extending from the right ankle to the tips of the right-hand fingers. The trunk, neck and head should remain parallel to the floor. Lower the trunk as far as possible and feel the pull throughout your right side. Look straight ahead. This is the final position (Figs. 33 & 34). (Note the two triangles that are formed with the limbs in the illustration.)

4. Hold out your breath and maintain this position comfortably and motionlessly for a few seconds in the beginning and increase the period gradually.

5. **Return:** Return gracefully to the upright position as follows: inhaling slowly, raise the trunk and head side-wise to the right till the right hand comes straight above the head, at the same time sliding the left palm up along the left calf and thigh. Now, exhale slowly and while exhaling, lower the right arm slowly to the side again, turning its palm inward at the shoulder level. Relax in the erect standing position with the feet still kept wide apart, ready to take the next turn (Fig. 28).

6. Repeat the entire exercise, bending the trunk and head to the right and holding the posture for the same length of time.

7. Take three turns on each side.

8. After completing the exercise, draw the legs together and finally relax in Savasana.

POINTS

1. The movements must be very slow and rhythmical.
2. Keep the knees and elbows straight throughout this asana.
3. Bend only to the sides. While bending, the trunk must not sway forward. Your hips should not move so that the pull comes from your waist. Do not twist the trunk or hips.
4. While bending, your feet should not slip.
5. Bend the trunk little by little by sliding the palm lower and lower towards the foot, going a little further each time you practise. The movement must be continuous without interruption at any stage.
6. Shift the weight of the body to the left when your left arm slides down on the left leg, and vice versa.
7. If you cannot touch the ankle-joint, hold on to any portion of the leg as near to it as you can manage.

Note

The technique for this variation is similar to Chakrasana, in standing, except for the position of the legs.

BENEFITS

Several benefits are derived by regularly practising this asana and its variations as almost all parts of the body are stretched.

A. Physical

1. Trikonasana is an all-round limbering exercise which does not cause any strain.

2. It effects a powerful lateral stretch and rotary twist to the whole vertebral column and keeps it flexible. All the lateral ligaments and muscles supporting the vertebrae are brought into play while executing the movements.

3. It alternately stretches and relaxes all the intercostal muscles.

4. The arms, shoulders, ribs, legs and feet are strengthened by stretching their muscles. The muscles and nerves of the neck are also toned up.

5. It removes tension from the neck and the side muscles and opens up the chest and expands it.

6. It exercises the hips and the buttocks. The eyes also are exercised.

7. It brings extra blood to the thyroid and parathyroid glands and the face. The circulation of the blood also improves.

8. The thymus and the adrenal glands are stimulated.

9. It massages the abdominal and pelvic organs.

10. It gently massages the liver, spleen, pancreas and kidneys.

11. This asana reduces excess fat in the abdomen, waist and hips and massages that area of the flank where fat accumulates. It thus gives the body a graceful form with minimum effort.

12. It increases the flexibility of the waist and the hip joints. It benefits women by slimming the waistline and giving shape and grace to the hipline besides exercising the pectoral muscles which hold the breasts in position.

13. This is an excellent exercise for correcting a faulty posture and for making the body well-proportioned.

14. Minor deformities of the legs and drooping shoulders can be set right. It also helps to keep the back straight and loosen the pelvis.
15. This asana will increase the height if practised regularly in the early years.
16. It will help a person to attain full stature.
17. Practising this asana regularly keeps the body in good trim.
18. Persons who have to sit for long periods at the workplace will find this posture invigorating, if it is practised during the period of work.

B. Therapeutical

1. Practising Trikonasana regularly improves the appetite. It also helps digestion and the assimilation of food.
2. It relieves constipation by invigorating the peristaltic action of the bowels.
3. It helps to cure enteroptosis and many urinary disorders.
4. It alleviates backche, pain in the neck, elbows, hip-joints, waistline and the knees.
5. It gives relief from sciatica if practised slowly.

Note

1. Everybody, except pregnant women, may practise this asana as it is very simple, though it may be a little strenuous in the beginning.
2. If you feel lazy before starting your daily round of asanas, you may practise this asana first and the lethargy will disappear.

3. There are several versions of this asana. The two given before are the simplest and are suitable to most people. Women generally do better in them than men.

4. Of the two versions given, you may learn the easier one first and then practise both.

5. Ensure that both sides of the body are equally exercised.

6. If you are able to do Ardha Matsyendrasana, this asana may be treated as optional as its principle is the same.

6. Bhujangasana
(The Cobra Posture)

अङ्गुष्ठनाभिपर्यन्मधो भूमौ च विन्यसेत् ।
करतलाभ्यां धरां ध त्वा ऊर्ध्वशीर्षः भणीव हि ।।

Let the lower part of the body from the toes up to the navel touch the ground. Place the palms on the ground and raise the head (the upper part of the body) like a cobra.
—*Gheranda Samhitts* II—42–43.

'Bhujanga' means 'cobra' in Sanskrit. This asana is called 'Bhujangasana' as the raised trunk, neck and head while practising it resemble a cobra rearing its hood and about to strike, while the joined and stretched legs resemble its tail.

- Lie flat on your abdomen. Keep your arms on the sides, feet together and insteps on the floor. Rest the forehead and the nose on the ground.
- Place the palms beneath the shoulders, and the chin on the ground.
- Bend the neck and head backward, keeping the chest close to the ground.

- Inhaling, bend backward your head, shoulder, chest and the upper abdomen up to the navel slowly and successively.
- Bend back the spine and arch the back as far as you can. Gaze upwards.
- Exhaling, return to the starting position in the reverse order in one flowing movement.

SEQUENCE

- Lie flat on your abdomen at full length. Stretch your arms on the sides with the palms turned upwards. Rest the forehead and nose on the ground. Keep your legs and feet together and the whole body straight. Soles must be turned upwards. Relax the whole body.
- Place the palms flat on the floor exactly beneath the corresponding shoulders with fingers close together. Keep the elbows close to the sides.
- Place the chin on the ground.
- Slowly bend the neck and head backward as far as possible, keeping the chest close to the ground.
- Supporting yourself lightly on the hands and forearms and inhaling, raise slowly your head, shoulders, chest and the upper abdomen (up to the navel) above the ground in a smooth backward movement, tensing the muscles of the back and the nape of the neck. Bend the head and neck as far back as possible.
- Arch the back and bend the whole spine further back as far as you can, putting very little pressure on the hands. Gaze upwards.
- Maintain this position comfortably, holding your breath.
- Exhaling, return slowly to the starting position in the reverse order.

TECHNIQUE

First Stage

1. Lie flat on your abdomen and chest with face downwards at full length on the carpet. Stretch your arms on their respective sides with the palms turned upwards. Rest the forehead and nose lightly on the ground. The abdomen, navel, knees and toes should touch the ground closely. Stretch your legs, keeping the legs and feet close together. Soles should be turned upwards. The toes of both legs should be extended and kept stretched backward on the floor, the big toes touching each other. Relax your body completely, particularly the back. Stay in this position for a few seconds, breathing normally (Fig. 35).

Fig. 35.

2. Bend the arms at the elbows and bring your hands slowly forward. Place the palms flat on the floor on either side of the chest and exactly beneath the corresponding shoulders. The thumb of each hand should be under the nipple. Both palms should be parallel. Fingers should be close together and their tips should point forward in line with the tops of the rounded shoulders. Bring the elbows close to the sides of the trunk and keep them high (Fig. 36). Breathe normally and relax all muscles thoroughly.

Fig. 36.

3. Slowly slide the nose forward along the floor. The chin will follow it, lightly brushing the floor. Lift your forehead and fix your chin on the floor as far forward as possible.

Second Stage

Lift your head slowly off the floor. Using only your neck muscles, slowly raise and bend your neck and head upward and backward as far as they go, thrusting the chin forward to the fullest extent (Fig. 37). This will stretch the front of the neck, while the nape will remain compressed. This position will help to arch your spine which is the next stage. Gaze upwards. At this stage, the chest is still kept close to the ground while the outstretched legs remain motionless on the floor.

Fig. 37.

Third Stage

1. Keep your head back and the elbows close to the sides. Exhale slowly and completely. Supporting yourself

BHUJANGASANA

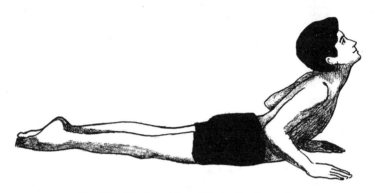

Fig. 40—Final position. The body above the
navel resembles the hood of a cobra.

Fig. 41. Beginners may place their palms flat on the floor on either
side of the head, with the tips of the fingers in line with the top
of the head and then raise their head and trunk.

lightly on the hands and forearms, inhale slowly and deeply and while inhaling, slowly raise your head, then the chest and finally the upper abdomen (up to the navel) above the ground in a smooth backward movement, tensing the muscles of the back and the nape of the neck. While raising the upper part of the body thus, look up and bend the head and neck as far back as possible, allowing the chest to expand. Raise only the portion of the body above the navel without straightening the elbows, pressing the body from the navel downwards to the tips of the toes closely on the floor.

The arms should remain folded. Use the arms and hands only for balance, depending mostly on the contraction of the neck and back muscles for raising the trunk and head and maintaining the suspended position. The body above the navel will now resemble a cobra raising its hood, as the name of the asana implies (Fig. 38).

Fig. 38.

2. Continuing to inhale, exert pressure on the small of the back and bend the whole spine further back as far as it goes, slowly and continuously, keeping the bent elbows close to their respective sides and putting very little pressure on the hands (Fig. 39). Raise the

Fig. 39.

trunk as high as possible and get the maximum
curvature of the spine until a slight strain is felt in
the lumbar region. Shoulders should be kept back and
on a level with each other. Arms should be kept
relaxed. Keep the navel region as close to the floor
as possible.

Legs and feet should be held together. Arch back
the neck right from its root and keep the head and
chin well up and the mouth closed. The body should
be supported on the legs, pelvis and hands. Gaze
upwards and try to see the ceiling without hunching
your shoulders. This is the final position (Figs. 40-41).

3. Completing the inhalation and holding in the breath,
    maintain this last position motionless for five to ten
    seconds, bending only the upper part of the body
    backwards, with the lower part, from the navel
    downwards, touching the floor closely. Allow the
    body, specially the legs and face, to relax; the more
    you relax, the more your back will bend. Concentrate
    your mind on the small of the back.

4. **Return:** When you have reached the limit of your
    flexibility and begin to feel a strong pressure in the
    lower part of the back, return to the starting position
    very slowly in the exact but reverse order as follows:

start exhaling slowly. While exhaling, lower the trunk and head very slowly, relaxing the pressure on the muscles of the back progressively from the sacral to the cervical region and that on the nape of the neck. First, let the abdomen touch the ground slowly, then the middle part of the chest, then the upper part of the chest and, finally, place the chin on the ground as far forward as possible. While bringing down the head and until the chin touches the ground, keep the head stiff, bent back and the chin up, using mostly the muscles of the back for support.

Relax the chest and lower your eyes as the chin touches the ground. Draw back the chin followed by the nose and, finally, rest your forehead and nose on the ground. Complete the exhalation and start breathing slowly and deeply. Bring your arms slowly back and stretch them again on their respective sides with the palms turned upwards as at the beginning. Take several breaths to recover and relax in this position completely until you are ready to repeat the exercise. After the asana is over, relax completely in Savasana.

MEASURE

This posture should be maintained from five to ten seconds at each attempt. Increase the time for retaining the posture gradually without discomfort. Take three to five turns according to your capacity and age, with a short period of rest between two turns.

BREATHING

1. A beginner should continue to breathe normally throughout. Since he will find the rising movement

difficult, he may take several normal breaths until the final position is reached.

2. After practising for a few weeks, inhale slowly while raising the head, chest and abdomen. Hold in the breath while maintaining the posture. Exhale slowly while returning to the starting position till the chin touches the ground. Then breathe normally.

3. If you can hold the posture without strain for ten second or more, breathe deeply and evenly during the period. While breathing thus, try to bend the back further without raising the navel off the ground.

4. It is customary to do this asana during one long inhalation while raising the trunk and head, and during one long exhalation while returning to the starting position, holding the breath in during the period maintaining the posture.

5. Breathing must be mostly thoracic because the abdomen is kept in contact with the floor, which to some extent impedes the action of the diaphragm.

POINTS

A. General

1. Though this asana seems to be simple, attention to details is very necessary to avoid mistakes.

2. Practise very slowly and in a relaxed manner in order to secure the maximum benefit. Avoid hasty and jerky movements as they may strain the back muscles.

B. Getting into the Posture

1. While practising this asana, the toes and heels must be kept together and the soles must be turned

backwards. At no stage of the practice should the feet be spread apart.

2. Palms must be kept parallel on either side of the chest. If the palms are not parallel, there will be unequal pressure on the body while lifting the trunk. Do not shake or move the palms while in action.

3. Before raising the trunk and head, ensure the correct positioning of the palms in relation to the shoulders since the arms act as an adjusting lever in this practice. The palms should not be placed too far above or too far below the shoulder but exactly beneath them. The tips of the fingers should be on a level with the line of the shoulders.

4. The forearms must touch the sides of the chest both while raising the trunk and while bringing it down.

5. The elbows should be bent and held close to the sides of the trunk. Do not separate them or spread them out during the practice.

6. Look up as far as possible both while raising your trunk and head and while maintaining the posture. It will help you to raise yourself higher and accentuate the curvature of the spine.

7. Concentrate your attention on the slow-curving spine while raising the head and trunk.

C. The Dynamic Stage

1. Before raising the trunk, bend the neck and head backward as far as possible, completely throwing out the chin. While doing this, the chest must be kept close to the ground, the trunk taking no part in the movement. After the head is fully bent backward, raise slowly your head, then chest and finally the

abdomen up to the navel, holding the head back. The
eyes and head should lead the way.

2.   While raising the trunk and head, the shoulders should
not be raised but kept rather low so that they move
gracefully back.

3.   Bring the shoulder blades as close to each other as
possible both during elevation and while holding the
posture.

4.   Raise the chin and head first, then chest and then the
portion of the trunk up to the navel in one flowing
motion, slowly and gracefully, as a cobra raises its
hood.

5.   Raise   the
trunk only up
to the navel
region   and
not beneath it
during   the
practice   of
this   asana.
The   body

Fig. 42.

from the navel downwards to the toes, namely the
lower abdomen, the navel, the front of the pelvic bone,
thighs, knees and toes, must stay on the floor and be
kept absolutely still and relaxed. When you look up
after raising your head, there will be a tendency to
raise the trunk below the navel region and the hips
but this should be avoided (Fig. 42). The knees should
not slacken or bend.

6.   All the bones in the spinal column, starting with those
in the neck down to the navel region, must be raised
slowly and curved up. Raise the spine very slowly

and not as a push-up so that you may get the full
benefit of this posture.

7. As your trunk and head are raised upwards and
    backwards, the spine should be continually curved
    and a steady pressure should be felt along the whole
    length of the spine, rolling down progressively from
    the cervical region to the dorsal, then to the lumbar
    and then to the sacral region at the base of the spine.

8. Do not give a full backward curve to the spine all at
    once; do so slowly. Also, go slow while returning to
    the starting position by straightening the curve of the
    spine from below upwards. Avoid jerks of any kind.

9. While raising the head to reach the final position, it
    must not tilt forward; it must be held stiffly. While
    coming down also, the head should be kept stiff, bent
    back till the chin touches the ground.

10. While assuming the posture and while returning, the
    hands should not change their positions. Do not put
    too much pressure on the hand and do not tense the
    arms. The arms should not be straightened. The legs
    should remain straight and together.

11. After mastering the practice, slowly raise the chest
    and abdomen and maintain the posture mainly by
    the strength of the deep muscles of the back and
    abdomen, and very little pressure should be put upon
    the hands. The hands and arms should be used only
    to keep your balance and give minimal support. The
    weight of the upraised trunk should not rest on the
    arms or hands which should be kept relaxed, though
    some strain may be felt in the beginning. Experience
    is the best guide in this matter.

D. Holding the Posture

1. While holding the posture, keep balance with the palms on the floor and with the upper arms and elbows close to the sides.
2. Hold the posture only as long as you feel comfortable and increase the time gradually as you advance in the practice. If you feel any strain or discomfort in the small of the back, relax at once, and return slowly back to the starting position.

E. Return

1. When you have reached the stage where your body can stretch no further without the assistance of your arms, start returning to the starting position.
2. Return without jerks, as slowly and steadily as you did, to attain the posture.
3. The back muscles must control the descent until the chin touches the floor.
4. While lowering your head and trunk, begin with the lowest vertebra of your spine. Do not allow the head to go down first.
5. Keep the elbows close to the body until the chin touches the ground.
6. While lowering the trunk, the spinal vertebrae should be relaxed and brought back to the starting position.

F. Caution

1. Do this asana on an empty stomach.
2. Persons with peptic ulcer, hernia or high blood pressure must not practise it.
3. Women must avoid it during pregnancy because of the pressure on the abdomen.

G. Beginners

1. Beginners, who find their spine stiff, should go through this asana slowly without jerking either the spine or the neck. The maximum stretch can be obtained only with long practise.

2. Beginners may place their forearms flat on the floor, with palms downward and fingers pointing forward in front of their shoulders and on each side of the head. The fingertips should be in line with the crown of the head.

3. At the start, beginners should raise their trunk and head only as far as they can do so comfortably. They should not attempt to go beyond the point where they feel the strain.

4. Beginners whose backs are very stiff will not be able to raise their head and trunk much but after a few weeks, they will be able to raise them to the maximum extent without strain if they try to do so a little higher each day. The stiffness of the back and the neck muscles will disappear gradually.

BENEFITS

A. Physical

1. Bhujangasana stretches and relaxes the vertebrae starting from the first vertebra just below the skull to the base of the spine. It alternately contracts and relaxes the deep muscles of the back while the full posture is being assumed. Thus, it develops the back muscles and keeps the spinal column elastic.

2. A regular practise of this asana will keep the vertebrae in good alignment. The progressive curving

of the spine, vertebra by vertebra, will set right slight displacements and restore or preserve the normal spinal curve. It also corrects minor deformities in the cervical, thoracic and lumbar regions of the spine and helps to set right slipped discs.

3. This asana promotes a liberal circulation of the blood in the back by inducing vigorous action in the muscular mechanism of the spine. Ordinarily, the deep muscles of the back are not exercised, but this asana exercises and tones them up.

4. It invigorates the parasympathetic and the sympathetic nervous systems and, indirectly, the brain. The spinal nerves are also toned up.

5. It relieves tension and stiffness in the neck and back.

6. The stretching back of the neck and head stimulates the thyroid gland.

7. It strengthens the arms, wrists, shoulders and the posterior.

8. The practice of this asana opens up narrow shoulders and expands the chest. It also develops the pectoral muscles of the bust as it stretches and realigns the spinal column.

9. This asana is specially beneficial to persons with a slight hump as the head, neck and back are bent in the reverse direction.

10. The heart benefits greatly as the circulatory system is invigorated.

11. The contraction of the shoulders and stretching the front of the neck facilitates the filling of the top lobes of the lungs. Hence, this asana is excellent for increasing lung power and improving the voice.

12. As the abdomen is well stretched, the abdominal muscles become supple and the viscera are toned up.

13. The alternate compression and stretching of the abdomen improves the digestive system and stimulates the appetite.

14. It gives a gentle massage to the liver, gall bladder, spleen and pancreas.

15. The kidneys are subjected to healthy pressure and flushed with fresh blood which stimulates their action.

16. It regulates the function of the adrenal glands.

17. It is very useful for removing excess fat in the abdomen and waist and reducing the hips. The body will thus become more beautiful and the limbs more proportionate.

18. It helps to reduce corpulence, improve the posture, and attain full stature.

19. The practise of this asana after office work will dispel fatigue.

20. The regular practise of Bhujangasana will help postpone old age and bring youthfulness by improving the elasticity of the spine.

B. Therapeutical

1. Bhujangasana alleviates the pain in the back and neck. It gives relief to an aching back if the pain is due to long hours of standing or bending over a desk or while sitting at a table.

2. It helps to expel gas from the stomach and intestines. Persons troubled by flatulence immediately after meals, may practise this asana along with Halasana to get relief.

3. This asana increases intra-abdominal pressure and brings down the faecal matter from the transverse colon to the rectum, thus improving bowel action.

4. It helps to cure low blood pressure.

5. Diabetic patients benefit by practising this asana as the abdominal organs press into the pancreas during the action of bending backward.

6. Women who suffer from irregularities of the menstrual cycle and various ovarian and uterine troubles will find this asana beneficial as the circulation in the ovaries and adjoining parts is greatly increased by the pressure on the lower abdomen.

Note

1. All persons can do Bhujangasana, though not perfectly at first. It is specially valuable for those who lead a sedentary life.

2. Bhujangasana should be followed by Shalabhasana and Dhanurasana to derive the maximum benefit. They form a good trio and are complementary to each other.

3. Halasana and Paschimotanasana are the counter-poses of Bhujangasana.

Source

Gheranda Samhita: II—42–43.

7. Ardha Shalabhasana
(The Half-Locust Posture)

अध्यास्य शेते करयुग्ममवक्षं आलम्ब्य भूमिं करयोस्तलाभ्याम् ।
पादौ च शून्ये च वितस्ति चोर्ध्वं वदन्ति पीठं शलभं मुनीन्द्राः ॥

Lie prone, pressing the ground with the palms placed on either side of the chest. Raise the feet together about nine inches in the air. This is called Shalabhasana by eminent sages.
Gheranda Samhita II—39.

'Shalabha' means 'locust' in Sanskrit. The final position of this asana resembles a locust when it lowers its head to eat and raises its tail. Hence the name. 'Ardha' means 'half' in Sanskrit.

- Lie flat on your abdomen and chest, arms on the sides, and chin on the floor.
- Clench your fingers into fists and place them on the floor facing upwards.
- Inhale and hold your breath.
- Pressing the fists down, raise backward your left leg as far up as you can, keeping the leg straight and outstretched.

- Exhaling, press the fists down and lower the leg without bending the knee.
- Repeat with the right leg.

TECHNIQUE

A. Starting Position

1. Lie flat on the carpet on your abdomen and chest with the face downwards. Stretch your body straight. Your forehead and nose should rest on the floor. Keep the hips close to the floor and the legs straight and close to each other. The stretched feet should be close together. Bring the heels also together. The toes must be extended backwards and the big toes must touch each other. The soles should be turned upwards and the front of the feet should be in contact with the floor. Arms should be stretched back along the respective sides, the entire length of the arms, from the shoulders to the fingertips, touching the body all along the sides of the thighs. Keep the elbows straight. Palms should be turned upwards, with fingers pointing towards the feet. The wrists and the back of the hands should rest on the floor. Relax all the muscles completely. Breathe normally (Fig. 35).

2. Raise your head a little and place your chin on the floor. Push it as far forward as possible, stretching the neck and bending the head back. This will stretch the front of the neck and compress the nape. Try to keep the shoulders touching the floor.

3. Hold down the chin, shoulders, chest, abdomen, hands, pelvis and knees firmly on the floor. Keep the knees rigid. Stiffen your arms and legs and remain steady in this position. This is the starting position.

B. Assuming the Posture

1. Ball your hands into fists with the thumbs tucked inside and fingers curled and pressing the palms. Place the fists close to your thighs. Fists should face upwards and knuckles should press the floor. Stiffen the whole body.

2. Breathe out fully and then, inhale slowly and deeply. While inhaling, clench your fingers tightly around your thumbs and raise the left leg straight up backwards from the navel downwards slowly and steadily as high as you can without bending the knee or flexing the ankle or tilting the trunk. While lifting the leg, it should be kept stiff and straight with the toes stretched out and pointing backwards. The legs should be lifted mainly by contracting the muscles of the lower dorsal and lumbar regions of the spine and those of the hips. Hands should be spared as much as possible, though a slight pressure may be applied on the floor with the clenched fists to give yourself more leverage to help lift the leg. The pressure of the uplifted leg will be felt on the clenched fists, the wrists, chin and chest. While lifting the left leg, the trunk and the right leg should be pressed down firmly on the floor. This is the final position (Figs. 43 & 44).

3. After raising the leg to the maximum extent without straining, keep it straight at the knee and press the abdomen on the floor to avoid any pelvic twist. Hold the breath and maintain the last position motionlessly and comfortably for about five seconds. Keep your attention on the pelvis and the lower vertebrae.

C. Return

1. When you can no longer hold your breath comfortably, exhale slowly and, while exhaling, relax the back muscles and gradually lower the raised leg to its original position on the floor without bending the knee and complete the exhalation.

2. After a little pause, raise the right leg also, adopting the same technique.

   Take three turns at ease, alternating the legs, taking sufficient rest before changing the legs and repeating the practice. Loosen the clenched fists. Breathe deeply a few times to allow your respiration rate to return to normal and finally relax in Savasana.

POINTS

1. The clenched fists must not be very tight or very loose.
2. If the blanket or carpet is not soft enough, you may place a folded towel underneath the chin.
3. While raising one leg, do not tilt the other leg. The leg on the floor must be in a straight line with the trunk.
4. The leg should be raised exactly above the spot where it lay at the start in a straight line with the body. It should not be raised beyond the point at which the pelvis starts tilting sideways.
5. While raising the leg, do not bend the knee or twist it sideways. Do not tighten the fists.
6. The raised leg must be kept steady; it must not shake. Keep the knee straight and the toes stretched out.
7. While raising one leg, do not move the other leg. The raised leg should not be supported by the pressure of the other knee on the ground.

8. While repeating on the other side, the weight of the body must not be shifted to the side of the outstretched leg.

9. Increase the period for maintaining the posture gradually for as long as you can hold your breath comfortably. Ten seconds should be the maximum.

8. Shalabhasana
(Locust Posture)

- Lie flat on your abdomen and chest. The forehead and nose should touch the floor. Keep the legs straight and together. Keep the feet also together. Soles should be turned upwards. Stretch the arms along the respective sides with palms turned upwards. Relax.
- Place the chin on the floor and slide it as far forward as possible.
- Clench your fingers into fists and place them close to the thighs.
- Keep the knees rigid and stiffen your arms and legs. Inhale slowly and deeply and hold your breath. Put mild pressure on the clenched fists and raise backward both legs together slowly as high as you can from the navel without raising the head or bending the knees.
- Hold this position for a few seconds.
- Exhaling, put mild pressure on the fists and lower the legs, slowly to the floor without bending the knees. Relax.

TECHNIQUE

1.   Lie flat on the carpet as for the Half-Shalabhasana posture, as described above. Clench your fingers lightly into fists and place them close to the thighs so that they give the maximum lift to the pelvis while raising the legs together. Place the chin on the floor and push it as far forward as possible, stretching the neck and bending the head back. Breathe normally and relax the whole body.

2.   Keep the legs straight and together and the arms fully extended. Breathe out fully and then inhale slowly and deeply and hold your breath. Tense the arms, legs and the back muscles. Putting mild pressure on the clenched fists and pressing the pelvis on the floor, raise backward both legs together slowly and steadily and as high as you can from the navel downwards in one continuous movement by contracting the lower back muscles and without experiencing strain. While raising the legs, the hips and the lower abdomen are also lifted a little, but do not raise the head or bend the knees or twist the trunk. Keep the arms stiff. Balance yourself, keeping the chin and fists pressing into the floor. This is the final position in which the body resembles a locust (Fig. 45A and B).

3.   Maintain this last position steadily and comfortably for a few seconds or as long as you can hold your breath comfortably. Direct your attention to the back muscles, the small of the back and the pelvis.

4.   **Return:** When you can no longer hold your breath comfortably, start exhaling very slowly and evenly. While exhaling, put mild pressure on the fists and

lower the legs very slowly to the floor without bending the knees, keeping complete control over the movement. Loosen the clenched fists. Take a few breaths to recover while still lying on the stomach with the arms by the sides. After this, totally relax in Savasana or Makarasana.

5. Beginners may take three turns with sufficient rest between the turns. After mastering the asana, take only one turn with a longer retention period. A second turn may be taken if desired.

POINTS

A. General

1. Practise this asana on an empty stomach.
2. The movements must be smooth. No pressure should be exerted on the legs to achieve a high lift.

B. Starting Position

1. Before starting the exercise, stretch the arms on their respective sides and hold them straight. Knuckles must be turned down and kept touching the thighs.
2. The chin, elbows, hands, chest and abdomen should rest on the floor in the same position throughout the practice; do not raise them. The shoulders should remain close to the floor.
3. While inhaling before assuming the posture, do not fill your lungs with air to their full capacity as it will make it more difficult to take the posture.
4. While raising the legs, the upper portion of the trunk above the navel must touch the floor closely and it must not move. Keeping the trunk straight, raise only the portion below the navel.

Fig. 43—Final position with the left leg lifted up.

Fig. 44—Final position with the right leg lifted up.

SHALABHASANA

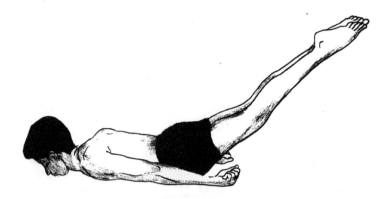

Fig. 45 (A)—Final position with both legs lifted up.

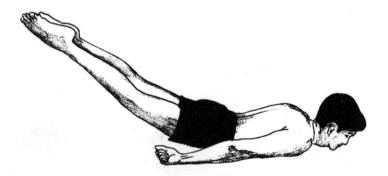

Fig. 45 (B)—Final position. The portion around the navel
is not touching the ground.

5. Raise the legs exactly above the place where they rested at the start. While raising them or bringing them down, do not bend the knees.

C. The Dynamic Stage

1. While raising the legs, press the chin on the floor and do not move it from that position. The head must not pop up.
2. While raising the legs, keep them stiff and straight like sticks throughout their length. Keep them close together so as to reduce the strain.
3. Keep the heels and the big toes together.
4. Keep the knees stiff during the asana; do not bend them.
5. Though the arms assist in raising the legs, the assistance of the arms should be progressively reduced and the main work should be done by the lower back muscles and those of the hips. Beginners, however, may push down their fists hard on the floor and use them as a lever.
6. Raise the legs right up from the hips and not at the knees.
7. Do not only raise the lower thighs, but also the upper thighs and pelvis up to the navel region which is possible only after some practice.
8. Raise and lower the legs very slowly, and do not tilt the pelvis sideways. Avoid jerks and sudden twists and turns.
9. Do not try to raise the legs too high which will put a strain on the lungs. About 45 degrees to the floor will be adequate for most people.

10. Raising the legs effectively is more important than the distance to which they are raised.

11. Beginners will be able to raise their legs only a few inches from the floor during the initial attempts. They should not strain and raise their legs abruptly, but very slowly, extending the distance a little each day and reach the final position gradually.

12. The stiffening of the back muscles while raising your legs and while holding your legs in the elevated position should be attempted only as you advance in the practice.

13. While elevating the legs, the pressure of the upturned legs should be felt on your clenched fists, the wrists, chin and chest. Try to put the maximum weight of the legs on the abdomen.

D. Maintenance

1. Increase the period for maintaining the posture gradually. To derive its full benefit, you should maintain the posture as long as your breath can be held comfortably.

2. Do not hold the posture so long that it becomes uncomfortable.

3. Care should be taken not to strain the heart and lungs by unduly prolonging the posture or raising the legs too high.

4. Initially, practise only Ardha Shalabhasana, and the full posture should be attempted if your physical condition permits.

E. Return

1. Bring down the legs very slowly and gently onto the floor in a controlled manner and in a continuous

movement. Take as much care while bringing down your legs as you did while raising them up. Do not drop them down which will nullify your effort in raising them.

2. While bringing down the legs, exhalation should be very slow and uniform. Air should not be allowed to gush out of the lungs forcefully.

CAUTION

1. Though this asana appears simple, it is a rather strenuous practice which calls for a sudden effort in raising the legs. Hence, aged and corpulent persons and beginners will find this asana difficult at first. They must not strain themselves to raise their legs very high from the floor. They must practise slowly according to their capacity, and each time they practise, they should try to lift the legs a little higher without strain and pause for a moment when they can go no further. They should practise Ardha Shalabhasana for a few weeks and strengthen their back and leg muscles before assuming the full posture which can be performed correctly only after long practise.

2. Beginners may tuck in their fists under the thighs which will enable them to lift their legs higher and more easily. They may also place their hands, palms up and fingers pointing towards the feet, under the thighs with elbows straight.

3. Breathing should be controlled while performing this asana.

4. After completing Shalabhasana and before starting the next asana, relax completely in Savasana until breathing returns to normal.

5. Persons with hernia, weak lungs, asthma, high blood pressure, cardiac complaints and pregnant women should not practise this asana.

BENEFITS

A. Physical

1. Shalabhasana is a good exercise for the legs, thighs, hips, buttocks, the lower abdomen, diaphragm and wrists. It also strengthens the muscles of the small of the back.

2. Because of the deep inhalation and holding of the breath in this asana, the lungs expand and become strong and the chest broadens. The blood circulation also improves.

3. The asana directly massages the heart and improves its action.

4. In this asana, intra-abdominal pressure is greatly increased and as a result, the bladder, liver, spleen, pancreas and kidneys get massaged and toned up. The solar plexus is also stimulated.

5. It greatly influences the activity of the adrenal and prostate glands and the reproductive organs and glands.

6. The lower lumbar and sacral regions of the spine become more flexible and the lumbo-sacral nerves are toned up.

7. Shalabhasana corrects any faulty curvature in the base of the spinal column.

8. It dissolves excess fat from the thighs, hips, waist, abdomen and the posterior. A protruding belly gets reduced and the waist becomes resilient and supple.

9. It regularizes the functioning of the intestines and promotes peristaltic action.

B. Therapeutical

1. Shalabhasana alleviates several gastric troubles and diseases of the stomach.
2. Persons who suffer from flatulence after meals may practise Shalabhasana in combination with Halasana and Bhujangasana to get relief.
3. It relieves sluggishness of the liver.
4. It prevents piles, fistula and varicose veins.
5. Persons suffering from bronchitis get relief.
6. This asana is used for the relief of rheumatic pain in the hips and knees, sciatica, slipped disc, lumbago and all forms of myalgia of the sacral and lumbar rigions of the spine except when the condition is serious.
7. Practise of this asana alleviates oedema of the ankles and feet.
8. It relieves constipation and dyspepsia and improves digestion.
9. Diabetic patients may practise this asana to control the disease.
10. Shalabhasana benefits women through its effect on the ovaries and uterus, helping to correct disorders of these organs.

Note

1. Practise the Full Locust posture after taking three turns of the Half-Locust posture which makes it easier to perform the full posture and derive optimum benefits from this asana.

2. Shalabhasana is a complementary posture to Bhujangasana and should be performed immediately after it. It should be followed by Dhanurasana which is a combination of Bhujangasana and Shalabhasana. The three asanas form a good combination.

3. Halasana and Paschimotanasana are the counterposes of Shalabhasana.

9. Dhanurasana
(The Bow Posture)

प्रसार्य पादौ भुवि दण्डरुपौ करौ च प ष्ठे ध तपादयुग्मम् ।
क त्वा धनुर्वत्परिवर्तितताड्.गं निंगद्यते वै धनुरासनं तत् ।।

Stretching the legs on the ground, straight like sticks (lying prostrate), and catching hold of the toes with the hands and curving the body like a bow is called Dhanurasana.
—*Gheranda Samhita* II—18.

'Dhanus' means 'bow' in Sanskrit. In the final position of this asana, the body takes the shape of a bow, drawn tight to shoot an arrow. The stretched arms and lower legs resemble the taut bowstring, while the trunk and thighs resemble the wooden part of the bow.

- Lie on your abdomen with the chin resting on the ground, arms on the sides.
- Keep the feet apart. Bend the legs backwards. Reach back and grasp the ankles.
- Bend your head and neck backward.
- Inhaling, pull the legs upward and, simultaneously, raise your knees, thighs, hips, the lower region of the

navel, chest, shoulders, chin, neck and head upward all together.

- Join the feet and knees. Look up.
- Balance the body on the navel region and arch the spine as much as possible.
- Exhaling, release.

SEQUENCE

- Lie with your abdomen, chest and chin resting on the ground. Stretch the arms on the sides. Keep the feet a little apart.
- Bend the legs backwards and grasp the corresponding ankles firmly. Hold the arms stiff and straight. Keep the knees sufficiently apart.
- Raise your chin and bend your head and neck backward without raising the chest.
- Inhaling, pull the legs slowly upward towards the ceiling (not the head). While pulling hard against the ankles, raise the knees, thighs, hips, the lower region of the navel, chest, shoulders, chin, neck and head upward all together until the body is balanced on the navel region which alone should touch the floor. Arch the back as much as possible with the arms and legs tugging at each other.
- Slowly bring the big toes, the inner edges of the feet and the knees closer and join them together.
- Keep your head up and backward as far as you can and look up.
- Hold your breath and maintain the posture until you feel the strain.
- Exhaling, return slowly to the starting position in the reverse order.

TECHNIQUE

1. Lie face down on the carpet with your abdomen, chest and chin resting on the ground and the legs stretched out straight. Stretch the arms along their respective sides, with palms turned upwards (Fig. 46). Keep your feet apart at about shoulder-width. Relax all the muscles completely, particularly the back muscles. Maintain this position and breathe normally.

Fig. 46.

2. Slowly bend the legs backwards at the knee-joints and fold them double over the backs of the respective thighs. Bring the heels back as close to your posterior as you can.

3. Extend your arms backward at full length and grasp the corresponding ankles firmly on the outer side by cupping all your fingers and thumb a little above the ankle bone of each leg, keeping the thumbs and fingers side by side. Hold the arms stiff and straight so that they link together the ankles and the shoulders. Keep the knees sufficiently apart and secure a comfortable position for raising them up. Keep the chin on the floor. This is the starting position. Relax the whole body, breathing normally.

4. Raise your chin off the floor and bend your head and neck backward as far as possible, keeping the chest close to the ground. Pull the ankles vigorously and look straight ahead (Fig. 47A).

5. Exhale completely and then inhale slowly and deeply. While inhaling, grasp the ankles firmly and pull the legs slowly and gently upwards towards the ceiling (not towards the head). While pulling hard on the ankles, pull

Fig. 47A.

your shoulder blades together and raise the knees, thighs, hips, the lower region of the navel, chest, shoulders, chin, neck and head upward from the floor, all together, slowly and without jerks.

6. Continue to inhale. Holding the ankles firmly and maintaining the upward pull, slowly bring the big toes and heels closer and join them together. Draw the knees also closer and join them together slowly. Expand the chest and hold your breath (Fig. 47 B and C).

7. Continue to inhale. Arching your back, continue to pull the ankles strongly upward and very slowly raise backward the knees, thighs, chest, chin, neck and head simultaneously to the maximum extent in one movement, without any jerk or strain. The arms should be straight and stiff. Hold your head back as far as you can, raising your chin as high as it goes, and look up. The body from the neck to the knees, curving upwards both ways from the navel, will now assume the shape of a bent bow. The arms and lower legs resemble the taut bowstring while the trunk and thighs which are well arched back resemble the bow.

DHANURASANA

Fig. 47B. Starting position, grasping the ankles. Note position of the hands and fingers.

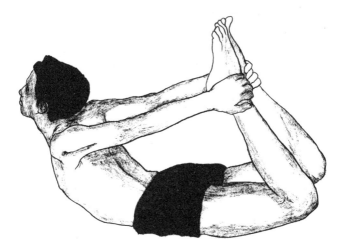

Fig. 47C. Starting position for Rocking Bow.

Fig. 48—Final position. Shoulders and knees are in a straight line.

The entire weight of the body should rest on the navel region, which alone should touch the floor. Balance the upper and lower halves of the body and stabilize yourself. This is the final position (Fig. 48).

8. In this final position, the extremities of the body should be fully stretched, with the arms and legs tugging at each other and the spine arched backwards.

9. Hold your breath and maintain this posture motionlessly and comfortably for five to ten seconds or until the strain is felt. Concentrate your mind on the small of your back and remain firm in the posture.

10. **Return:** Return slowly to the starting position in the reverse order as follows: relax the pressure on the hands and legs and also the backward pull of the legs. Exhale slowly. While exhaling, relax the limbs and still holding the ankles, lower the chin, chest and knees gradually and simultaneously till they return to the floor all together. Release the hands from the ankles and let go the feet slowly till they touch the ground together. Place the arms again at their respective sides. Bring the legs close together and stretch them straight again. This is the starting position. Take several breaths to recover and relax before repeating the asana. After the final repetition, relax in Savasana.

MEASURE

Take only three turns of this asana, but do them thoroughly. To start with, practise only twice and judge yourself whether you should make one more attempt. If you repeat the asana, relax lying on the abdomen during

the interval with the chin resting on the ground and still
grasping your ankles.

BREATHING

1. Breathe normally in the initial stages of this practice.
2. In the advanced stage, breathing should be done in
    only one round of inhalation, retention and exhalation
    as follows: inhale slowly while raising the chest, head
    and legs; hold your breath while maintaining the
    posture, and exhale slowly while returning to the
    starting position. You may breathe deeply and
    rhythmically if you can hold the posture comfortably
    for more than ten seconds.

POINTS

A. General

1. Have the picture of a bow in mind while performing
    this asana so that you may do it effectively and obtain
    the maximum benefit from it.
2. Do this asana on an empty stomach.
3. Perform very slowly and avoid jerks.
4. Practise this asana without any strain, and take care
    not to sprain any joint.

B. Starting Position

1. While reaching back to grasp the ankles, keep the
    trunk horizontal and do not lean over to one side.
2. The ankles should be grasped in the correct way. They
    should not be grasped too high from the ankle-bone.
    The grip of the hands on the ankles should be firm.
3. After grasping the ankles, the arms should be held
    straight and stiff and must not be bent at the elbows.

Do not spread out the elbows since it will lead to an insufficient arching of the back.

4. After joining the feet, keep them together and on a level with each other throughout the practice. If they are at different levels, the spine cannot be arched properly.

C. Position of the Knees and Ankles

1. Keep your knees and ankles a little apart while raising them from the floor so that you may lift the thighs more easily and secure a greater curve of the spine and neck.
2. As the muscles of the thighs become more supple, the knees, heels and the big toes should be drawn closer after raising them from the floor till they touch each other in the final position. This will increase the effectiveness of the posture.
3. Do not join the knees and feet while raising them from the floor since the legs cannot be lifted high enough. Join them only after raising the trunk and head and the full backward stretch of the body has been achieved.
4. Avoid strain while raising the knees and feet and drawing them closer to each other.
5. In the advanced stage of this practice, the shoulders and knees are brought in a straight line and the inner edges of the feet touch each other.

D. Final Position

1. To attain the final position, raise backward the knees, thighs, chest, chin, neck and head simultaneously and balance the whole body on the navel region. Do not rest the chest, pelvis and thighs on the floor.

2. Do not raise the chest and head first as you will find the raising of the thighs and legs difficult and the maximum arch of the spine may not be obtained.

3. Hold the legs firmly at the ankles and pull them up in such a way that your thighs are raised off the floor as high as possible, enabling you to secure a greater curvature of the spine and maximum pressure on the abdominal region.

4. Do not pull the legs down towards the head but upwards by intensifying the pull of the arms and using the muscles of your legs and thighs.

5. By exerting pressure on the ankles and pushing your feet higher and higher, raise the chest, head and thighs simultaneously to the maximum extent so that the body curves like a bent bow. While lifting your trunk and legs from the floor, bend your head and neck back.

6. Thighs, trunk and neck should be curved to the maximum extent so as to deepen your stretch. The feet should be pulled higher than the head, and while pulling them, it should feel as if they want to get released from your hands. The importance of this asana lies in securing the maximum backward curve of the body.

7. Look up as high as possible while lifting as it will help you in lifting yourself and holding the posture at the highest point.

E. Maintenance

1. Look up as high as possible as soon as the final position is reached.

2. When the final position is attained, there will be a tug-of-war between the legs and the arms which should be maintained while holding the posture. Keep the arms

and legs well stretched, and do not allow the legs to slip down by loosening the grip on the ankles.

3. Do not jerk up or down; be steady.
4. Increase the period for maintaining the position gradually according to your capacity, but do not maintain the posture too long as it will cause strain.

F. Return

1. Lower yourself to the floor very slowly and in a controlled manner.
2. While lowering your legs, trunk and head, do not release the grip on the ankles, and take care that the legs and arms do not spring apart. Hold the ankles firmly and do not let go of your feet.
3. Do not let go of your feet while holding your breath as it may cause residual tension in the back.

BEGINNERS

1. Beginners and bulky persons will find the practice of this asana difficult at first due to the stiffness of their back, hips or knees, but they should not give it up as the stiffness will disappear with regular practise. They may perform the preliminary positions of this asana in the beginning.
2. Beginners will experience some strain in the thighs, knees, shoulders and spine in their first attempts, but it will decrease and disappear with regular practise for a few weeks.
3. Beginners who are unable to reach back with their hands and grasp their ankles may take hold of the instep of each leg and try to improve on it each time until they are able to grasp their ankles.

4. Beginners may allow their knees and feet to spread apart slightly while maintaining the posture so as to reduce the tension on the thighs and secure the maximum curve of the spine. As proficiency improves, the space between the knees should be gradually reduced and they should be drawn closer till at last they are joined together. Keeping the knees and feet together is the correct method and enhances the effectiveness of the posture.

5. Beginners will find it easier to lift their knees off the floor by pulling the ankles up and away from each other with their hands and raising their head at the same time.

6. Beginners will find it difficult to raise their thighs and chest together from the floor. They may raise their thighs and legs first as it is more difficult and then raise the chest and head which will be easier by pulling the legs by the arms and pushing the feet backwards. After practising thus for a few weeks, the beginners will manage to raise their head, chest and thighs all together.

7. Beginners would be able to raise their head and knees only a few inches from the floor, but as they continue the practice, they will be able to lift them higher and higher and reach the final position gradually without strain or jerks. It takes several weeks or regular practise for their body to adapt to this posture.

CAUTION

1. Persons who suffer from high blood pressure, heart ailments, stomach ulcer, colitis, hernia or slipped disc must not attempt this posture.

2. Those who have undergone any abdominal operation must give it up until they have recovered fully.

3. Women should not practise this asana during pregnancy.

BENEFITS

A. Physical

1. Dhanurasana arches both halves of the body at once from head to foot and provides good exercise to the arms, shoulders, thighs, legs, ankles, back and neck.

2. It removes the rigidity in the joints and makes the body flexible.

3. Dhanurasana strengthens the muscles of the thighs and buttocks. It makes the abdominal, lumbar and pelvic muscles supple and strong. The two recti as well as the muscles that flex the hip-joints are more fully stretched in this posture than in Bhujangasana and Shalabhasana.

4. It improves the elasticity of the entire spine and, at the same time, tones up the spinal nerves and muscles. It corrects minor vertebral defects and alleviates slipped disc troubles. It also prevents the premature calcification of the vertebrae.

5. It expands and develops the chest and increases lung capacity. It is of special benefit to women in developing and firming the muscles of the bustline.

6. This asana has a beneficial effect on the heart, liver, spleen, bladder, the genital organs and the solar plexus. It has also a stimulating effect on the glandular system including the prostate and the adrenals.

7. The kidneys are squeezed and relaxed alternately and this causes them to be flushed out.

8. Dhanurasana promotes digestion by stimulating gastric secretions and relieves congestion of blood in the abdominal viscera.
9. It reduces excess fat around the abdomen, waist, hips and thighs and is specially beneficial to women.
10. It improves the posture. It also rectifies slouching.
11. For persons accustomed to a sedentary lifestyle, it is a blessing as it eliminates fatigue. It also wipes out laziness.

B. Therapeutical

1. Dhanurasana helps to cure rheumatism of the legs, knee-joints, hands, relieves pain in the neck and back, and also certain types of lumbar pain. It also alleviates sciatica.
2. It helps to set right slipped disc.
3. The intense intra-abdominal pressure will aid the elimination of gas in the stomach and intestines. It also helps to cure flatulence after meals.
4. It will eradicate dyspepsia, sluggishness of the liver and urinary troubles.
5. It relieves constipation by improving the peristaltic action of the intestines. It prevents or gives relief in piles.
6. It can be specially prescribed for those suffering from diabetes as it stimulates pancreatic action.
7. It prevents sterility.

Note

1. As the pull of the arms and legs can be adjusted according to one's capacity, all persons can do this asana, whether strong or weak.

2. Dhanurasana is a combination of Bhujangasana and Shalabhasana and produces a complete arch of the spine. To get the maximum benefit from these postures, perform Bhujangasana, Shalabhasana and Dhanurasana, one after the other, as one complete set of practice. They form a good trio to exercise the entire spine.

3. Paschimotanasana, Halasana and Chakrasana (Lying) are the counterposes of Dhanurasana as they stretch the spine in the opposite direction.

Source

1. *Hatha Pradipika*: I—25.
2. *Hatha Sanketa Chandrika*: Ch. 2 (Asanas), Verse 63.

THE ROCKING BOW

1. Assume the Dhanurasana posture with your trunk and knees well raised from the floor. While holding the posture at its maximum stretch, make gentle and slow rocking movements with the bow-shaped body forwards and backwards and from side to side without strain. Rock the body on the abdominal wall very slowly to and from without stopping, like a rocking chair or a rocking horse. Keep the knees together and do not straighten the spine throughout the practice.

2. Rock backward first and use its momentum to rock forward again.

3. While rocking yourself forward, lower the head and chest and raise the legs backward as high as possible without releasing the grip on the ankles until the chin touches the ground. While rocking backward, the groin, thighs and knees must touch the ground, while

the trunk must be brought up and back as far as possible without strain and the head held high.

4. During the rocking movements, concentrate your attention on the abdominal muscles.

5. A forward and backward movement together may be considered as one turn. Take up to ten turns at a time without stopping the motion. Then rest at the starting point of Dhanurasana and relax for about half a minute before making the next attempt. Make two to three attempts according to your capacity.

6. After rocking back and forth as stated above and without disturbing the posture, roll over to the left side. Pause for a few seconds and then repeat on the right side. Rolling over once to the left side and then to the right may be considered as one turn. Take three to six turns consecutively and roll back onto the stomach. Advanced students may roll to both sides without pause. After the side-to-side movements, you may also rock forward and backward on one side only and then on the other, taking care not to fall off on the side. Then rest at the starting point of Dhanurasana and relax for about half a minute before making the next attempt.

7. After completing all the movements, bring back your knees and chin simultaneously to the floor. Release the hands and legs and lie down in Savasana. Take a few deep breaths and relax completely until your breathing returns to normal.

BREATHING

While swinging the body as stated above, match your breathing so that it is in rhythm with the to-and-fro movements as follows: inhale when the body swings backward and exhale when it swings forward. Do not hold your breath at any stage.

POINTS

1. Before starting, make sure that there are no zippers, hooks or buckles in the dress which may cause pain while rocking.
2. Holding the ankles firmly and keeping the back arched stiffly, move the body forward and backward and from side to side with the help of the hands, rhythmically. Swing to the rhythm of your breathing.
3. After lifting the knees off the floor, beginners will find it easier by separating the knees and pulling the ankles away from each other with their hands before rocking to and fro and from side to side.
4. Do not use your head to rock.
5. In the initial stages of the rocking movement, only the abdomen will touch the ground but you will benefit even if you move a few inches either way. As the movements gain momentum, try to roll further back and forth each time until the chin and knees touch the ground alternately.
6. Do not rock back and forth too slowly or pause between each back and forth swing. If you do so, you will lose your momentum and get stuck.
7. Do not rock too far which will strain the back and neck.
8. Have control over your swinging movements and maintain balance when the rocking gains momentum.
9. Do not keep rocking until you become breathless. Stop before you are out of breath. About ten turns each,

with sufficient rest periods, will suffice when done along with other asanas.

BENEFITS

1. The rocking movements in Dhanurasana provide brisk massage to the abdomen and gradually reduce excess fat in the waist, hips and abdomen.
2. The to-and-fro movements massage the vertebral column and limber up the spine.
3. The lower back, the muscles of the chest and those at the front of the thighs get strengthened.
4. The rocking movements massage and stimulate the solar plexus and remove any congestion in that region.
5. The ankles become more supple.

Note

1. Rocking in Dhanurasana is a simple exercise and with a little practise everyone can do it.
2. Do this exercise only when you are able to perform Dhanurasana with ease.

10. Ardha Halasana
(The Half-Plough Posture)

'Ardha' means 'half' and 'Hala' means 'plough' in Sanskrit.

- Lie flat on your back, keeping the legs together.
- Inhaling, press the palms down and raise first one leg and then the other, alternately. Then, raise both legs together perpendicular to the ground without bending the knees.
- Exhaling, return to the starting position.

SEQUENCES

- Lie flat on your back. Stretch your legs at full length. Keep the heels and the big toes together. Stretch your arms on the respective sides with palms turned down.
- Inhaling, press the palms down and raise first one leg slowly as high as possible without bending the knee, keeping the other leg flat on the floor.
- Hold the leg straight up until you complete the inhalation.
- Exhaling, bring the leg down slowly.
- Repeat the process with the other leg also.

ARDHA HALASANA

Right leg is raised.

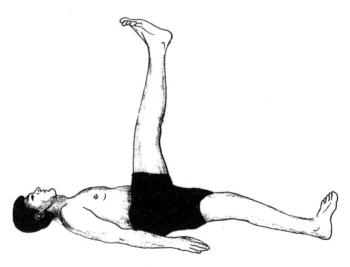

Left leg is raised.

- Take three turns, alternating the legs.
- Inhaling, press the palms down and, without bending the knees or raising the hands, raise the legs together slowly till they make an angle of 30 degrees to the ground, then 60 degrees, and, finally, bring them perpendicular at 90 degrees to the ground. Complete the inhalation. Fix your gaze on the big toes.
- Remain in this position as long as you can hold your breath comfortably.
- Exhaling, press the palms down again, and without bending the knees, bring down your legs together slowly, pausing for five seconds each as they reach 60 degrees and 30 degrees to the ground.
- Execute three turns, raising both legs together.

TECHNIQUE

1. Lie flat on your back on the carpet. Stretch your legs straight in line with your trunk. Bring your heels and the big toes together. Stretch your arms at full length and hold them close to your sides. Elbows should not bend. Palms should be turned down on the floor with fingers close together and the thumbs touching the respective thighs. Toes should point outwards and should be kept relaxed. The whole body must be straight from head to foot (Fig. 49). Relax the muscles of your legs completely. Rest for about a minute in this position, breathing normally.

Fig. 49.

2. Secure a steady position of the head, arms and legs. Keep the knees rigid. Keep the arms also stiff.

3. Inhale slowly and deeply and, while inhaling, press the palms down on the floor and raise first one leg through the hip-joint as slowly as you can and as high as it goes without bending the knee and keeping the other leg flat on the floor. The back should also remain flat on the floor.

4. Hold the leg straight up and as relaxed as possible until you complete the inhalation. Fix your gaze on the big toe.

5. Bring the leg down slowly from the hip-joint to the floor while exhaling. Relax for a few seconds.

6. Repeat the process with the other leg also and relax for a few seconds.

7. Perform three turns, alternating the legs.

8. Join both legs closely, heels and the big toes touching each other. Inhale slowly and deeply. While inhaling, press the palms down on the floor and without bending the knees or raising the hands and head and using your abdominal muscles mostly, raise the fully stretched legs together slowly and

Fig. 50.

Fig. 51.

steadily through the
hip-joints till they make
an angle of 30 degrees
to the ground (Fig. 50).
Hold the legs steady in
this position for about
five seconds and,
continuing to inhale,
raise them further till
they make an angle of
60 degrees to the
ground (Fig. 51). Hold
the legs steady in this

Fig. 52.

position again for about five seconds. Continuing to
inhale, raise the legs further till they are perpendicular
at an angle of 90 degrees to the ground (Fig. 52).
Complete the inhalation. While raising the legs, keep
the toes pointing outwards.

9.   Hold your breath and keep the legs together and
     straight up at right angles to the trunk and head.
     Knees should be straight so that the legs are not bent.
     Keep the back flat, pressing the floor. Also, keep the
     back of the head touching the floor. Arms and elbows
     should be close to the trunk. Fix your gaze on the big
     toes. This is the Ardha Halasana posture.

10. Stay balanced in this position as relaxed as possible
     and as long as you can hold your breath comfortably,
     keeping the legs steady with the feet and toes relaxed.
     Concentrate your mind on the big toes.

11. **Return:** When you can no longer hold your breath
     comfortably, exhale slowly. While exhaling, press the
     palms down again on the floor and without bending

the knees, bring down your legs to the floor, keeping them close together and as slowly as you can in the same manner as you raised them up, pausing for five seconds each as they reach 60 degrees and 30 degrees to the ground. Complete the exhalation.

12. After resuming the starting position, relax the body before taking another turn. After completing the exercise, relax in Savasana.

MEASURE

In the initial stages, this exercise may be done three times without stopping and resting. It may be dropped later as it is only a preparation for full Halasana.

BREATHING

Breathe normally until you pick up the practice. After mastering it, breathe as stated above. Breathe normally in the final position if you can stay in it comfortably for about a minute.

POINTS

1. Do not alter the position of your head, neck, shoulders and arms during the practice.
2. Do not raise the trunk and head at any time during the practice. The body above the hip-joints must lie still on the floor, undisturbed.
3. Keep your back as close to the floor as possible throughout this practice, and do not use your shoulders to help lift your legs.
4. Arms must be kept at their respective sides with palms turned down; do not move them from the position held at the start of the practice. They should not be raised while lifting the legs.

5. Knees must be kept straight, both while lifting the legs and while bringing them down.

6. In the initial stages, you may press down with your hands to facilitate the upward movement of the legs. As you advance in the practice, you can raise your legs and bring them down slowly without the slightest help of the hands by pressing your lower back down on the floor to straighten the spine and by tightening the muscles of the abdomen and legs.

7. When one leg is raised, the other leg must lie straight and motionless, the whole length touching the ground. Do not twist other parts of the body; let the whole body remain on the floor.

8. While raising both legs together and while bringing them down, they should be close together and straight like sticks.

9. Tense the muscles of the legs while raising them and while bringing them down.

10. The legs should not shake while performing this asana.

11. Raise and lower the legs as slowly as you can in the same slow rhythm. Avoid strain and jerky movements.

12. After raising the legs, the toes should be stretched outwards and they must not be kept stiff or pointed. Pointing the toes creates tension in the legs.

13. Lower the feet to the floor in one smooth movement.

14. Relax the legs completely as they reach the floor from the vertical position. As they come close to the floor, do not lose control and drop them down.

BENEFITS

1. Ardha Halasana builds up elasticity of the muscle in the abdominal area.

2. It prevents the prolapse of the abdominal organs, such as the uterus in women and the rectum in men.
3. It has a curative effect on menstrual disorders.
4. It helps to rid the stomach and intestines of gas and eliminate constipation.
5. It prevents hernia.
6. Persons who have varicose veins can practise this posture several times a day to get relief.

Note

1. You may perform this exercise in bed also before rising in the morning if you are plagued by constipation.
2. This is a simple asana which any person can perform.

11. Halasana
(The Plough Posture)

'Hala' means 'plough' in Sanskrit. This posture is called 'Halasana' because in the final position the body resembles the Indian plough.

- Assume Ardha Halasana.
- Pressing the palms down and without bending the knees, raise the posterior, hips and lower back.
- Lower and move your legs forward with knees kept straight until the toes touch the ground behind and beyond the head.
- Slide away the toes to the farthest point.
- Press the chest against the chin and form a chin-lock.
- Form a fingerlock and keep it encircling the top of your head.
- Release in the reverse order.

SEQUENCE

- Assume the Ardha Halasana posture without much support from the hands.

- Exhaling slowly, press the palms on the floor and raise your posterior, hips and lower back off the floor and, simultaneously, lower and move your legs right over your head without bending the knees until the toes touch the ground at the nearest point beyond your head. Inhale and breathe freely.
- Slide away the toes together straight along the floor, curving the spine to the maximum extent.
- Press the chest against the chin and form a firm chin-lock.
- Lift your arms and move them slowly until they rest on the floor on either side of your head. Form a finger-lock and keep the clasped hands encircling the top of your head. Keep the legs straight and together.
- Hold this position as long as comfortable, breathing freely.
- Restore the arms to their original position on the respective sides.
- Inhaling, bring back the legs together to the perpendicular position without bending the knees.
- Exhaling, bring down the legs until the heels rest on the floor.

TECHNIQUE

First Stage

1. Lie flat on your back. Stretch your legs at full length and keep them together. Stretch your arms on the respective sides. Palms should be turned down with fingers close together and the thumbs touching the thighs.

2. Inhaling slowly, push down on your hands and, without bending the knees, raise the legs together

slowly till they are perpendicular to the floor. Complete the inhalation. This is Ardha Halasana.

3. Keep the legs perpendicular to the ground and close together. Keep the toes relaxed. Breathe normally and relax for a few seconds.

4. Take a deep breath. Exhaling slowly, press the palms on the ground and, while pressing them, raise your posterior, hips and lower back off the floor and, simultaneously, lower and move your legs forward slowly towards your head, bringing the thighs towards the chest. While doing this, stretch your neck fully and lower your chin, but do not bend your knees or raise your head.

5. Continue pressing the palms on the ground. Pushing the torso up, move the legs over and beyond the head until

Fig. 53.

they come almost parallel to the floor. The body balances itself on the hands now (Fig. 53).

6. Without any pause in the movement of the legs and without bending the knees or raising the hands, bend your body slowly at the waist and, contracting the abdominal

Fig. 54.

muscles, bring the legs and thighs down slowly together till the knees come just above the forehead. Keep the toes pointing outward (Fig. 54).

7. Pressing the palms on the ground and keeping the arms straight, raise the hips and the lower back slowly without strain so that your feet continue to move downward and the tips of the toes just touch the ground at the nearest point behind and beyond your head. The toes must be kept pointed outward. The arms must not move and should be kept straight along the ground in the

Fig. 55.

opposite direction to the legs with the palms turned down (Fig. 55). Stabilize yourself in this position and complete the exhalation. Breathe slowly and deeply and remain in this position comfortably and relaxed for about ten seconds with the legs fully outstretched, feet together, and toes touching the ground lightly. Secure this position well before proceeding to the next stage.

Second Stage

1. Keep the arms straight in their original position with the palms flat on the floor. Take a deep

Fig. 56.

breath. Exhaling slowly, straighten the legs and slide away the toes together straight along the ground and away from the head, curving the spine at the same time. Slide away the toes till the legs are straightened out completely and the lower parts of the thighs are brought opposite the forehead. In this position, the abdomen is pressed further. Press the toes down on the floor and remain in this position for about ten seconds (Fig. 56). Inhale and breathe normally a few times through the nose.

2. Keep the knees straight and the arms in their original extended position. Take a deep breath. Exhaling, slide away the toes together still further along the ground, curving the spine further, till the upper parts of the thighs are brought opposite the forehead. Inhale and breathe normally.

3. Press the chest against the chin and form a firm chin-lock.

4. Lift your arms from the sides and move them slowly until they rest on the floor behind your head. Form a fingerlock and keeping the clasped hands on the top of the head, exert a slight pressure on it so that the nape of the neck and the shoulders touch the ground closely and adjust themselves. Keep the elbows and toes pressing the ground. The upper arms should rest on the floor (Fig. 57).

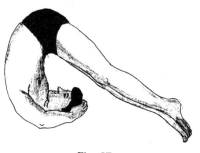

Fig. 57.

5. Take a deep breath. Exhaling, slide the toes forward again as far away from the head as possible till pressure is felt at the cervical region of the spine. Keep the chin pressed even tighter against the chest. Keep the legs from the thighs to the feet perfectly straight and together. Keep the knees stiff and the toes pressing the ground without creating tension in the legs. Slide the toes still further and secure the maximum curve of the spine. The weight of the body will now rest on the shoulders, the back portion of the upper arms, neck and head and the big toes. In this position, the pelvic region is also curved. This is the final position (Fig. 58B).

6. Keep your balance and relax the whole body, particularly the neck and shoulders.

7. Maintain this fully-stretched position comfortably and motionlessly for about ten seconds in the beginning and increase the period gradually. Concentrate your mind on the spinal column. Breathe deeply and rhythmically.

   Return: Resume the starting position slowly and gradually in the reverse order by adopting the following procedure: slide back your toes nearer the head without bending your knees so that your back comes down slightly. Unlock your fingers and bring your arms back slowly to the sides. Restore the arms to their original extended position on the respective sides and parallel to each other. Keep the palms turned down on the respective sides and parallel to each other. Keep the palms turned down on the floor.

   After your toes have come near the head as in the first position, inhale slowly and while inhaling, press the palms down and raise the toes from the floor. While raising them, lower your hips and bring back the legs together slowly without bending the knees until they are almost parallel to the floor. Continue to inhale. Pressing the palms down again on the floor and uncoiling the spine, bring back the legs again slowly over your head towards the vertical position without bending the knees and without any strain. When your lower back is nearing the floor, straighten out your legs so that they are once again at right angles to your trunk and head. Complete the inhalation and pause for a few seconds. Keep the toes relaxed. Exhale slowly and while exhaling, press the palms down again and, without bending the knees, bring down first your back and then your legs slowly and steadily until the heels rest on the floor, pausing at 60 degrees and 30 degrees to the ground as before. The entire body will now lie flat on the floor at full length in the supine position. Breathe normally and relax completely in Savasana.

MEASURE

1. Repeat this asana three times, relaxing in-between and maintaining the posture for only five to ten seconds in the beginning. Increase the holding period gradually to fifteen seconds, adding five seconds every week. In the advanced stage, maintain the posture for a maximum of two minutes.

2. No repetition beyond three is necessary if you are able to maintain the posture comfortably for two minutes at a stretch.

BREATHING

Breathe as stated above while doing this asana. There should not be any constraint or retention of the breath at any stage. Breathing will be mostly in the thorax as the ribcage is moved to its fullest extent.

POINTS

A. General

1. Practise Ardha Halasana to perfection before starting Full Halasana so that the spine becomes more flexible and the recti muscles are toned up for the later stage of the practice.
2. No strain should be felt anywhere in the body while practising this asana.
3. Avoid haste. The slower the movements, the greater the benefit.

B. Getting into the Posture

1. First, keep the legs close to each other. Raise them by stages up to 90 degrees to the ground. As soon as this position is reached, slowly bring the legs forward and without any pause at the different stages, place the toes on the floor at the nearest point beyond the head.
2. Both while raising and bringing down the legs, hold them together, straight and stretched without bending. Keep the feet also close together. The knees, thighs and hands should not be spread out.
3. The head should not be turned or raised from the floor during the practice since it may sprain the neck and disturb the posture.

4. While taking the legs towards the head, the arms should not move from their original position. They should be kept straight along the ground (Fig. 58A).

5. The elbows should not be raised at any time during the practice, except when placing the fingerlock behind the head in the final stage.

6. Keep your palms flat on the floor with the fingers close together. Do not move your hands to support the hips.

7. Both while raising the legs and while bringing them down, keep the palms pressing the floor and do not tilt the body. Press the palms firmly on the floor for keeping your balance and also to aid the lifting of the legs like a fulcrum. As you progress in the practice, use your abdominal muscles as much as possible and the arms as little as possible.

8. Do not bend the knees throughout this practice. The thighs and calves must be in a straight line.

9. Raise the legs and bring them down very slowly to avoid undue strain on the back. The movements must be smooth, steady and controlled. Do not bob up and down after raising the legs and while attempting to reach the floor with your toes. Balance your weight on the hands, and allow your legs to move down to the floor by their own weight. While returning also, use your hands for balancing your body.

10. The entire movement, from raising the legs to touching the floor with the toes beyond the head, should be without any jerks since they may injure the rigid muscles. Also, there should not be any spasmodic movements when bringing down the legs.

HALASANA

Fig. 58A—Toes touch the ground at the nearest point beyond the head.

Fig. 58B—Final position. Note the fingerlock behind the head
and the chin pressing the chest.

11. Relax the legs after placing them behind the head and while maintaining the posture. Relax them also after bringing them back and placing them on the floor.

C. Final Position

1. The toes must be stretched outwards and kept relaxed till they touch the floor above the head.

2. After the legs come parallel to the floor, allow them to lower themselves gradually of their own accord until the toes touch the floor. The toes should be fixed firmly on the floor only in the subsequent stages of the practice.

3. Do not strain your legs or your spine to exert pressure on your toes beyond the head to attain the final position quickly. The toes will reach the floor only with regular practise.

4. First, touch the nearest point beyond the head with your toes. Then, gradually slide them away together on the floor. The greater the distance of the toes from the head, the greater the spinal curve. The clasped hands on the top of the head will help you to inch forth a short but significant distance with your toes.

5. After resting the toes beyond the head, maintain the first and the last stages of the stretch for a longer period to derive a full benefit out of this posture.

6. When the final position is attained, the stretch of the back muscles must be maintained for some time comfortably.

7. Whatever little bend of the spine has been achieved at first should be maintained for some time. After a few weeks, you will be able to bend it more and more.

With daily practise, the stiff muscles of the back and the spine will become more flexible. (This also applies to Bhujangasana, Dhanurasana, Paschimotanasana and Yoga Mudra.)

8. Increase the spinal stretch gradually day by day without feeling the strain. As the practice advances, try to bend the base of the spine also.

9. The hands should be clasped on top of the head, and not under the head at the base of the skull.

10. Do not gulp down saliva during the chin-lock period.

D. Return

1. Have complete control while coming out of the posture.

2. While returning to the starting position, keep the back of your head firmly on the floor and the legs straight until the toes touch the floor.

3. Return from the final position very slowly as if your legs are being pulled back. Feel the stretch of the vertebral column as your legs are being lowered and your back curls down slowly on the floor.

4. Use mostly your abdominal muscles while lowering your legs to the floor.

5. When your lower back and the posterior are nearing the floor, do not allow your legs to fall back heavily on the floor.

BEGINNERS

1. It will be difficult for beginners to practise even the first stage of this asana. They should move slowly stage by stage. They should proceed to the second stage only after they are able to hold the first stage

comfortably for about fifteen seconds. They should not try to get to the final position right away which should be reached only in three or four attempts, extending the legs a little further in each attempt. After mastering the practice, they should avoid going by stages.

2. Persons with stiff muscles, inelastic or deformed spine or those who are overweight should practise this asana slowly. They will find it difficult in the beginning to place their toes on the ground beyond their head without bending the knees. After lifting their legs over the head as far as they can, they should stop at whatever point the movement becomes a strain and simply hold the legs at the farthest position reached, letting their feet hang in the air behind them as low as they are able to and for as long as it is comfortable.

   As their spine becomes more supple, the weight of their legs will gradually pull their feet down and they will be able to place their toes on the floor at the nearest point beyond the head that they can comfortably reach. Even the final position will become easy for them as their body adjusts itself to the posture. Everybody can attain the final position with persistent practise.

3. To help raise the lower back and the posterior from the floor and extend the legs beyond the head, beginners may bend the arms and push their posterior up from behind with their palms to help lift the trunk and propel the legs while the arms take the weight. While returning also, they may hold the back and the posterior with their palms and slide the palms down the back of the thighs as the legs are being lowered. Pressing the elbows on the ground also helps.

4. Beginners may feel some strain in the abdominal region on account of the pull on their abdominal muscles. They should then stop and begin again the next day. The strain will disappear as they progress with their practice.

5. Bulky persons with a protruding belly can practise Halasana better if they regularly practise Bhujangasana, Shalabhasana, Dhanurasana and Paschimotanasana and reduce their abdomen gradually.

CAUTION

1. Practise this asana on an empty stomach.

2. This asana should be stopped if it causes pain continuously in the liver or spleen or exerts excessive pressure on the abdomen.

3. Persons suffering from hernia, high blood pressure or heart ailments must not practise it.

4. Women should not practise it during menstruation and after the third month of pregnancy.

BENEFITS

A. Physical

1. Halasana stretches and exercises the posterior muscles of the entire body. The asana keeps the intercostal muscles healthy. The asana exerts alternate pressure on the heart muscle and thus strengthens the heart and improves circulation. It is helpful in developing the muscles of the back, hips, shoulders, abdomen, recti and thighs. The muscles at the back of the neck are stretched and relaxed. The hamstrings are also well stretched.

2. The alternate contraction, relaxation, stretching and the slow unwinding of the spinal column provide complete exercise for the different areas. If practised slowly and smoothly, the entire spine becomes flexible and the spinal nerves, muscles and ligaments are toned up and fed with extra supply of arterial blood.

3. Slight deformities of the spine are set right and its natural curve is maintained by the regular practise of this asana, besides preventing the early degeneration of the vertebral bones.

4. The brain and face receive a richer blood supply.

5. The regular practise of Halasana makes the lungs more elastic.

6. This asana develops healthy thyroid and parathyroid. It will also keep the gonad (sex) glands healthy.

7. Musicians and teachers benefit by performing this asana as the region of the throat is given a good massage. The throat gets cleared up after the practice and the neck muscles become strong.

8. The pelvic region and the legs are stretched and exercised by this practice.

9. It helps to maintain the abdominal and pelvic organs in their correct positions and strengthens them.

10. It helps to reduce the congestion or enlargement of the liver and spleen.

11. Persons desirous of reducing deposits of fat in the chest, lower abdomen, hips, thighs, legs and the backside may practise this asana regularly. It will help them to reduce weight and trim a flabby abdomen.

12. It makes the waist slim and the hip-joints flexible.

13. It helps a person to maintain a correct standing posture and grow to his full stature.

14. The practise of this asana will relieve fatigue almost immediately.

15. Halasana is an excellent remedy for physical and mental laziness.

B. Therapeutical

1. Systematic practise of Halasana releases the tension in the back, neck and legs and helps to cure lumbago, spinal rigidity and various kinds of rheumatism.

2. It alleviates pain in the shoulders and the waist and neuralgic pain in the back. Pain in the joints of the legs and ankles will also subside.

3. It is very effective in eliminating myalgia, neurasthenia, arthritis, sciatica and varicose veins.

4. It helps to eradicate belching, gastritis, flatulence and enteroptosis.

5. It improves digestive power and is conducive to smooth bowel movement.

6. It gives relief in cases of headache, bronchitis and asthma.

7. It is recommended for those suffering from some types of diabetes since it aids the rejuvenation of the pancreas. It also regulates the secretion of adrenalin in the system.

8. It is good for persons with a tendency for high blood pressure, but those already having it, should not practise it until they get cured by other yogic or non-yogic methods.

9. The pressure exerted on the palms while raising and bringing down the legs and the stretching of the palms and fingers in the fingerlock cures cramps in the hands.

10. Disorders of the uterus and ovaries and menstrual ailments are set right by the regular practise of this asana.
11. The early stages of piles respond well to Ardha Halasana.

Note

1. Attempt this asana only after mastering Viparita Karani and Sarvangasana.
2. Paschimotanasana is complementary to Halasana, while Matsyasana, Chakrasana (Supine) and Bhujangasana are counterposes of Halasana as the spine is bent in the opposite direction.

12. Sarvangasana
(All-Parts' Posture)

'ऊर्ध्वाधः स्थितयोः चन्द्रसूर्ययोः अध ऊर्ध्वकरणेन
अन्वर्था ... ... विपरीतकरणी मुद्रा'

—*Jyotsna on Hathapradipika* III—79.

प्रथमं शवासनं क त्वा ततः कूर्परद्वयं प ष्ठभागे प थिव्यां
निधाय करतलाभ्यां कटिभागत आपादं शरीरमूर्ध्वमुन्नेयम्,
स्कन्धद्वयेन कूर्परद्वयेन च यत् प थिव्यां व्यवस्थानं तदिति।।

—*Yogasutra: 'Kirana' Tika,*
Srikrishnavallabhacharya, P—250.

'Sarva' means 'all' and 'Anga' means 'part' in Sanskrit. Almost all parts of the body are involved and derive benefit from this asana and hence the name.

- Lie on your back with the arms on the sides and palms turned down.
- Raise the legs perpendicular to the floor, keeping the knees straight.

- Raise your legs over your head.
- Place the palms beneath the hips and prop up the trunk and legs.
- Sliding the palms higher on the trunk, push the hips and the small of the back and bring the trunk and legs to a vertical position. Keep the palms at the back of the ribs and support the trunk and legs with the palms, forearms and elbows.
- Sliding the palms higher, raise the hips and legs further till the trunk and legs are in a straight line.
- Push the chest forward towards the chin and form a chin-lock. Fix your gaze on the big toes.
- Return slowly in the reverse order.

SEQUENCE

- Lie on your back with arms on the sides and palms turned down. Keep the legs together.
- Pressing the palms and elbows down and keeping the knees straight, raise the legs together till they are perpendicular to the floor.
- Raise your hips and lower back off the floor and move your legs towards your head.
- Place the palms beneath the hips and prop up the trunk and legs.
- Sliding the palms higher on the trunk, keep on pushing the hips and the small of the back higher and raise the whole trunk off the floor till it is vertical. While doing this, bring the legs also back to the vertical position.
- Place the palms at the back of the ribs and support the raised trunk and legs with the palms, forearms and elbows.

- Sliding the palms higher and higher again, raise the hips and legs further till the trunk and legs are in a straight line.
- Push the chest forward towards the chin and form a chin-lock. Fix your gaze on the big toes and keep the balance.
- Breathe deeply and rhythmically and maintain this posture for about three minutes.
- Return slowly to the starting position in the reverse order.

TECHNIQUE

1. Lie flat on your back on the carpet. The head must be well stretched out as also the vertebrae of the neck. Stretch your legs at full length. Keep the heels and the big toes together. Stretch your arms along the respective sides of the trunk, touching the sides of your body. Palms should be turned down. Toes should be stretched outwards. Keep the whole body straight from head to foot (Fig. 49). Breathe normally and relax the whole body completely, particularly the leg muscles.

2. Keep the head, arms and legs steady. Put your heels and the big toes together and keep the knees rigid. Press the palms and elbows down on the floor. Inhale slowly and while inhaling, slowly raise the fully stretched legs together from the hip-joints, keeping the knees straight and without pointing the toes, till they are perpendicular to the floor, as in Ardha Halasana (Fig. 52). While raising the legs, tense the abdominal and leg muscles. Complete the inhalation. Keep the legs straight up at right angle to the trunk

and head. Hold the arms and elbows close to the trunk. Remain in this position for a few seconds, keeping the legs steady with the toes turned outwards and relaxed. (See also 'Points' in Ardha Halasana.)

3. Exhale slowly and while exhaling, increase the pressure of your palms and elbows against the floor and using the muscular power of your abdomen and back, raise your posterior, hips and lower back off the floor and slowly move your legs back over your head from the perpendicular position, keeping the knees stiff. While raising the posterior, hips and trunk from the floor, curve up the lower part of the spine till the legs bend over and beyond the head at an angle of about 45 degrees to the ground. This can be done easily by applying pressure on both the palms and on the arms which are stretched along their respective sides and by elongating the neck (Fig. 59).

Fig. 59.

4. As soon as the hips leave the floor, bend the arms at the elbows and raise the forearms without widening or shifting the elbows. Resting the elbows on the floor, place the palms firmly a little above the small of the back like brackets and prop up the trunk and legs

with the hands and upper arms. Keep your fingers
pointing upward towards the spinal column. The back
of the upper arms should rest firmly on the floor, close
to the trunk, to provide steady support. Relax the
face, neck and shoulders (Fig. 60).

5. Inhale slowly and while inhaling, slide the palms higher
and higher on the ribcage on either side of the spine.
Utilizing the pressure
exerted by the palms
and with the support of
the elbows, push the hips
and the small of the back
gently higher and higher
with the palms and raise
the whole trunk till it is
vertical. As the trunk
straightens up, slowly
extend the legs upwards
in line with the trunk
and bring them back to
the vertical position

Fig. 60.

again without bending the knees. Exhale completely
and start breathing normally.

6. As your body rises, slide the palms on the back of the
ribcage and support the raised trunk from behind with
the palms. While the thumbs grasp the sides of the
trunk, one on each side, the fingers should be spread
out and grasp the back part on either side of the spine
for better support. Keep the trunk and legs erect and
perpendicular to the floor, the elbows and shoulders
fixed firmly on the floor, and the forearms propping
up the body at the back like pillars. The back of the

head and the nape of the neck must remain pressing the floor. Your body is now in a straight line and upside down from your shoulders. Balance yourself well in this position.

7. Put more pressure on the palms and elbows and raise the trunk, hips and legs further up vertically without bending the knees. As the back, hips and legs rise up, support them by slowly sliding the palms higher up the back. Raise and stretch your trunk till both the legs and the trunk are at right angle to the neck and head lying on the floor.

8. Pushing your lower back upward with your palms and giving your body an extra lift with the hands, push the upper chest forward towards the chin till the latter is fixed in the jugular notch, and thus forms a firm chin-lock. Keep the fully stretched legs together and in line with the trunk. Rest the shoulders on the floor. Keep the back of your upper arms up to the elbows firmly on the floor and use your hands to steady yourself. Breathe normally and remain in this position for a few seconds.

9. **Final Position:** Continue to breathe normally. Push the back up with the hands so that the legs are stretched out and the trunk is straightened up completely. As the palms catch the back as high as possible, slide them up gradually, pushing up and supporting the trunk and helping to raise the legs higher. Lift the back as high as possible, keeping the legs and knees straight. Raise the legs vertically to the maximum extent, the trunk following them, till the trunk and legs are in a straight line and perpendicular to the ground.

The whole body, from the midpoint of the feet down to the shoulders, should be straight and vertical. Balance evenly the entire weight of the body upon the hands, forearms, elbows, the back of the upper arms, shoulders and the back of the neck and head. Continue pressing the upper chest against the chin and maintain balance with the help of the hands, the forearms propping up the trunk and legs and keeping them vertical. Extend the legs and keep them straight and together. Stretch the feet and toes outward as high as possible and keep them together and relaxed. Adjust the position of the neck and hands. The shoulders, elbows and the back of the neck and head must press the floor. Keep the mouth closed. Maintain balance with the help of your hands. Fix your gaze on the big toes. This is the final position (Fig. 61).

10. Breathe deeply and rhythmically and keep the legs relaxed in this position. Focus your attention on the thyroid gland at the base of the throat.

11. Maintain this posture comfortably and motionlessly for fifteen seconds as a beginner and gradually work up to three minutes, adding fifteen seconds more every week.

12. **Return:** Return very slowly to the starting position, reversing the order of the movements, keeping the back of your head against the floor and the body stretched out throughout. The reversal procedure is as follows. Exhale slowly and while exhaling, lower the legs slowly over the head to an angle of about 45 degrees as before, thereby reducing the weight on the elbows. While doing this, slide down the palms

until they are behind the waist, and then lower your knees towards your forehead without bending them.

When you are confident that you can come down without the support of your hands, remove them from the waist and stretch your forearms again on the floor on the respective sides of the trunk with the palms turned down (Fig. 59). Press the palms down on the floor to support the trunk and legs. Keep the knees straight. Maintain this position for a few seconds and steady yourself. Inhaling slowly and balancing yourself on your hands, bring down the upper back, the lower back, hips and the posterior gradually till the legs are perpendicular to the floor. Exhale slowly and while exhaling, lower the legs very slowly to the floor, keeping the feet together and without bending the knees. After your back and heels rest again on the floor, turn the palms upwards and stretch out your neck and legs. This is the starting position. Take a few deep breaths and then breathe normally. Relax the body completely in Savasana for a few minutes and allow the blood circulation to return to normal. Rise slowly to a sitting position again.

BREATHING

1. Breathing should be normal throughout this practice in the initial stages. After you have made progress, breathe as stated above.
2. Do not force the pace of breathing while holding the posture as pressure is exerted on the thorax.
3. There should not be any retention of the breath at any stage of the practice.

MEASURE

1. Beginners may take three turns, maintaining the posture for only about thirty seconds. Advanced students may take only one turn when they are able to hold the posture for a longer period.

2. After mastering the posture, the maintenance period may be increased gradually from one minute to three minutes when done along with other asanas. No repetition is necessary as one derives greater benefits by maintaining the posture for a while, rather than by repeating it.

3. Three minutes is the average maximum for this posture. It must not be prolonged beyond three minutes as holding the posture for quite a long time will not bring proportionately greater benefits.

4. Beginners should first learn the technique thoroughly and only then increase the period of the asana's duration.

POINTS

A. General

1. Perform this asana on an empty stomach and after emptying the bladder and if possible the bowels, which will facilitate the movements.

2. Do not cough or sneeze during the practice. If it is unavoidable, resume the starting position quickly and begin again.

3. Do not gulp down saliva in the chin-lock period.

4. Practise this asana slowly and in as relaxed a manner as possible with complete control over the movements.

5. Maintain the continuity of the movements, avoiding jolts and jerks.
6. Keep the heels and the big toes together and do not separate the legs throughout this practice.
7. Do not keep your toes pointed; keep your feet relaxed.
8. Knees should not be bent at any stage as this will alter the position of the spine.
9. Throughout this practice, the back of the head must rest on the carpet.

B. Getting into the Posture

1. Raise the legs in a slow and steady movement and reach the final position without straining yourself. After maintaining the posture, bring down the legs slowly to the floor without jerks. Do not drop them down.
2. While raising the legs, press the palms down on the floor and again at the back to facilitate the upward movement of the legs.
3. Do not keep your feet stiff while raising them.
4. Beginners and obese persons who are unable to raise their posterior from the floor may push them up with the palms in the initial stages.
5. Pushing the trunk with the hands towards the head will be helpful in executing the chin-lock.
6. Bring the upper chest forward to touch the chin. Do not push the chin towards the chest. Do not raise the head to form the chin-lock.
7. While holding the posture, press the upper chest to the chin to effect pressure on the thyroid region.

C. Final Position

1. In the final position, the head and neck should be at right angle to the trunk and legs in case you are of a

normal build. The trunk and legs should be in a straight line and perpendicular to the floor with no angle at the hipline. An exact vertical position is not possible for bulky persons with bulges in the front or the sides, and they may slightly incline their legs over the top of their head so that they may hold the posture comfortably.

2. The back of the head, the shoulders and the upper arms up to the elbows should remain on the floor.

3. After supporting the trunk with your palms, ensure that the elbows are placed neither too far out from the sides nor too near them. If the elbows are wider than the width of the shoulders, the trunk cannot be raised properly.

4. The palms should hold the trunk lightly so as to maintain a balance. They should not slip down in which case the body may slant to one side.

5. Do not put too much weight on the elbows alone. There should be more weight on the shoulders than on the arms and elbows.

6. While maintaining the posture, hold the legs straight like sticks but not tense.

7. While supporting the trunk lightly with the palms, take care that the legs do not move towards the head from their perpendicular position to gain balance.

8. In the initial stages, there will be a tendency for the legs to swing out of the perpendicular position. To correct this, press the back with the palms, tighten the knee and thigh muscles and stretch up vertically.

9. Keep the heels and the big toes close together while maintaining the posture.

10. Keep the toes exactly above your eyes. They should be turned outwards and remain relaxed. Do not stretch the feet up or keep the toes stiff as it will cause tension in the feet and legs.

11. Keep the neck straight and do not put pressure on it. The neck must not move sideways during the practice as it will cause pain.

12. Pressing the upper chest against the chin and forming the chin-lock is the most important part of this practice as the thyroid is well massaged in between them with an increased arterial supply. Those who are unable to set the chin against the jugular notch may press their chin against any part of the sternum which is nearest, but this is not the correct position and the benefit derived will be less.

13. In the final position, do not allow the body to move to and fro or sag at the waist.

14. Maintain the full stretch of the entire body, balancing perfectly and without any discomfort.

15. If the legs begin to shake, return to the starting position and relax in Savasana.

16. Performing eye exercises during the holding period will be extremely beneficial.

D. Return

1. Return to the starting position with grace and balance, using your abdominal muscles as much as possible.

2. Ensure that the downward movement of the legs is very slow and controlled at every stage by pressing your hands against the floor.

3. The spine should slowly uncoil on the carpet and the legs should not drop down. The tailbone and the posterioɪ must not land heavily on the floor.

4. While bringing down the legs, as they near the floor, do not raise the shoulders or the head from the floor. The nape of the neck should cling to the floor.

5. While bringing down the legs, beginners may support them by placing their palms on the posterior and sliding them down along the back of the thighs until the back touches the floor.

6. Do not get up to the standing position immediately after Sarvangasana or any other inverted posture. Relax in Savasana, allowing the blood circulation to return to normal.

CAUTION

1. Do not attempt Sarvangasana if you have any history of serious cardiovascular disorders or high blood pressure.

2. Avoid it if you are suffering from cold and your nostrils are blocked or if you have a thyroid disorder.

3. Persons suffering from eye trouble should avoid this asana.

4. Young persons below fourteen years should not practise this.

5. Women should not do it during menstruation as the blood released at this time is often very acidic and a back-flow could damage the womb.

6. Do not practise it if you feel dizzy or have palpitation while performing it.

SARVANGASANA

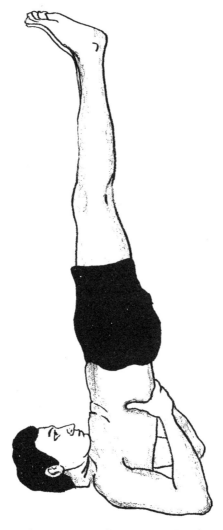

Fig. 61 (A)—Final position. Hands are supporting the trunk and legs from behind.

SARVANGASANA

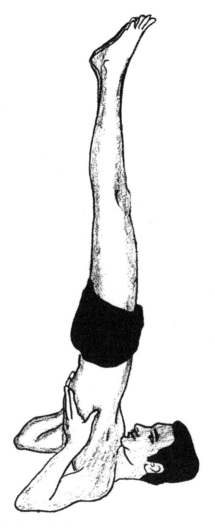

Fig. 61 (B)—Final position. Trunk and legs are at right angles to the head. Note the chin-lock.

BENEFITS

A. Physical

1. The principal physical benefit of Sarvangasana lies in keeping the thyroid and parathyroid glands healthy which regulate the functioning of many vital organs of the body and stabilize the metabolic processes. A healthy thyroid will reduce nervous tension. Signs of old age, due to the faulty functioning of the thyroid, are counteracted by performing this asana regularly. It also activates the pituitary and thymus glands and keeps the prostate gland healthy.

2. It prevents the untimely wrinkling of the face and premature ageing.

3. The inverted position of the body in Sarvangasana, in which the feet and legs are kept higher than the heart, promotes an increased flow of blood to the thorax, neck and head on account of the reversal of the gravitational pull on the blood flow. A rich flow of blood to the brain, the scalp, face, the organs of the chest, the roots of the cranial and spinal nerves, and other vital organs and glands is ensured. Most circulatory congestions are relieved besides promoting the free flow of hormones into the blood. The reverse flow of blood also relieves the work of the heart.

4. A regular practise of this asana will keep the vertebral column supple. A stiff spine can be made pliable and minor defects in its curvature are corrected. The spinal nerves are also toned up.

5. The muscles of the upper arms, shoulders, neck and thighs get strengthened.

6. The inversion of the body relieves any congestion of the organs in the lower part of the abdomen and the pelvis.

7. The liver and kidneys get massaged and function better.

8. It improves digestion and pancreatic secretion.

9. It prevents the accumulation of fat around the abdomen, waist and hips.

10. This asana prevents sagging of breasts in women.

11. It improves the functioning of the throat vessels and the vocal cords. The voice is enriched on account of the pressure exerted on the neck and the massaging of the larynx and pharynx and all the organs of the throat.

12. It enables the practitioner to have good eyesight.

13. Persons engaged in sedentary occupations or whose work demands long hours of standing will find this posture ideal for easing the legs.

14. A regular practise of this asana will help to regulate and normalize the weight of the body because of its effect on the thyroid gland.

B. Therapeutical

1. Sarvangasana gives relief in cases of dyspepsia, gastritis, constipation, visceroptosis and enteroptosis or at least prevents them from becoming worse. It also helps to cure many diseases of the spleen and bladder.

2. The practise of this asana gives relief to those suffering from palpitation, bronchitis, tonsillites, tuberculosis, headache, insomnia and epilepsy.

3. The deep breathing and the strong action of the diaphragm, induced by the inverted position of the

body, benefit the victims of some types of asthma. The increased circulation of the blood to the neck and chest also helps them.

4. Doing this asana regularly will prevent goitre.
5. It will prevent or give relief from varicose veins in the legs for it helps to drain accumulated blood from these areas.
6. It relieves pain in the back of the neck.
7. The continued practise of Sarvangasana prevents cold and other nasal disturbances by clearing the congestion in the sinus cavities.
8. It prevents hernia and gives relief in cases of bleeding piles and urinary disorders.
9. This asana has often been found helpful in the treatment of leprosy.
10. It prevents the prolapse of the uterus by decreasing pressure in the abdomen. Prolapse of the rectum and any displacement of the abdominal organs are also set right.
11. If women practise Sarvangasana a few months after childbirth, the inverted position of the body will help the organs and glands related to childbirth to easily regain their proper positions.
12. This asana keeps the gonads and ovaries functioning properly. Loss of sex drive in males and various uterine and menstrual disorders in females can be overcome by practising this asana. It also enhances the power of sex control.
13. Sarvangasana counteracts nervous fatigue and exhaustion.
14. This asana brings back lost vitality even after prolonged illness.

Note

1. Every person with normal health can include Sarvangasana in his daily schedule as it will have a rejuvenating effect upon his whole system and improve his concentration.

2. This practice is particularly beneficial for persons who start yoga exercises after the age of forty.

3. Sarvangasana becomes easier if Viparita Karani is mastered first. Advanced yoga students may combine both by switching over to Sarvangasana from the Viparita Karani posture.

4. Sarvangasasna is a good substitute for those who are unable to do Sirshasana. It is easier to perform and its benefits are essentially the same as that of Sirshasana without any of the harmful effects which Sirshasana sometimes brings due to wrong practise.

5. Even those who have mastered Sirshasana should not omit Sarvangasana from their daily practise on account of its unique benefits.

6. Matsyasana is the counterpose of Sarvangasana as unlike Sarvangasana, it frees the front of the neck while compressing its nape. It also releases the tension in the dorsal and abdominal sinews which may have been felt during Sarvangasana.

7. Matsyasana must be performed after Sarvangasana followed by Halasana to get the maximum benefit out of these postures. Good health is maintained by regularly doing Sarvangasana, Matsyasana, and Halasana one after the other.

13. Savasana
(The Dead Body Posture)

उत्तानं शववद् भूमौ शयनं तच्छवासनम् ।
शवासनं श्रान्तिहरं चित्तविश्रान्तिकारकम् ।।

Lying supine on the ground like a corpse—that is Savasana.
Savasana wards off fatigue and brings mental repose.
—*Hatha Pradipika* I—32.

'Sava' means 'dead body' in Sanskrit. To practise this asana, the student should lie motionless on the floor like a dead body in order to secure complete relaxation of all parts of his body and remove tensions, both physical and mental.

NEED FOR RELAXATION

Modern life is full of stress and tension. The hectic pace of life leads to tension both at home and at the workplace. This is particularly the case in big cities where people with ambition and drive are always tense in their anxiety to get ahead in their lure for wealth and fame.

While modern living and lifestyle increase stress and tension, the ability to cope with them with poise and balance is decreasing. As tension drains away the energy, people get tired easily and both their body and mind need relaxation. They will collapse like an overworked horse if not given timely rest.

To relieve physical strain, remove the in-built tensions of modern life, and to quieten the mind, Savasana or the corpse-like posture is the best. The technique is simple but difficult to master as both body and mind have to work in unison.

SEQUENCE

- Select a quiet place. Spread your carpet on a firm and flat surface. Wear only minimum clothing.
- Lie flat on your back at full length. Rest your head in a comfortable position. Legs should be kept sufficiently apart. Keep the knees slightly flexed.
- Extend the arms fully and rest them lightly on their respective sides with the hands about a foot away from the thighs. Palms should be turned upwards and fingers slightly curled.
- Allow your mouth to fall open slightly. Drop your chin and let your lower jaw sag a little. Allow your teeth to part a little. Close your eyes gently.
- Lie perfectly still like a corpse and persuade all your muscles to relax completely. Relax your mind by freeing it from immediate cares, conflicts, worries and fears.
- As you relax, allow your mind to run over every part and organ of your body from head to toe. Get a

picture of each part in your mind and 'let go' without any conscious effort.

- If there are any parts of your body that still feel taut, relax them by releasing the muscles.
- Be aware of only your breath and follow its rhythm until you lose consciousness of your body.
- As you regain consciousness of the body, take a few deep breaths. Join your legs slowly and bring back your arms to their respective sides. Open your eyes gently. Stretch your limbs and get up slowly to the sitting position and then to the standing position.

TECHNIQUE

A. Preparing for Relaxation

1. Select a quiet and well-ventilated place where you will not be disturbed during the practice. The surroundings must be pleasant and free from flies and insects.

2. Select a soft thick carpet. Spread it on the hard floor and lie down slowly flat on your back at full length. Roll your head gently side to side a few times and rest it in the most comfortable position with the face turned upwards. The back of the head should rest comfortably on the carpet to avoid any tension in the back and cramping of the neck. The head should be in line with the spinal column and the whole body should be straight and symmetrical.

3. Stretch out your legs at full length. Keep a comfortable distance in between the feet with the heels about 14 inches apart. Both legs must rest on the ground; keep them relaxed and comfortable. Allow your feet to fall a little to the sides, with the

inside edges of the heels in contact with the floor. Your feet must be turned outwards and drooping. Bend the knees slightly and keep them relaxed.

4. Extend your arms and let them lie passively on either side of your body in the most comfortable position, with the hands about a foot away from the thighs. Leave your arms loose. Slightly bend the elbows so that the weight of the arms and hands is taken by the floor. Palms should be turned upwards and kept relaxed. Fingers should be slightly curled in and loosely held.

5. Adjust your arms, legs, back, shoulders and head so as to make yourself as comfortable as possible. Your arms and legs should be spread symmetrically.

6. Keep your lips just touching each other; do not close them firmly. Drop your chin and let your lower jaw sag a little. Allow the two rows of your teeth to part a little. Let your tongue lie limp with its tip resting behind your lower teeth or in whatever way you find most comfortable. Do not move your head or allow your mouth to drop open. Relax your facial muscles in this position.

7. Lie perfectly still in an attitude of total surrender.

8. Start to develop your awareness of different parts of your body which are in contact with the floor.

9. Gradually transfer your awareness from the outside world to inside your body. Imagine that nothing else exists in the world but your body and start relaxing every part and organ as if you have no control over them. When you feel perfectly relaxed, slacken your hold on your body and let it go limp and 'sink' into the floor. Abandon yourself completely and feel that

your body is a dead mass and that you are not its owner.

10. Lower your upper eyelids slowly and close your eyes gently. The eyelids should be closed loosely, not firmly, and the eyeballs must remain passive without any movement as though you are in peaceful slumber (Fig. 62).

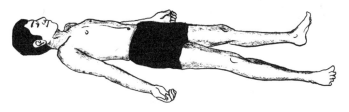

Fig. 62—Final position in which both body and mind are totally relaxed.

11. Breathe naturally through the nose and do not attempt to regulate your breathing. Just follow your incoming and outgoing breath in your mind without any effort to lengthen or shorten them or interfere with their rhythm or sound. Allow respiration to occur naturally and feel the sensation of the breath in the nostrils without widening them. As breathing slows down, the mental activity also quietens.

12. Remain motionless in this position like a corpse but stay inwardly alert, and determine to relax thoroughly. Switch off your mind from your work and lay aside all your worries and conflicts with complete confidence in yourself. Shake yourself free from all negative emotions such as anger, anxiety, fear, guilt, resentment, frustration, depression and phobias as they all bottle up and produce tension in

the body. Eliminate gradually from your mind all rambling thoughts and distractions. As the last train of thought leaves your mind, do not think of anything whatsoever—past, present or future. Turn your attention inward and give yourself up to peace and rest.

B. How to Relax

1. Relaxation cannot be induced straightaway. Start relaxing the body slowly and part by part as effortlessly as possible. Relax each segment of your body—the legs, abdomen, chest, arms, neck and head—one after another without moving them. Take a particular part and, directing your consciousness to that part, relax it thoroughly by loosening the muscles and joints gradually.

2. While relaxing any part of your body, turn your attention only to it and feel the relaxation before withdrawing your consciousness from that part and proceeding to the next. As your attention travels in logical sequence from part to part, do not be impatient and move on hurriedly from one part to another.

3. After relaxing each part of the body by turn, make an attempt to relax more than one part conjointly, such as from the toes to the groin, from the fingertips to the shoulders. Relax the entire back and then the front of the body. Finally, relax all parts of your body simultaneously and continuously and relieve tensions more quickly. Such overall relaxation, however, can be achieved only by practise.

4. After relaxing the voluntary muscles, namely those attached to the skeleton, the involuntary organs such

as the heart, lungs and brain, whose functions are automatic, can be relaxed by turning your attention to them.

5. Complete relaxation of the whole body at one and the same time should be achieved in the final stage, eliminating all tensions, nervous or muscular, in any part of the body.

6. Awareness of the parts of the body by rotation should be neither too fast nor too slow.

First Stage

1. As mentioned above, stretch yourself on the carpet. Arms and legs should be stretched to their full length and passively rested. The back of the legs, arms, trunk and head should touch the floor and feel the contact. Adjust your head finally on the carpet. Close your eyes as if you are falling asleep. Be completely at ease and try to secure the stillness of a corpse.

2. Relaxation should be done in stages initially, taking one particular part of your body at a time. Start with relaxing, say, the chest. The abdomen should be taken up next. The lower extremities should follow this and then the upper ones, and the head should come last.

3. This is the general practice but need not necessarily be followed as the route of relaxation along which your mind should travel securely. This should be determined by yourself. You may start from the tip of the toe and with the active cooperation of the mind, a wave of relaxation should pass from every part of the body to the top of the head.

4. First, direct your consciousness to the lowest part of your body and proceed gradually upwards without

missing a single part until the whole body has
received attention. Start from the tip of the right big
toe and work upwards inwardly to the instep, heel,
sole, ankle and lower leg one by one and reach up to
the knee without moving it even slightly. Proceed
upwards mentally from joint to joint, from the knee
to the thigh and then the hips. Make the same
progression with the left leg. Then, relax the anus,
rectus muscles, the genitals, the loins and the posterior,
one at a time, and proceed, in turn, to loosen the pelvis
muscles and the navel. Pass your attention slowly to
the solar plexus and from there to the muscles at the
base of the spine and the abdominal wall.

From the internal organs of the abdomen, move
your awareness towards the organs in the chest,
circling the heart and lungs and relax them. Then
relax the spinal column from the bottom upwards,
relaxing the individual vertebrae and the muscles on
both sides of the spine.

Slowly come to the sides, relaxing each muscle
on the way. Pass on little by little from the shoulder
girdle to the armpit and then right up to the tips of
the fingers, feeling your way to each tip and relaxing
each finger, joint by joint, without moving them.
Carry on in this way by taking up the palm, back of
the hand, wrist, forearm, elbow and the upper arm
one by one. Move back to the other arm and making
the same progression, reach up to the neck in your
upward exploration of the body. Relax the front of
the neck as also the nape completely. Then carry on
with a similar relaxation of your throat, the lower
jaw, the muscle under the chin, mouth, tongue, the

upper and lower lips, the tip and inside of the nose, right cheek, left cheek, right ear, left ear, right temple, left temple, right eyebrow, left eyebrow, facial muscles, forehead, the top of the head, the muscles of the scalp, and the back of the head, letting your attention dwell easily on these parts.

The precise sequence of the rotation of awareness is irrelevant as long as all the body areas are 'treated' to the relaxation procedure.

5.   After relaxing each part and organ consciously one by one in isolation from the rest of the body and after loosening every joint and relaxing every taut muscle and limb, come to the eyelids and the eyeballs. Let your eyelids droop and close your eyes gently without any muscular effort. As your eyes turn back under the lids, focus your awareness finally on the spot between the eyebrows. Slowly dissociate your awareness from the various parts of your body and the body as a whole and start listening to your breathing while in a semi-conscious state until finally the consciousness of the body fades away, leaving only pure awareness.

6.   Another method is to start relaxing all controllable parts of your body one by one like the arms, legs, neck, face and so on, the mind dwelling on the parts which are being relaxed. Then do likewise with the non-controllable parts like the stomach, heart and brain. After this, cease to think of specific areas or parts and relax the whole body as a coordinated unit. By releasing all knots of tension in the body as they show up one by one, you can achieve complete relaxation.

7. Yet another method of relaxation involves your becoming conscious of the weight of each part of your body which is supported by the floor. Imagine that the limbs of your body are very heavy as if they are made of lead and that you are dropping them down one by one on a soft cushion as if they are not yours. This will induce the relaxation of those parts. Finally, surrender your whole body to gravity and feel you are sinking into the floor though you feel light at the end of the practice.

8. Try out all the above relaxation patterns and choose the one which suits you the best. Practise it regularly, keeping to the same sequence and relaxing each part of the body as completely as possible.

9. After you work out a sequence of relaxation techniques and develop your own style, it should not be changed so that it becomes a habit when the parts relax by themselves without your having to go through every step of the process.

10. Imagination plays a vital role in all these relaxation processes.

Second Stage

1. After completing the relaxation routine as described above, locate and release the residual tension in the voluntary and involuntary muscles, the major muscle groups, joints, nerve plexuses and every part and organ of your body, from the tips of the toes to the top of the head, and feel the sensation of relaxation as you 'let go' every part. As relaxation proceeds progressively, each part and organ receiving its quota of rest, feel as if every organ of your body is

'collapsing' one by one and that you are slowly sinking down and becoming lifeless. 'Let go' the body completely and finally give yourself up as a corpse. There will not then be any consciousness of the body as it will be functioning merely as a machine.

2. Maintain this state of psychosomatic relaxation in which the consciousness of the body is progressively lost and you lose your own identity for the time being.

POINTS

A. Preparing for Savasana

1. As you have to look inward throughout this asana, it is always best to practise Savasana in a solitary place where the distractions of noise and light are within your tolerance level.

2. If you are practising relaxation at night, it will be easier in dim light. Do not practise under glaring lights.

3. Always relax on a firm and flat surface covered with a blanket, carpet or rug which alone permits the spine to be kept completely straight. Do not relax on a springy mattress or in bed as they are too soft and yielding and you may fall asleep. Do not use a pillow as your head should be no higher than your body and it is best to have the head resting on something firm. A thin cushion may be used if you like, in the initial stages.

4. Wear as little clothing as possible which is light and loose-fitting and which does not press on any organ of the body. You may cover up your body with a light blanket or sheet if the weather is cold.

5. Remove your collar and tie if you are wearing any. Take off your belt and shoes so that they do not impede the circulation of your blood. Remove your watch, glasses, dentures and jewellery so that you may be comfortable during the relaxation period.
6. Lie down slowly in a mood to relax.
7. Lie flat on your back, keeping your head, neck and trunk straight. Your lower back should rest as close to the floor as possible. The head should be placed in such a way that the face is turned straight upwards. The face may be turned a little sideways by rotating the head on its own axis if this position is more comfortable, but the head must not slant to either side or get out of alignment with the spinal column during the practice. Your eyes must not be exposed to strong light.
8. When you lie down, ensure that one limb does not touch the other.
9. Do not keep your hand under your head or on your chest. The legs should not be crossed as this puts the burden of supporting one leg on the other, instead of on the carpet.
10. Get into the most comfortable position which offers the least resistance to gravity.
11. After settling down in the most comfortable position, it must not be altered until the exercise is over as it may disturb your mood. Initially, you will be tempted to shift position or move a muscle or limb due to discomfort, but with practice, this can be got over. Allow each part and organ of your body to remain where it is and function naturally.

12. Lie perfectly still and do not move your limbs since every movement, however slight, will create muscular tension.

13. Except the rhythmic rise and fall of the abdomen and chest, no part of the body should make the slightest movement while relaxing as it breaks the sequence of relaxation and re-tense the muscles.

14. Do not yawn at any stage of the practice and let the breath make its own rhythm.

B. Step by Step Relaxation

1. After lying down and stretching completely, become conscious of your body and start relaxing systematically, in a pleasant frame of mind, as many muscles as you can consciously trace.

2. Do not allow your muscles to sag or force yourself to relax by using will power as it will only make you more tense. The ability to relax will develop only gradually.

3. Relax leisurely and never be in a hurry. There will be no special sensation in the early minutes of relaxation, but do not become impatient as it will bring about a feeling of tension.

4. Try to keep your mind focused on your body. Reflect that your body is made of bones, sinews, nerves, muscles, blood, mucus, fat and skin.

5. Revive your knowledge of anatomy and try to locate the internal organs of your body. Become 'aware of your body' and start relaxing its parts one by one.

6. Forget the parts which are already relaxed which should remain motionless. All parts which are tense should then be located and relaxed as you run through

them in your mind. If, in the end, you find that certain parts, muscles or joints, are not completely relaxed or have unconsciously re-contracted, persuade them also to 'let go'. If you thus relax progressively every part of your body, from the toes to the top of the head, all residual tensions will disappear.

7. While attempting to relax one specific muscle or part, focus your mind's eye on it and do not think of or proceed to another before completely relaxing it. Do not, however, stay on any one part for a long time.

8. Take care not to contract any muscle already relaxed when trying to relax another. Avoid particularly the tendency of the relaxed facial muscles to tense up again by concentration.

9. As your mind travels from part to part, do not review or check up whether you are succeeding or not in your attempt as the mind will not proceed further and the tension you dropped may creep up again.

10. Do not give up the relaxation process if you reach only half way at first.

11. As you relax and move on from one part to another, say from the toes to the head, if your mind wanders when you reach a particular part, do not pick up from that part when the mind returns but start working from the toes again and go over all the areas of your body quickly, locating any spots of tension and relaxing them immediately. If you practise like this for several weeks or months, you will not lose the thread of relaxation and will get accustomed to relaxing from the toes to the head in a single round. A habit of relaxation can also be built up this way.

12. Practise to relax the body from the toes to the head slowly and successively in a single round which alone will bring complete relaxation. If you relax the body thoroughly in the first round itself, there will be no need for a second round. If you feel the need for a second or a third round, they should be gone through more quickly than the first, relaxing any tensions you find on the way with intensified awareness.

13. When starting the practice, keep the eyes focused on some fixed spot on the ceiling. The eyeballs should not dart around restlessly. Keep the eyelids half-closed for some time.

14. In the final stage of the practice, relax the eyelids and the eye muscles as it helps a general relaxing of the body. Allow the upper lids to droop gently over the eyeballs. As the lids fall with natural ease and come together, keep the eyeballs and eyelids passive and relaxed without any flickering or blinking. You may now feel as if you are lulled to sleep, but do not slip off to sleep or drowse. Be conscious while relaxing since Savasana is a twilight state just prior to falling asleep. Even if a wave of drowsiness sweeps over you and you sink unawares into sleep or a semi-conscious nap, when the whole process is completed and you are in a truly relaxed state, it will be beneficial and refreshing owing to the calming of the nerves, but do not make it a habit since this sleep will be short-lived. Conscious relaxation will be more satisfying than dozing off in this asana.

15. Your eyes get half-closed or fully closed of their own accord as you proceed with your relaxation in this pre-sleep period. When your eyeballs become

motionless and your awareness of the environment diminishes gradually, turn your mind inwards, when you become oblivious of your surroundings. As you become unconscious of the operations of your body, relaxation will be complete.

C. The Relaxed Condition

1. There are degrees of relaxation. Complete relaxation is as much mental as physical and can be developed only by constant practise.
2. If the practise of this asana is successful, there will not be any tension in any part of the body. This can be achieved by relaxing the parts of the body and loosening the muscles and joints gradually to such an extent as to induce total relaxation.
3. While lying still in a deeply relaxed state, you will feel that your body has become as light as air. You will eventually lose the sense of gravity and feel as if you are out of the body and floating in space like a cloud.
4. While you are in a state of total relaxation, you will feel that you have 'collapsed' altogether, that your body has become lifeless and that you are only looking at it.
5. If you are perfectly relaxed, every limb and organ will become completely passive, as if dead, and the consciousness of the body will be completely lost. In this condition, if someone raises your forearm and lets it go to observe its flaccidity, it will flop back to the ground like that of a dead body and you will feel its movement or impact on the floor only very slightly.
6. If you are perfectly relaxed, there will not be any kind of activity, whether physical or mental, as your

senses are attuned to duty and you are doing nothing. Perfect quiescence is attained with complete cessation of all thoughts, imagination and feeling.

SILENCING THE MIND

1. Even if the body is perfectly relaxed, the mind often continues to be restless. To gain the full benefit from this asana, the mind too should be relaxed along with the body as both are intimately interrelated and interact with each other constantly and ultimately. One reflects the other, both under normal and abnormal conditions.

2. Relaxation of the body will also bring some repose to the mind in sympathy, but mere mechanical relaxation of the parts and muscles of the body will not bring about a complete relaxation. The mind should be freed from all tensions, both conscious and subconscious, since thoughts and emotions have a strong effect on the body complex.

3. After persuading every part of your body to become limp and releasing any tension that may linger on or creep back in some of the sensitive zones of your body, close your eyes gently and tell yourself: 'I am dead tired'; 'I need rest'; 'I am relaxing now'. Do nothing which will disturb your mood and try to keep the feeling of mental quiet you may get thus for as long as you can.

4. As your body relaxes, try to empty your mind of all cares, conflicts, worries and fears so that they die out for lack of attention. Divert your mind from the problems that preoccupy it, but do not switch it off to something else, however pleasant it may be, since

it may wander off in daydreams and end up in worthless fantasy, making it difficult for you to turn your mind back from the phantasmagoria of fleeting thoughts.

5. After going completely limp from head to toe, try to detach your mind from the world around you as much as possible. If it is occupied elsewhere or runs around in circles, wean it gently and listen passively to a sound which is continuous and low-pitched like the ticking of a clock or the 'hum' of an electric fan. While your attention is diverted to the sound and your mind gets absorbed in its rhythm, all unwanted thoughts arising from sense perceptions will disappear automatically. The roaming mind will be brought back into focus and prevented from running loose like a wild horse. If troublesome trains of thought again enter and seize control of your mind like uninvited guests and your imagination runs riot as the stimuli of the outer world such as noise and light impinge on your senses, allow your thoughts to wander at will while continuing to listen passively to the first sound. The mind, after its non-stop wanderings, will gradually settle down by dwelling more and more on the monotony of the sound and finally merges itself in it.

6. Allow the sounds of the outside world such as birdsong and the noises of the town to make their impact on your ears and just ignore them. Since sounds in the environment cannot be shut off, listen to those that reach your ears with complete indifference. Assimilate them, remaining neither absorbed nor engrossed in any one sound. The sounds around you will then have no significance. Acquire a passive

attitude while relaxing thus so that you gradually overcome the normal tendency of the mind to react to all sensory stimuli. This will induce an 'impulseless condition' in which the mind does not respond to anything but simply registers everything; this state of mind will be conducive to total relaxation and mental repose.

7. The five senses of hearing, sight, smell, taste and touch should be gradually made to withdraw their traffic with outside objects and events so that they become passive. When the habitual tendency of the senses to flow out towards their specific objects is reversed, you will no longer be swayed by their tyranny and a decreasing sensitivity to sensory stimuli will occur. Gradually, the sense organs will cease to receive inputs from without and a stillness will creep over them. When the fretful mind does not register anything through the channels of the senses, the external world ceases to signify and the mind gradually turns inward.

    When the mind turns back upon itself and becomes introspective, try to become its boss and not its slave. When the mind is introverted thus and the senses stay put, give up all visual imagery and even 'silent speech' and look inwardly at yourself. The perception of the world through the senses will then cease altogether and the trinity of the perceiver, the perceived and the act of perception will disappear and you will become oblivious to your surroundings and 'dead' to the outside world. Since you are practically shut off from the world and all external and internal stimuli are eliminated, the activity of the mind will remain suspended temporarily.

Memory, reasoning and associative thinking gradually cease and passive awareness alone remains. As the consciousness of the body also fades away gradually, the relaxation of the body will come naturally. This state, however, will not continue for long, as the mind never rests for long. It becomes uneasy again and the senses make efforts to re-establish contact with the outer world when a host of thoughts again invade the mind and entice it to project outwards. When this happens, a myriad impressions from the senses and the deeper levels of the mind again bombard the mind for attention which tries its best to sort out and correlate them. The practice of sense-withdrawal for longer and longer periods can overcome this tendency of the vagabond mind to go round and round and get engrossed in whirlpools of thoughts.

8. Remaining in the relaxed state of the body, try to make your racing and ever-restless mind still, by giving up all thoughts about the outside world one by one and finally refusing to think about anything. Tell your mind to be quiet repeatedly when thoughts flow in of their own accord and seize control of your mind. Restrain your oscillating mind as much as possible by slackening the mental processes and consciously shutting out your thoughts as soon as they leap into your consciousness, just as a watchman drives out a thief. When the mental processes slacken, thoughts and memories get fewer in number and intensity. The control of the mind will then become easy by making it one-pointed and you may ultimately transcend it.

9. As your nimble mind flits from thought to thought linked by association, allow it to become more and more placid without making any conscious effort of the will. When thoughts, which are but modifications of the mind, become fewer and space themselves out, feel perfectly at ease during the blank period. Be conscious only of your true self in the short spell between two successive thoughts. Try to extend the duration of this state by persistent practise.

    When new waves of thought again intrude on your mind and trigger the imagination, do not try to shut them out but divert them at the start by applying counter thoughts at once. If this is not successful and your mind overpowers you with a vengeance, simply step back and observe your thoughts and images as a witness as though you are watching a movie and do not associate yourself with them or interpret them inwardly. Just let them have their full run and watch them pass by as a passive spectator. When thoughts unattended to drift by and eventually leave the observing mind in peace, it will become calm, passive and still.

10. If your mind still plays the monkey and you start once again mulling over your problems or list in your mind the engagements for the day and all the chores you have to do immediately, do not get frustrated but simply shift your attention back gently to your breath. Just observe or listen passively to the smooth passing of the air in and out of your nostrils without interfering with the natural rhythm of your breathing cycle. Just watching every phase of your breath and noticing its length or shortness without attempting

to regulate it in any way will slow down the rhythm of your breath and the heart rate. As the cardio-respiratory rate slows down by itself, a peaceful state of mind will be attained and this, in turn, will relieve mental tension and gradually arrest the flow of your darting and unconnected thoughts. The act of observing or feeling the spontaneous movement of your breath will also cease of itself so that you no longer hear it or even notice it. Even your awareness of breathing will disappear gradually and you will relax automatically.

11. Yet another method to subdue the mind is to silence the thought streams by just observing the passing parade of your thoughts and images without judgement or comment or interfering with their flow. By allowing your never-ending thoughts and thought patterns to come and go as they please without getting involved in them, the turbulence of the mind will decrease and the mental processes will slacken down. Thoughts will become fewer and pass in slow motion and every time your mind gets mired in memories of the past or the unborn future, guide it back.

Cut down the number of thoughts that pop up automatically in your mind and clamour for attention until at last conceptual thinking ceases altogether. When the mind has no object to associate with, it dissolves in itself and not even a ripple of thought will disturb your tranquil 'mind-lake' since thoughts arise only from mental effort. When all thoughts, subjective and objective, drop out gradually, the mind loses its content and a stillness sets in. When the mental apparatus is silenced thus, all messages to and from the brain cease and passive awareness alone remains. There will be no body consciousness then. You lose your identity for the time being as the ego is temporarily transcended. This is Savasana.

12. The mind has always a vicious hold on the body and vice versa. In the final stage of this asana, break this hold as much as possible. Remove the correlation between body and mind and slowly detach your mind from your body by assuming that only your body is lying on the floor like a deadweight and that it does not belong to you. This will make the relaxation of the mind easy and complete, which, in turn, will provide adequate rest to the body.

GETTING UP

1. After relaxing in this trance-like posture, when you slip back from it into the fully wakeful state, you will feel as though you are returning to this world from the threshold of another. As the body's sensations return gradually, you will feel the force of gravity in every limb, if the relaxation is perfect.

2. After your consciousness has been brought back to your body and thoughts start to show up, turn your attention to the breathing and take a few deep breaths. Become aware of the parts of your body which are in contact with the floor. Move your toes gently and join your legs. Move the arms also gently and keep them on their respective sides again. You may turn your head to one side and then roll your head gently on both sides and bring it back slowly to the centre. Assume the most comfortable position and lie quietly for some time. Open your mind to the outside world and become aware of

the surroundings. Slowly open your eyes wide and look around. You will feel refreshed when you open your eyes and come out of the depths of relaxation.

3.   To get the maximum benefit out of this posture, you may, if you like, roll over onto your left side gently with your head turned to the left, your left arm stretched under your head, your left knee slightly drawn up and your right knee brought over your left leg to rest on the floor on the left side. Place your right hand flat on the floor by the chest for support, and take a comfortable relaxed position. Do likewise on your right side. Bring the hands and legs back and roll over on to your back again and, lying flat, relax for a short while. If it helps, you may fold your arms loosely and place your hands lightly on your abdomen for some time. All these, however, are optional, and not imperative.

4.   Stretch your arms above your head and take a deep breath. Holding your breath, stretch your limbs to their very limit, making as much muscular effort as possible, and then 'let go' your body gradually while exhaling.

5.   Bring your arms closer to your body and keep the palms down touching the thighs. Bring the legs also a little closer towards each other. Slide the right foot up and place it flat on the floor in a comfortable position. Pressing the right foot and the left elbow on the floor, roll over on the left side and place your right hand on the floor on your left side to lean on. Pressing your left elbow and right palm on the floor, get up very slowly to the sitting position with as little muscular effort as possible. Stretch back the right foot and keep both legs together.

6. After composing yourself for half to one minute in a comfortable sitting position, get slowly to your feet, avoiding all abrupt movements and consequent strain. Never jump to your feet since you may feel dizzy due to a sudden change in the blood pressure. Then, move around slowly before resuming your normal routine.

7. After mastering this asana, you will not need any outside assistance or an alarm clock to wake you up.

BREATHING

1. At the beginning of this practice, keep your attention on the incoming and outgoing breaths which will be slightly deeper than normal. As you become more relaxed, abandon all attempts to observe your breathing. You may forget breathing altogether, as the breathing apparatus regulates itself and your pulse will stabilize eventually. The breath will take care of itself, and the rhythm of the heart will be maintained naturally.

2. Savasana induces a natural rhythm in the flow of breath and hence no attempt should be made to control or regulate breathing even if it is uneven. Breathing will spontaneously become slower, deeper and rhythmic in the final stage without any conscious effort on your part and rhythmical breathing will contribute to further relaxation. As the rate of breathing slows down, the mind will become more relaxed and calm.

3. In this practice, breathing is done mostly in the abdominal area which allows the diaphragm to expand downward and fill the lower lungs with air.

DURATION

1. Practise Savasana at least once a day. It can be done at any time of the day whenever you get a chance, but do not do it when your stomach is full.
2. You may do Savasana whenever you feel tired or tense. You may do it as often and as long as you like as the threshold of stress varies from person to person.
3. Practise Savasana whenever there is physical, mental or emotional tension or at times of crisis when it will be immediately effective.
4. It can be done prior to undertaking any activity which requires sustained attention for long periods. It can also be done after coming home from work and you can feel the tension draining away.
5. Savasana if done for less than five minutes will have very little effect. Doing it effectively for ten to fifteen minutes will remove all traces of tension.
6. Persons suffering from high blood pressure may do it for about ten minutes at a time at frequent intervals and increase the period up to half an hour as the ability to relax improves and the practice becomes habitual.
7. Note the difference in feeling before and after the practice and prolong the feeling of relaxation you have developed before you return to your normal routine.
8. Do not continue the practice if your legs grow numb.

BENEFITS

A. Physical

1. Savasana, rightly practised, pacifies the body and quietens the mind by discharging muscular, nervous, mental and emotional tensions almost immediately.

2. Persons who are tense by temperament and who find it hard to relax may do it whenever they are restless or agitated and they will gain stability and balance besides feeling more rested.

3. The debilitating effects of anxiety, frustration, fear, insecurity and restlessness, both physical and mental, are minimized.

4. Fits of depression and emotional conflicts which are the consequences of stress will be eliminated gradually and inner peace regained quickly.

5. The restful repose of Savasana imparts new vigour to the body and mind simultaneously. The whole body gets conditioned and the physical and mental capacity are considerably increased.

6. Rest and calmness and the sense of well-being by Savasana repairs the overworked parts of your body and they start working again more vigorously as they are recharged with energy. Your reserves of energy make good the losses resulting from the stresses of everyday life. Efficiency in work improves.

7. A regular practise of this asana will enable you to strike a balance between rest and work.

8. Conscious relaxation in this posture between spells of work in office or at home will counteract fatigue and refresh the tired limbs quickly and completely. It gives the maximum renewed strength in the minimum time.

9. Relaxation in Savasana when you are mentally fatigued after prolonged work will improve concentration.

10. Savasana enables you to overcome fatigue in a few minutes. After playing strenuous games, doing intense

physical exertion, or long-distance walking, you may do this asana till your breathing resumes its normal rhythm and your heart regains its normal beat. This will eliminate fatigue and you will feel refreshed since the exercised and overtaxed parts and muscles of the body are given adequate rest and thorough relaxation.

11. It is imperative that this asana is done both at the beginning and at the end of every yoga session: it should also be interspersed with other exercises to get the best benefit. If it is practised for a brief period between any two strenuous asanas or a group of asanas, it will work off the pent up tension in the muscles and revitalize the limbs. You may also round off a session of yogic exercises by relaxing in this asana for about ten minutes to cool down the body.

12. Persons who are tired after a sleepless night will feel refreshed if they do this asana for a few minutes at frequent intervals during the day. They will sleep well at night as deep relaxation helps to promote sounder sleep.

13. A few minutes of psychosomatic relaxation in this asana is more beneficial for the body and mind than many hours of restless sleep.

14. If Savasana is practised for longer spells during the day at frequent and regular intervals, the hours of sleep during the night could be reduced. The need for daytime dozing will also decrease.

15. By practising this asana, any difficulty in going off to sleep can be overcome and the need for sedatives can be gradually reduced and finally eliminated as this asana is a natural tranquillizer.

16. Savasana provides adequate rest to everyone, particularly to persons of middle age and those of advanced age. It has also a remarkable regenerative effect.

17. Persons who are sick, aged, lack the capacity for work, get easily tired and those who are unable to do any exercise or asana may practise Savasana for increasingly longer periods in order to maintain physical and mental health and cope more fully with the problems of everyday life.

18. Savasana builds up and conserves energy and slows down the ageing process.

19. It develops strong will power.

B. Therapeutical

1. Savasana provides relief from various aches and pains and often proves dramatically effective.

2. Any part or organ of the body which is diseased or gives pain may be relaxed thoroughly for a longer time when its turn comes during the practise of this asana and the benefit will be immediate. The chances of recovery also improve.

3. Savasana removes all stress from the spine and restores its natural symmetry.

4. It is very efficacious in reducing high blood pressure and bringing it to normal. Those suffering from this condition should stay longer in this posture.

5. Practise of this posture will help to cure neurasthenia, asthma and many psychosomatic diseases.

6. Metabolic activity slows down due to the relaxed musculature.

7. Savasana slows down the respiratory rate. The slowing of the breath slows down the heart and a slow heartbeat gives the heart more rest and calms the nerves. Since the strain on the heart is considerably reduced, it helps to cure many cardiac complaints.

8. It gives relief during giddiness, nervousness and irritability.

9. It alleviates headache, angina pectoris, arteriosclerosis, colitis and dyspepsia.

C. Spiritual

1. The systematic practise of Savasana will heighten your awareness.

2. Control over your body and emotions can be gained and the natural harmony between body and mind maintained.

3. Relaxation in Savasana tames the mind and makes it calm and alert. Greater equanimity and a capacity for overcoming stress are also developed.

4. It helps to withdraw the senses from their objects and makes concentration and meditation easy.

5. It helps to cultivate an attitude of detachment to the world and develops introspection.

Note

1. To master Savasana as a neuromuscular skill, you should make repeated attempts daily and persevere. It takes constant repetition and prolonged habituation to do the asana naturally and easily. You will experience a feeling of euphoria after each attempt even if it is not a complete success.

2. After mastering the technique of Savasana, and as skill in relaxation develops, learn to relax your body

and mind at will in any comfortable position anywhere, anytime instead of for a specific period lying down on the floor. You may relax in the horizontal posture as described above or when lying down on one side. Learn to relax also in the cross-legged postures, while sitting at your desk, leaning against a wall, while standing or in any other convenient position, though the benefit in all these cases will be partial and less than in the supine position. Lying flat on your back on the carpet or rug is the most restful position since it is the only one which allows the total relaxation of the entire body.

3. For inducing deep relaxation of body and mind, you may have someone check your posture and read slowly in a soothing voice the step-by-step instructions given earlier in this chapter. After mastering the asana, all outside help should be dispensed with.

4. The technique described under the head 'Silencing the Mind' can also be used as a meditative technique while sitting in a cross-legged position. It will help to still the mind.

Source

1. *Gheranda Samhita* II–19.
2. *Hatha Sanketa Chandrika* by Sundaradasa-II Asana Verse No. 11.

14. Sukhasana
(The Comfortable Posture)

'Sukha' means 'pleasant' or 'comfortable' in Sanskrit. Any cross-legged sitting position which you find comfortable, in which the body does not shake and in which you can remain at ease for a long time, is called Sukhasana.

SEQUENCE

- Sit erect.
- Stretch out your legs loosely in front of you.
- Fold the left leg and draw in the foot towards the body. Raise the right knee and slide the left foot under the right thigh with the sole tilted up and touching the back of the right thigh near the knee.
- Similarly, fold the right leg and draw in that foot

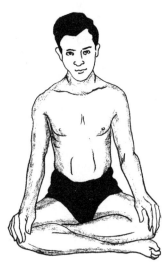

Fig. 63.

towards the body. Raise the left knee and slide the right foot under the left calf (not thigh) with the sole tilted up and the edge of the foot supporting the left shin.

- The legs now cross loosely at the ankles. Adjust the position of the legs with the hands and assume the most comfortable position.

- Rest the hands on the respective knees. Hold the head, neck and spine erect. Maintain this position as long as you like.

- Stretch forward both the legs and release the posture.

- The position of the right and the left legs could be interchanged.

BENEFITS

- This is the easiest of all asanas and the simplest of the crossed-legged postures and can be practised by all.

- This is a basic sitting posture. You may start your daily yogic practices by first sitting in this position.

- This is a very comfortable posture and you may remain in it for long periods of time without any discomfort in the legs or pain in the knee-joints. The entire body will be at ease.

15. Chakrasana (Standing)
(The Wheel Posture)

'Chakra' means 'wheel' in Sanskrit.

SEQUENCE

- Stand erect. Place the feet slightly apart. Keep the hands on the sides of the respective thighs with fingers close together and touching them. Look straight ahead.

- Inhaling, tense and raise the right arm slowly and laterally and bring it above the head, the inside

Fig. 64.

of the upper arm touching the right ear. While raising the arm, keep the palm inwards up to the shoulder level and then turn it upwards till it is brought straight above the head.

- Exhaling, raise the right shoulder and bend the trunk and head together along with the raised right arm sideways to the left till the right arm is parallel to the floor. While bending thus, slide the left palm down your left thigh until it reaches the left knee; knees should be kept straight, and the right arm must follow the ear without bending the elbow.
- Hold this position comfortably as long as you can hold out your breath.
- Inhaling, bring back the trunk, head and the right arm together till the right hand comes straight above the head. Exhaling and keeping the head erect, lower the right arm again to the side, turning the palm inward at the shoulder level.
- Repeat the exercise on the right side also.

BENEFITS

Chakrasana gives a good lateral bend to the spine and improves its elasticity.

It increases the flexibility of the hip-joints which get very little lateral exercise in daily life.

With regular practice of this asana, the body becomes resilient and supple, the waist slim and the chest broad.

It is useful in removing the rigidity of the joints of the ribcage and thus increases the capacity of the lungs.

16. Utkatasana
(The Half-Squat)

'Ut' means 'raised' and 'kata' means 'hips' in Sanskrit. This posture is known as 'Utkatasana' because while practising it, the heels and hips are raised.

SEQUENCE

- Stand erect, keeping the feet apart at a slight angle to each other.
- Stretch out your arms in front of your chest at shoulder level with palms turned down.
- Inhaling, raise your body slowly until you stand on tip-toe. Keep your balance.
- Keeping the trunk and head erect, lower you body very slowly while exhaling till the back of your thighs press against the respective calves. Squat on your heels without lowering the latter to the ground.

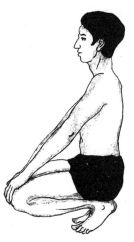

Fig. 65.

- Squat erect on your toes and keep balance.
- Spread the knees apart and keep them parallel to the floor.
- Rest the palms on the respective knees and find your balance.
- Bring the knees closer and stretch out the arms straight again in front of your chest.
- Inhaling, rise up slowly on tiptoe, keeping your trunk and head straight, until you are standing on tiptoe. Exhale.
- Return to the starting position with the foot flat on the floor.

BENEFITS

This asana provides good exercise to the lower portion of the body, particularly the muscles of the hips, thighs, calves, ankles and feet. The tendons at the back of the legs are stretched. It also strengthens the toes and the muscles which support the arches of the feet.

It loosens stiff knees and hip-joints and enhances their mobility.

17. Talasana
(Palm-tree Posture)

'Tala' means 'palm tree' in Sanskrit. In this posture, the body is held upright like the trunk of a palm tree. Hence the name.

SEQUENCE

- Stand erect. Keep your feet slightly turned out and sufficiently apart according to your height and build. Look straight ahead.
- Inhaling, slowly raise your arms overhead with the palms facing each other.
- Raise your heels slowly, keeping your balance.
- Lift yourself on your toes slowly until you stand on tiptoe. Exhale slowly and keep balance.
- Inhale slowly again. Balancing the body on tiptoe, pull up and stretch

Fig. 66.

your arms upwards from the shoulder-blades with the fingers outstretched. Raise your heels also simultaneously as high as possible and stretch your body to the maximum.

- Stretch your neck and head backwards and look up. Hold your breath and keep your balance.
- Keep yourself firmly in this position as long as you can hold your breath comfortably.
- Exhaling, relax the body and return to the starting position by slowly lowering the arms and heels simultaneously, bending the neck and head forward.

BENEFITS

Talasana fully stretches the upper portion of the body. It stretches the spine vertically in particular and straightens out unnatural curves if any.

By practising this asana, the body becomes well-built, well-proportioned, nimble and agile.

It expands the ribcage and increases the capacity of the lungs.

It firms up the respiratory muscles and the muscles of the neck, lower back, abdomen and pelvis.

18. Padahastasana
(The Hands-to-Feet Posture)

'**P**ada' means 'foot' and 'Hasta' means 'hand' in Sanskrit. You have to catch your big toes with your hands in this posture.

SEQUENCE

- Stand upright with the feet parallel and the heels about six inches apart.
- Inhaling, raise your hands straight above your head, palms outwards.
- Exhaling, bend your head and trunk from the waist as far back as you can without tipping over, with upper arms touching the ears.
- Inhaling, bend forward from the waist, keeping the knees straight and the upper arms touching the ears.
- As soon as the arms extend straight above your head, start

Fig. 67.

exhaling and continue to bend your head and trunk forward from the waist.

- Reach forward and catch hold of the big toes with your thumbs, index and middle fingers.
- Holding out your breath, pull the big toes and move your forehead into the space between the knees. Keep the legs straight and the knees stiff.
- Maintain this position for a few seconds while holding out your breath.
- Start inhaling and return slowly to the upright position in the reverse order.

BENEFITS

Padahastasana secures the maximum stretching of the posterior muscles, from the legs to the neck. The lateral muscles of the trunk are also brought into play to some extent.

The tendons and ligaments of the thighs and legs are well stretched and the hamstring muscles at the back of the thighs are strengthened by this practice. It also gives a good pull to the sciatic nerve.

The ankles, calves, the back of the thighs, hips, waist, back, shoulders and neck are all well exercised and blood is rushed to all these parts.

19. Vrikshasana

(The Tree Posture)

'Vriksha' means 'tree' in Sanskrit. In the final position of this asana, you have to stand still like a tree.

SEQUENCE

- Stand erect. Keep the feet together and the knees straight with arms on the respective sides.
- Without bending the left knee, lift the right foot and grasp the ankle with the right hand.
- Fold the right leg double at the knee-joint.
- Without losing your balance, place the right heel at the top of the left thigh, using both hands. The right sole must press the inside of the left thigh with the toes pointing downwards. The folded leg must be at right angle to the other leg and

Fig. 68.

both thighs must be in alignment. Balance yourself on the left leg.

- Join the palms and fingers and touch the middle of the chest. Fingers should point upwards.
- Keeping your hands together, raise them slowly a little above your head. Keep the arms slightly bent.
- Stretch up and stand erect. Keep your balance. Look straight ahead and be relaxed.
- Lower the hands slowly to the middle of the chest again.
- Return to the starting position, lowering your right leg.
- Practise reversing the legs.

BENEFITS

The joints of the legs, knees and ankles become flexible by the regular practise of this asana. It also loosens the pelvis.

It tones up the leg muscles and strengthens the arches, tendons and ligaments in the feet.

Numbness and rheumatic pain in the legs will be alleviated.

Neuromuscular coordination can be gained by the regular practise of this asana.

20. Akarshana Dhanurasana
(The Pulled Bow)

'Akarshana' means 'pulling' and 'Dhanus' means 'bow' in Sanskrit. In this posture, the big toes are pulled up to the ear (alternately) as an archer pulls back the string of his bow and gets ready to shoot an arrow.

SEQUENCE

- Sit erect.
- Stretch out the legs and keep them close together. Place the palms on the floor at the sides.
- Bend the right leg at the knee and crossing the left leg, place the right heel on the ground beside the left ankle.
- Grasp the right big toe with the thumb, index and middle fingers of the left hand and the left big toe with the right thumb, index and middle fingers.
- Inhaling and keeping the head erect, pull up the right foot till the right knee comes near the right armpit and the right big toe touches the left ear. While doing this, the right hand should pull the big toe of the left

leg. While pulling the toes, fix your gaze on the big toe of the stretched left leg (Fig. 69A).

- Exhaling, bring back the right foot to the floor on the left side of the outstretched left leg. Release the hands and stretch the legs straight again side by side.

- Practise reversing the position of the legs (Fig. 69B).

- **Variation:** Stretch out the legs. Pull the big toes straight towards the ears on the same side of the body, one after the other (Fig. 69C).

BENEFITS

The arms, shoulders, chest, waist, back, thighs and calves come into play in Akarshana Dhanurasana, and they become well developed, well proportioned and strong. In few of the asanas are so many parts of the body exercised in so short a time and so effectively.

Fig. 69A: Right toe is pulled up to the left ear.

Fig. 69B: Reverse position of the legs.

Fig. 69C: Left toe is pulled up to the left ear.

21. Bhadrasana
(The Beneficial Posture)

'B hadra' means 'beneficial' in Sanskrit.

SEQUENCE

- Sit erect in Sukhasana.
- Stretch the legs forward and keep them together.
- Pull the legs inward and bring the feet towards the body, bending the knees outward.
- Join the soles and keep the heels and toes together.

Fig. 70.

- Form a fingerlock and clasp your fingers around the toes and the forepart of the feet. Keep the trunk and head erect.

- Bending your elbows outward, draw in the feet little by little until the heels are in front of the genitals. While doing this, widen the thighs and allow the knees to bend gently downward.
- Lower the knees gently until they touch the floor.
- Draw in the heels further and fix them on either side of the perineum. Sit erect.
- Release the fingerlock, stretch forward the legs and resume the starting position.

BENEFITS

Bhadrasana strengthens the muscles of the groin and the pelvis.

The weight of the flexed knees stretches and tones up the adductor muscles running along the inner thighs.

It has a beneficial effect on the muscles and ligaments of the urogenital region, promoting in it a supply of fresh blood.

It restores elasticity to stiff knees, hips and ankle-joints.

It relieves tension in the sacral and coccygeal regions of the spine.

It keeps the kidneys, the prostrate, and the urinary bladder healthy.

22. Baddha Konasana

'**B**addha' means 'locked-up' and 'kona' means 'angle' in Sanskrit.

SEQUENCE

- Assume the Bhadrasana posture, holding with your clasped hands the forepart of your feet which are placed firmly on the floor on their outer edges. Keep the back straight and look straight ahead.

Fig. 71.

- Bend forward and place the elbows on the thighs and press them down gently.
- Inhale deeply and exhale slowly. While exhaling, draw in your abdomen and bend your pelvis and trunk forward from your posterior bones slowly without jerks, at the same time lowering your elbows outside the shin. When you have bent forward as

much as you can, place your forehead gently on the floor in front of your feet without raising your seat and rest your forearms and elbows on the floor. Keep the elbows in a line. This is the final position.

- Maintain this position motionlessly for about five seconds or as long as you can comfortably hold out your breath. Breathe normally if you can increase the duration of the posture.

- Inhale slowly and while inhaling, release the feet, straighten the arms, stretch out the legs, raise the trunk and head together and resume the erect sitting position slowly.

- Take only two turns as this is a strenuous posture. After completing the practice, relax for a few minutes in Savasana.

BENEFITS

Baddha Konasana keeps the spine and the hip-joints supple.

It removes tension in the back and thighs and relieves pain in the hip-joints.

It tones up the organs in the abdomen and pelvis.

It reduces excess fat in the thighs.

23. Ardha Matsyendrasana
(Half-Spinal Twist)

This posture was first promoted by the great Yogi Matsyendranath, one of the founders of Hatha Yoga, and hence the name. 'Ardha' means 'half' in Sanskrit. Since the full posture is difficult to be practised, the half-posture, which is easier, is followed widely.

SEQUENCE

- Sit erect.
- Stretch out your legs.
- Place the right heel in the perineum. Keep the right thigh straight.
- Place the left foot flat on the floor, crossing the right knee. The left heel should rest close to the right side of the right knee.

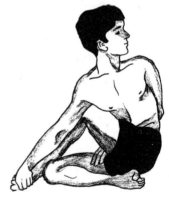

Fig. 72.

- Pass the right arm over the left side of the left knee and line it up with the left calf.
- Grasp the left big toe with the index finger, middle finger and thumb of the right hand.
- Slide the left hand across the small of the back and grasp the root of the right thigh.
- Turn round your head, neck, shoulders and the whole trunk to the left and bring the chin in line with the left shoulder. Look as far behind you as you can. Keep the head and spine erect.
- Maintain this position until strain is felt.
- Release in the reverse order.
- Repeat on the other side.

BENEFITS

Ardha Matsyendrasana is considered to be the best of the twisting postures as it rotates the spine around its own axis besides giving two side-twists to the spine throughout its length with the greatest efficacy, using one's own arm and knee as a lever. As the spine is twisted spirally, each movable vertebra rotates in its socket, as a result of which the spinal column, particularly the lumbar vertebrae, becomes more flexible.

24. Ushtrasana
(The Camel Posture)

'Ushtra' means 'camel' in Sanskrit.

SEQUENCE

Fig. 73.

- Assume the kneeling position. Keep the knees shoulder-width apart and the big toes about eight inches apart. Only your knees and toes should touch the floor.
- Place the posterior between the heels and sit comfortably.
- Grasp the heels with the corresponding hands. Press the heels with your palms. Inhale and exhale a few times.
- Inhaling, raise your posterior off your heels and come up on your knees and toes.

- Pulling the shoulders back, push the hips forward. Exhaling, raise the chest and bend the trunk and head back as far as you can, curving the spine backwards. Keep the arms straight. Turn your face towards the sky. Complete the exhalation and take a few deep breaths.
- Invert the feet and place the toes and the upper part of the feet flat on the floor. Slide your hands down and grasp each ankle with the corresponding hand. Bend backwards further on the arms and make a curvature of the body by arching the spine and neck.
- Maintain this posture, breathing deeply and rhythmically, until strain is felt.
- Inhaling, release the hands and return slowly to the upright kneeling position. Resume the sitting position between the heels and then the original sitting position.

BENEFITS

The alternate flexion and extension of the spine in this asana makes it more flexible and particularly so, the lumbar area.

It improves the tone of the muscles and nerves attached to the entire spine besides the deep muscles of the thighs, trunk, neck and face.

It expands the lungs to their maximum capacity and develops the ribcage. The elasticity of the diaphragm also improves.

25. Vajrasana
(The Adamant Posture)

'Vajra' means 'Adamant' in Sanskrit. Sitting in this asana will provide firmness or stability to the sitter like that of an adamant person. Hence the name.

SEQUENCE

- Sit erect in Sukhasana.
- Stretch out the legs in front of you.
- Fold the legs back one by one along the respective thighs.
- Drawing in the feet one by one, place them by the sides of the posterior with soles upturned.
- The posterior should be planted firmly on the floor between the upturned heels. Toes should point to each other behind the posterior.

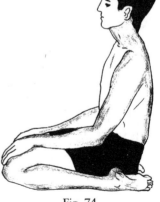

Fig. 74.

- Bring the knees close to each other.
- Rest the palms on the respective knees.
- Sit erect and look straight ahead.
- **Variation:** Instead of keeping the upturned feet on the sides of the posterior, place the heels beneath the posterior so that you sit back in between the heels with the big toes crossing each other. The posterior rests between the inner edges of the upturned heels and does not touch the ground. The rest of the practice is the same.

BENEFITS

Vajrasana loosens the stiff joints and ligaments of the legs and strengthens the hips, thighs, knees, calves, ankles, insteps and toes.

It firms up and strengthens the muscles of the vertebral column. It also strengthens the pelvic region.

It holds the abdominal organs in their correct position.

It reduces excess fat in the thighs.

The spine will be kept erect in this posture.

26. Supta Vajrasana
(The Reclining Vajrasana)

'Supta' means 'asleep' in Sanskrit. 'Supta Vajrasana' is lying down supine in Vajrasana.

SEQUENCE

- Sit in Vajrasana.
- Lean back slowly from the waist with the support of your elbows till

Fig. 75.

your head, shoulders and back touch the ground in easy stages without raising your knees from the floor or changing the position of the legs. Allow your back to come close to the ground and lie supine.
- Cross the arms and place the palms beneath the opposite shoulders so that the crossed wrists serve as a cushion for the head.
- Keep the knees together and touching the ground. Close your eyes.

- Catch hold of the ankles and return slowly to the starting position in the reverse order with the help of the elbows.

BENEFITS

All the benefits of Vajrasana accrue from this asana also.

The importance of Supta Vajrasana lies in the fact that it exerts pressure on the utero-abdominal and genito-urinary organs. This gives a better muscular tone and brings in a fresh supply of blood to the abdominal viscera, particularly to the kidneys, liver, pancreas and bowels.

It stimulates the adrenal glands through pressure in the small of the back.

In the final position, the muscles of the spine, abdomen, pelvis, thighs and legs are stretched fully which tones them up.

It improves circulation of blood in the thighs, backside, knees and neck. It has a beneficial effect on the pelvic organs and the gonads.

The asana expands the chest and increases the mobility of the thorax.

27. Mandukasana
(The Frog Posture)

'**M**anduka' means 'frog' in Sanskrit. The arrangement of the legs in this posture resembles the hind legs of a frog. Hence the name.

- Assume the Vajrasana posture with the posterior planted firmly on the floor between the upturned feet. The inner edges of the feet should encircle the posterior. Spread the knees as wide apart as possible and rest them on the floor. The feet point towards each other with the soles facing upwards. The big toes should touch each other behind the posterior.

Fig. 76.

You will now be squatting between your heels. Rest the hands, palms down, on the respective knees. Straighten the spine and look straight ahead. Sit erect in this position for about ten seconds without strain.

28. Aswini Mudra
(Anal Contraction)

'Aswini' means 'mare' and 'mudra' means 'symbol' in Sanskrit. Just as a horse, while expelling its bowel contents, relaxes and contracts its anus muscles, you relax and contract these muscles rhythmically while practising this Mudra.

TECHNIQUE

- Assume the Janu Vakshasana posture.
- Take a few normal breaths.
- Contract and relax the sphincter muscles of the anus slowly, evenly and tightly—contract while exhaling, and relax while inhaling. The contraction and relaxation of these muscles close and open up the anus alternately. The repeated alternation of this process is Aswini Mudra.
- Repeat the action seven times to begin with and increase it by two times every week up to eleven times.
- After completing the practice, revert to the sitting position.

BENEFITS

The practise of this Mudra strengthens the rectum and the muscles and nerves surrounding the anal sphincters.

29. Yoga Mudra
(The Symbol of Yoga)

'**M**udra' means 'symbol' in Sanskrit.

SEQUENCE

- Sit erect in Padmasana.
- Extend the arms behind your back and grasp the right wrist firmly with the left hand.

Fig. 77.

- Take a deep breath. Exhaling, bend the head and trunk forward and downward from the hip-joints very slowly over the heels. Slowly bring down the lower abdomen, the upper abdomen, the lower part of the chest, the upper part of the chest and the shoulders towards the floor and finally rest your forehead gently on the floor. Relax the body completely.

- Maintain this posture comfortably and motionlessly, breathing slowly, deeply and rhythmically.
- Stretch your neck and head forward a little. Inhaling, bend the trunk and head backward slowly and revert to the Padmasana position.
- Practise alternating the legs.

Variation

- Assume the Padmasana posture.
- Keep the fingers of both hands interlocked behind the back.
- Exhaling, bend forward and rest your forehead on the floor.
- While bending forward, raise your arms upward as far as you comfortably can, keeping the arms straight behind your back. The arms should act as a lever and accentuate the stretch of the shoulders and the chest.
- Remain in this posture for a few seconds.
- Inhaling and lowering the arms, return slowly to the upright position. Release the fingerlock.
- Execute three turns, striving to raise your arms higher with each repetition.

BENEFITS

Yoga Mudra stretches fully the muscles of the back and relaxes the spinal ligaments. The entire spinal column, from the neck to the coccyx, is stretched fully and becomes more supple.

30. Gomukhasana

(The Cow-Face Posture)

'Go' means 'cow' and 'Mukha' means 'face' in Sanskrit. When this asana is performed, the final position of the legs resembles the face of a cow.

SEQUENCE

- Sit erect in Sukhasana.
- Stretch out the legs straight in front of you.
- Fold back the left leg a little. Raising the right knee, draw in the left foot beneath the right thigh and set the heel on the side of the right buttock, just touching it. The toes and the lower edge of the left foot must lie flat on the floor with the sole turned upwards and

Fig. 78.

the toes pointing away from the body. Keep the thigh of the folded left leg straight in front of you.

- Drawing in the right foot and crossing it over the left thigh, set the heel on the side of the left buttock, just touching it.

- Bring the knees exactly one above the other and both of them should be directly in front of you. Sit erect.

- Twist the left arm from the elbow and bring the forearm upwards behind the back, moving up the back of the hand along the spine. Push the forearm up as far as it will go.

- Raise the right arm straight up, the upper arm touching the ear. Folding it back at the elbow, slide down the forearm behind the back over the right shoulder, palm and fingers facing inward, till the right hand meets the left hand. Lock the forefingers of both hands together.

- Keep the head, neck and spine erect. Look straight ahead.

- Return to the starting position in the reverse order.

- Repeat the entire procedure by reversing the positions of the legs and arms.

BENEFITS

The practice of Gomukhasana strengthens the muscles of the upper back, upper arms, shoulders, chest, hips and thighs.

Forefingers are locked behind the back.

31. Janusirasana
(The Head-to-Knee Posture)

'Janu' means 'knee' and 'Siras' means 'head' in Sanskrit. The head is made to rest on the knee in this posture, hence the name.

SEQUENCE

- Sit erect in Sukhasana.
- Stretch the legs forward.
- Spread the legs and keep the heels about fifteen inches apart.

Fig. 79.

- Bending the right knee outward and sliding the outer edge of the right foot along the floor, draw it in towards the left thigh. With the help of the hands, press flat the right sole against the inside of the left thigh. The upper end of the right heel must press the perineal space and the bent right knee must rest on the floor. Keep the trunk and head erect.

- Inhaling, raise the hands above the head with the palms facing outwards. Exhale completely.
- Keep the knees stiff. Take a deep breath. Exhaling, draw in your abdomen and bend the trunk and head forward and downward from the waist against the left thigh, keeping the head between the upper arms. While doing so, extend forward the forearms and fingers towards the extended left foot and clasp the ball of the foot firmly with the interlaced fingers of both hands.
- Inhale deeply again. Exhaling, press the knee of the extended left leg on the floor and bending the elbows outward, slowly bend down the head and trunk further. Pulling the trunk forward, rest your forehead on the left knee-joint. Lower the elbows gradually and rest them on the floor. The entire back of the stretched leg and the back of the knees must touch the floor closely.
- Maintain this position comfortably as long as you can hold out your breath or until any strain is felt at the back of the extended leg.
- Inhaling, get back slowly to the starting position in the reverse order.
- Repeat the identical movements with the right leg stretched out.

BENEFITS

Janusirasana has a beneficial effect on the sciatic nerve and on the solar plexus.

32. Sasankasana
(The Hare Posture)

'Sasanka' means 'hare' in Sanskrit. The final position of this asana resembles a bounding hare.

SEQUENCE

- Sit in Vajrasana. The posterior should rest between the inner edges of the heels. Keep thighs and knees together and soles upturned.

- Inhaling, raise the arms over the head and keep them stiff and straight. Palms should be turned outwards.

Fig. 80.

- Keeping the inside of the upper arms touching the ears and holding your breath, lean backward as far as possible.

- Exhaling and keeping the inside of the upper arms touching the ears, bend your pelvis and the whole trunk slowly forward from your posterior bones without raising your seat from the floor. While doing so, bring your head and arms down till the palms rest on the floor.
- Slide the hands forward along the floor to the maximum extent and rest your forehead on the floor in front of your knees. Keep the palms together and thighs pressing the abdomen.
- Hold out your breath and maintain this position for about five seconds or as long as comfortable.
- Inhaling, return slowly to the starting position in the reverse order, keeping the inside of the upper arms touching the ears and without raising your seat.

BENEFITS

Sasankasana stretches the shoulder girdle and the sacral region of the spine.

The arms, shoulders and the upper back are well stretched. Stooping shoulders are set right.

This posture offers good traction to the spine, relieving spinal problems. It also gives relief in cases of slipped disc.

It brings a copious flow of blood to the brain and face.

It strengthens the knees, ankles and insteps.

Leaning backward tones the abdominal muscles and organs and improves digestive power.

33. Matsyasana
(The Fish Posture)

'**M**atsya' means 'fish' in Sanskrit. If a person lies steadily on water in this posture, he can keep floating on it easily like a fish without the help of the hands and legs, as the name of the asana suggests.

SEQUENCE

- Form a footlock in Padmasana with the knees touching the ground.
- Lean back gradually on your elbows and lie flat on your back with the support of the hands and elbows.
- Bring the hands backward towards the head and place your

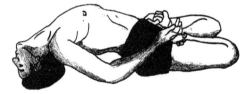

Fig. 81.

palms flat on the floor under the corresponding shoulders in the reverse direction.

- Pressing down the knees and palms and pushing your chest and abdomen forward, raise the shoulders, back and hips from the floor, supporting the body with your hands. While raising them, make an arch of the spine and, simultaneously, bend your head and neck backward as far as you can to place the crown of your head perpendicularly on the floor.

- Bring your hands forward and grasp the back of your thighs with your palms. Using your elbows for leverage, raise your chest and abdomen and, accentuating the arch of the spine, place the crown of your head in position on the floor.

- Make hooks of the index finger, the middle finger and thumb of each hand and catch in each of them the opposite big toes and pull them gently.

- Maintain this position comfortably, breathing deeply and rhythmically.

- Return slowly in the reverse order to the starting position of Padmasana.

BENEFITS

Matsyasana tones up the spinal column. The cervical and dorsal regions are fully extended and become more flexible. If the spine has become habitually curved by sitting incorrectly, it will again become straight by the regular practise of this asana.

The chest expands and the capacity of the lungs increases by the abundant supply of fresh air.

34. Chakrasana (Supine)
(The Wheel Posture)

'Chakra' means 'wheel' in Sanskrit. In the final position of this asana, the body is arched backward and resembles the rim of a wheel. Hence the name.

SEQUENCE

- Lie flat on your back. Keep the feet sufficiently apart. Stretch your arms on their respective sides with palms turned down.

Fig. 82.

- Fold the legs and draw the feet back so that the heel of each foot touches the corresponding buttock. Keep the soles flat on the floor.
- Bring your hands backwards and place them on either side of your head. Rest your palms and fingers flat

on the floor in the reverse direction beneath the corresponding shoulders. The palms should be in line with the heels.

- Inhaling, press down the hands and feet and raise the thighs, hips, abdomen, trunk and shoulders slowly and simultaneously from the floor. Arch the back and neck and rest the crown of your head firmly on the floor.

- Exhale and inhale a few times and again take a deep breath. Hold your breath and press the hands and feet down on the floor. Supporting the weight of your body on your hands and feet, raise your thighs, hips, abdomen, trunk, shoulders and head slowly and simultaneously as far as your spine allows them to do so. The elbows should be straight. Bend the whole body backwards as much as possible. The head should drop back between the shoulders.

- Maintain this posture for about ten seconds, holding your breath.

- Exhaling, lower the body gradually to the floor and resume the starting position.

BENEFITS

Chakrasana exercises several parts of the body simultaneously in a very short time. It strengthens the neck, arms, wrists, fingers, spine, backside, thighs, knees, ankles and feet. It also strengthens the muscles and organs of the pelvis and the abdominal area.

35. Pavanamuktasana
(The Wind-releasing Posture)

'**P**avana' means 'wind' and 'Mukta' means 'release' in Sanskrit. As the name suggests, this asana massages the digestive organs and gives relief from excess wind in the stomach and intestines.

SEQUENCE

- Lie flat on your back. Stretch your arms on the respective sides with palms turned down.
- Fold the legs back and place the feet flat on the floor.

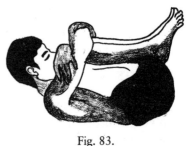

Fig. 83.

- Draw the feet in so that the legs are folded against the thighs and the heels come near the posterior.
- Pressing the palms down on the floor, lift your feet off the ground and bring the knees towards the chest.

- While pressing the palms down again on the floor, raise your head and shoulders off the floor.
- Then, pressing the palms down once again on the floor, raise your hips and buttocks and move your knees further towards your chest, keeping the knees and feet together and without lowering the head.
- Fold your arms and embrace the folded legs a little below the knees.
- While exhaling, press down the knees together on top of the chest with your folded forearms. While doing this, raise your head, shoulders and the upper portion of the chest and bring down your nose in the space between the knees.
- Maintain this position for about five seconds while holding out your breath.
- Inhaling, bring back the head to the floor, relaxing the pressure of the arms on the legs and keeping the arms still folded below the knees.
- After taking the necessary turns, stretch out your arms and legs and relax.

BENEFITS

It benefits persons suffering from flatulence by releasing the gas which is the main object of this asana. Even persons of advanced age can practise it if they have any wind in the abdomen, specially in the colon. The confined wind is pressed out through the ano-rectal passage.

36. Janu Vakshasana
(Knee-Chest Posture)

'Janu' means 'knee' and 'Vaksha' means 'chest' in Sanskrit.

SEQUENCE

- Kneel down. Curl the toes inward and keep the feet perpendicular to the ground.
- Sit back slowly between the heels.
- Get down on 'All Fours' as follows. Raising your posterior and leaning forward slowly from your hip-joints, move your hand forward and place your

Fig. 84.

palms flat on the floor in line with your knees and parallel to each other.

- Lift your chin and keep your head back. Arch your spine and hollow your lower back. Look forward. This is the 'All-Fours' position, technically known as the 'Prone-kneeling' position.
- Without moving the hands, knees and toes from the 'All-Fours' position, bend the arms at the elbows sideways and stoop forward. Lower your shoulders towards the floor while keeping the hips high. Arching your back into a slight concavity, rest your forehead gently on the floor.
- Slide forward your palms and rest your forearms on the floor, leaving your feet, knees and head exactly where they were.
- Lift your head a little. Wrap the hands, holding with the right hand the left upper arm a little above the elbow, and with the left hand, the right upper arm a little above the elbow.
- Rest your forehead gently on the forearms at the centre without moving your knees and feet. Keep the abdomen relaxed and allow it to sag towards the floor. Remain motionless and breathe normally. This is the final position.
- Resume the kneeling position and stand upright again.

BENEFITS

In this posture, the position of the back will help the proper alignment of the vertebrae as the compressed inter-vertebral discs are stretched.

37. Makarasana
(The Crocodile Posture)

'**M**akara' means 'crocodile' in Sanskrit.

SEQUENCE

- Lie flat on the carpet with the chin, chest and a b d o m e n touching the ground. Stretch

  Fig. 85.

  out the legs together at full length. Keep the arms on their respective sides.
- Spread the legs comfortably apart and rest them on the floor. Heels must point towards each other and the edges of the feet must touch the floor. The feet should be at right angles to the legs and the toes pointing outward.
- Raise your trunk and head. Bring one hand beneath the opposite shoulder and grasp it lightly and place

the other hand on the opposite shoulder and grasp it lightly. Do this in such a way that a 'double triangle' is formed with the folded elbows resting exactly above one another and the forearms crossing the opposite upper arms.

- Rest your forehead on this 'double triangle' and dip your face in the space in between. Close your eyes and relax.
- Do abdominal breathing and maintain this position as long as comfortable.
- Lie on your back and resume the sitting position slowly.

BENEFITS

Makarasana induces a complete relaxation of the body and mind.

It relaxes the muscles and relieves the fatigue after doing a strenuous asana.

The asana relieves and helps correct many breathing troubles and disorders in the genito-urinary system.

It helps to reduce high blood pressure.

Makarasana stimulates the small intestines which, in turn, helps the digestive processes.

It prevents scoliosis and flatulence.

ERECT SITTING POSTURE

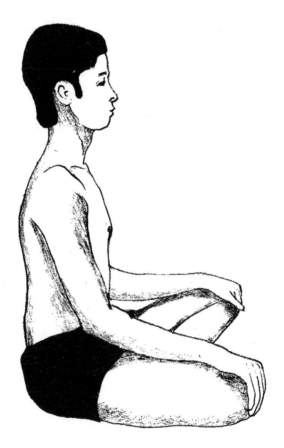

The back is erect and in line with the back
of the head and the posterior.

ERECT STANDING POSTURE

The back of the head is level with the spine. Shoulders and pelvis are also level. The abdomen is drawn in and the chest open.

38. The Erect Posture

Asanas help to cultivate correct postural habits.

- Maintain an erect and balanced posture while sitting, standing or walking, bending your hips and backbone, using your full stature. Hold an erect position naturally, without effort or tension. Do not adopt a stiff military posture.

- Check occasionally with your back kept right up against a wall and correct faulty posture so that you neither slump forward or become stiff in your bearing. You may check in a full-length mirror until you acquire and maintain a correct posture.

- Do not allow yourself to habitually stand or sit stoop-shouldered and hunchbacked as the thoracic section of the spine will become affected.

- The following asanas help to correct postural defects:

- 1. Matsyasana 2. Halasana, 3. Bhujangasana, 4. Dhanurasana 5. Ardha Matsyendrasana 6. Paschimotanasana 7. Padahastasana 8. Ushtrasana 9. Talasana.

BENEFITS

The upright posture keeps the body in correct alignment while standing, sitting and walking and helps prevent a protruding abdomen.

It helps to balance all parts of the body and prevents straining any one or more postural muscles.

All the internal organs function correctly and actively as they are well supported in the pelvic region.

An upright posture allows the lungs to expand fully, ensuring balance between the muscles of the abdominal wall and the diaphragm. It also contributes to the firming up of the abdominal, shoulder and back muscles.

Good posture enables the process of breathing, circulation and digestion to function efficiently and lessens the strain on the muscles and joints.

39. Sitting Upright

- Sit up comfortably on your posterior with your weight evenly distributed, using the muscles of the flanks and lower back. Sit with a minimum of tension.
- Sit well balanced and relaxed and without any support for your back. Do not slouch as it leads to overstretching of the ligaments of the spine and the consequent backache. Do not sit stiffly upright with shoulders thrust back, accentuating the curve in the back.
- While sitting, your head must be held up and well in line with the spinal column. Keep the shoulders straight in their natural position. The chin must be parallel to the floor. The chest should not cave in. The abdomen must be held in naturally and should not protrude. The spine should be held naturally upright and not allowed to droop. The back must be erect but not rigid and in line with the back of the head and the posterior. The upper back should not be humped or the shoulders rounded as they will create a bulge below the waistline and exert pressure on the abdominal viscera. The low back must also be

kept straight. The pelvis should be erect. (See also Sukhasana.)

- In an erect sitting posture, there is the minimum of burden on the spine: the shoulders do not hunch, the abdominal organs do not get cramped, the diaphragm moves freely and no part of the body is held rigid.

40. Standing Upright

- Stand upright while well balanced, with as little effort as possible.
- In the correct standing posture, the back of the head should be level with the spine and the head must not be tilted backwards, forwards or sideways. Shoulders should not be raised or hunched; they should be kept relaxed. Ears must be in line with the shoulders. The abdomen should be held in and the chest naturally lifted. The back should be straight but not stiff.
- Shoulders and pelvis should be level. The pelvis should not be tucked in nor should it stick out.
- Legs should be straight without tightening the knees. Knees and hips should also be straight.
- Arms should hang freely by the sides, palms facing inward towards the body.
- Feet should be slightly parted so that it feels comfortable. Toes should be uncurled and not gripping the ground.
- The weight of the body should be evenly distributed over the heels, the outer sides of the feet, and the two weight-bearing points of each foot: one at the base

of the little toe and the other at the base of the big toe. If the weight of your body is thrown on the inner borders of the feet, it will weaken the feet and ankles and strain the calf muscles.

- In the correct standing posture, the whole body will feel light.

41. Walking Upright

- Walking calms the nervous system, aids the work of the heart and lungs, strengthens the muscles and raises the rate of metabolism.
- Always walk with an upraised head and a measured tread, without misaligning the body.
- The shoulders should be held back a little; do not hunch them.
- Look straight ahead and walk with a steady rhythm, keeping the feet parallel and the toes straight.
- Swing your arms naturally from the shoulders.
- Raise your heels and take even steps, moving from the top of the feet. Make sure you use your whole foot—heel and toe.
- Distribute the weight of your body evenly over the feet, holding the back and head erect.
- Try to walk straight, without swaying from side to side.

42. Viparita Karani
(The Inverted Posture)

'Viparita' means 'inverted' and 'Karani' means 'action' in Sanskrit. The usual posture of the body is inverted in this practice.

SEQUENCE

- Lie flat on your back and keep your legs together. Keep your arms on their respective sides.
- Inhaling, press your palms down and raise your legs slowly together without bending the knees or raising the hands till they are perpendicular to the floor. Exhale completely.
- Inhale deeply and exhale slowly. While exhaling, press the palms down again and without bending

Fig. 86.

the knees or raising the head, move the legs towards the head. While doing this, raise the hips and the small of the back also from the floor and curve up the lower part of the spine. Bring the legs parallel to the floor. Take a deep breath and breathe normally a few times.

- Bend the arms at the elbows and support the slanted trunk with the palms which should press the upper portion of the posterior on each side.

- Inhaling, bring back the legs again perpendicular to the floor, using the elbows as a fulcrum. Exhale and breathe normally.

- Keep the knees straight and the feet together. Fix your gaze on the tips of the big toes. Maintain this position for about three minutes.

- Return to the starting position in the reverse order.

BENEFITS

One who practises this Mudra regularly becomes healthy and strong and attains longevity due to the secretions of the thyroid, pituitary, gonad and adrenal glands which are stimulated by this practice.

This posture promotes inner harmony through the regulation of pelvic circulation and increasing the supply of blood to the thorax, brain, face and neck.

43. Parvatasana

(The Mountain Posture)

'**P**arvata' means 'mountain' in Sanskrit. As the arms are raised high and the fingers are joined together above the head in this posture, the body resembles a mountain peak and hence the name.

SEQUENCE

- Sit erect in Padmasana.
- Form a firm fingerlock.
- Inhaling, stretch the arms with the finger-lock vertically above the head without raising the seat and knees.
- Turn the palms up exactly above the centre of the head. Exhale.

Fig. 87.

- Inhaling again, stretch your arms upwards from the shoulder blades and stretch the trunk to the maximum without moving from your seat.

- Maintain this posture, holding your breath. (Fig. 87.)
- Exhaling, resume the starting position.
- **Variation:** Instead of forming a fingerlock, both palms may be joined together with the fingers well stretched out above the head. (Fig. 88.)

BENEFITS

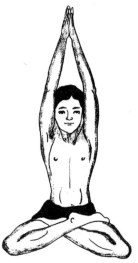

Fig. 88.

Parvatasana pulls up all the abdominal, pelvic and side muscles, stretches the spine and ribs, loosens the hips, stretches and exercises the usually inactive waist zone and helps to reduce a fat, flabby and protruding abdomen. As a result, the body becomes slim and its balancing power increases.

The chest expands to its full extent and the lung's capacity improves by the regular practise of this asana. It also aids correct breathing.

The asana strengthens the muscles of the back of the diaphragm.

44. Oordhwa Pada Hastasana
(Hands-to-Raised-Feet Posture)

'**O**ordhwa' means raised, 'Pada' means 'foot' and 'Hasta' means 'hand' in Sanskrit. You have to touch your raised feet with your hands in this posture.

SEQUENCE

- Lie flat on your back. Stretch out your legs fully and keep them together.
- Place the palms on the respective thighs with fingers pointing to the feet. Join the heels and the big toes. Keep the knees stiff.
- Breathing gently, raise your head, neck, shoulders, trunk and legs together slowly and simultaneously without bending

Fig. 89.

the knees and elbow; keep the toes pointing outwards. While doing this, slide down the palms along the thighs, keeping the arms fully stretched over the corresponding thighs.

- Hold the legs straight at an angle of about 60 degrees to the ground.

- Without altering the position of the legs, bend the trunk and head further forward and reach out to touch the ankles with the tips of your fingers. The back should be well arched. Balance the entire weight of the body on the posterior. Focus your eyes on the big toes.

- Maintain this posture as long as comfortable, breathing gently (Fig. 89).

- While breathing gently, return very slowly to the starting position in the reverse order.

BENEFITS

Oordhwa Pada Hastasana exercises well the neck, shoulders, diaphragm, arms, posterior, thighs, knees, calves and feet. It keeps the uterus healthy.

The lower back, hips and the pelvic region become more flexible.

This position strengthens the hamstring tendons and the muscles in the back of the knees.

It strengthens the organs of the abdomen and tones up the solar plexus.

45. Naukasana (Supine)
(The Boat Posture)

The technique of this asana is the same as that of Oordhwa Pada Hastasana with the following difference:

Lie flat on your back. Instead of placing your hands on the respective thighs, stretch out the arms above the head and keep the upper arms touching the ears. While inhaling, raise your arms,

Fig. 90.

head, neck, shoulders, trunk and legs all together to an angle of about 60 degrees to the floor. The arms should be held straight at the same level as the toes, and the tips of the toes should be level with the tips of the fingers. Focus your eyes on the big toes. The body is now balanced on the posterior and resembles a boat, as the name of the asana suggests. Maintain the posture steadily while holding your breath. While exhaling, return slowly to the starting position (Fig. 90).

46. Jnana Mudra

(The Symbol of Knowledge)

'Jnana' means 'knowledge' and 'Mudra' means 'symbol' in Sanskrit.

TECHNIQUE

- Sit in Padmasana or in any other meditative posture with the spine erect. Rest the back of the hands on the corresponding knees, with the palms turned upwards and the fingers fully stretched out.
- Fold the index finger of each hand inwards and join it with the thumb of the same hand, tip to tip, and form a rough circle, the other three fingers stretched out straight and kept close together and loose. While the index finger is being curved to meet the thumb, the latter should advance a little to meet it. Do not press them together.
- This gesture of the hand in which the forefinger and the thumb of each hand form a rough circle while the other fingers are spread out and held straight close to each other is known as Jnana Mudra, also called Chin Mudra. It is practised as an accompaniment to many meditative postures.

47. Naukasana
(The Boat Posture—Prone Lying)

'Nauka' means 'boat' in Sanskrit. The final position of this asana resembles a boat. Hence the name.

TECHNIQUE

- Lie straight on your abdomen and chest with your forehead resting on the floor. Keep the feet together and the arms on the sides.

Fig. 91.

- Stretch out the arms straight on both sides of the head and keep them parallel. Turn down the palms on the floor with fingers close together. Keep your forehead on the floor between the upper arms.

- Inhaling, raise the arms, head, neck, shoulders, trunk and legs all together slowly and simultaneously as high as possible without bending the knees and elbows and without any jerk. While doing this, keep the upper arms touching the ears and the feet together.
- Bring the head up as high as possible and keep it between the raised upper arms.
- Bend the extremities as far back as possible, and the back should be well arched. The whole body should be curved from the fingertips to the toes, both of which should be on the same level.
- Balance the entire weight of the body on the lower part of the abdomen which alone should touch the ground.
- Maintain the posture motionlessly, as long as you can comfortably hold your breath. (Fig. 91.)
- Exhaling, return slowly to the starting position.
- Relax completely in Savasana.

BENEFITS

Naukasana bends the middle of the spine and makes it flexible. Deformities of the spinal column are corrected.

It strengthens the hips, arms, thighs, knees, calves, feet and the pelvic region.

It expands the chest and strengthens the lungs.

It strengthens the muscles of the back, abdomen, the lower limbs, neck and shoulders.

48. Jalandhara Bandha
(Chin-lock)

'Jala' means 'net' or 'web' and 'dhara' means 'an upward pull' in Sanskrit. The chin is pressed against the jugular notch in this Bandha (lock).

TECHNIQUE

- Sit comfortably in Padmasana or in any other sitting posture in which the legs are crossed. The spine and the head must be held erect. Place the palms on the knees.
- Exhale completely and then inhale slowly and deeply, at the same time expanding the chest fully. Hold your breath.
- Raise your chin as high as possible without tilting the head.
- Bend your head and neck forward and downward slowly towards your chest, at the same time contracting the muscles of your neck and throat.
- Bring the chin down slowly to the chest and press the point firmly into the jugular notch. Keep your chin

tucked in with the maximum contraction of the muscles of the neck and throat, with the back still held erect.

- Fix your gaze on the tip of the nose.
- Close your nostrils with the thumb, ring finger and the little finger of the right hand and hold your breath.
- Maintain the lock as long as your breath can be held comfortably.
- After holding your breath, release the chin-lock and fingers, raise the neck and head to the erect position, straighten up the spine and exhale slowly. Take a few breaths of normal duration.

BENEFITS

Jalandhara Bandha benefits the thyroid and the parathyroid glands and the carotid sinuses.

The pressure on the carotid sinuses facilitates intracranial circulation and helps in lowering the blood pressure.

It has a stimulating effect on the muscles of the throat and improves the blood circulation in that region.

It exercises the neck muscles and stimulates the spinal nerve centres.

This Bandha is useful to persons with a double chin and helps them to get rid of it.

It cures many disorders of the throat.

The practise of this Bandha helps to awaken one's latent spiritual force, according to the classical textbooks on yoga.

49. Moola Bandha
(Anal Contraction)

'Moola' means 'root', 'basis', 'source', or 'cause' in Sanskrit. It also means 'anal region'. 'Bandha' means 'lock'. 'Moola Bandha' means 'Anal lock'.

TECHNIQUE

- Sit erect on the carpet in Siddhasana, pressing well the perineum with the left heel. Look straight ahead.
- Take a deep breath. Exhale slowly and as the abdomen contracts, close the anal aperture tightly, and then contract both the internal and the external sphincter muscles vigorously and continuously and draw them upwards.
- Intensify the contraction and lifting of the anal sphincter muscles after completing the exhalation. Try to get the maximum contraction but do not contract violently.
- Hold the contraction from five to ten seconds without discomfort.
- Inhale slowly and, while inhaling, relax the anal sphincter muscles slowly. This completes the Moola Bandha.

- Perform five turns of this Bandha in succession in the beginning, and increase by one turn every week up to a maximum of ten turns for gaining the maximum amount of physical benefit. Relax for about five seconds between the contractions.

BENEFITS

Moola Bandha benefits the prostate gland, the gonads, the perineal body and the pelvic muscles. The pelvic floor receives an increased blood supply.

It gives relief in several disorders of the urogenital and anal systems.

It prevents piles, fistula and prostatic hypetrophy. If the ailments are already present, it reduces their severity and prevents further complications.

It prevents a prolapse of the rectum.

50. Siddhasana
(The Posture of an Adept)

'Siddha' means a spiritually enlightened person in Sanskrit.

- Sit erect in Sukhasana. Stretch out your legs. Place the left heel against the perineum and the right heel above the root of the generative organ. Insert the toes of both legs between the opposite thighs and calves. Knees must touch the floor. Head, neck and the spine should be kept erect.

BENEFITS

This asana is one of the classic meditative postures and is practised mostly for its spiritual values. The advanced yogis favour it for practising meditation and Pranayama.

51. Brumadhya Drishti
(Frontal Gaze)

'**B**ru' means 'eyebrow' and 'Madhya' means 'centre' in Sanskrit. 'Brumadhya' means 'the point halfway between the two eyebrows'. 'Drishti' means 'gaze'.

'Brumadhya Drishti' is a frontal gaze in which the eyeballs are gently turned upward and converge centrally on the point between the eyebrows just above the root of the nose where the olfactory nerve receptors lie. The mind should also be fixed on this imaginary spot between and behind the eyebrows.

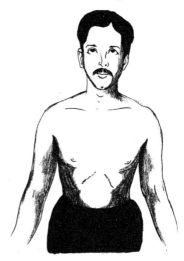

The eyeballs are turned upward and converge centrally on the spot between the eyebrows.

TECHNIQUE

First, keep the eyes wide open and look in

front at a fixed point. Then, looking up as high as possible without moving the head, focus the eyes and concentrate on the spot between and behind the eyebrows. Breathe normally. Then lower the eyes.

Gaze steadily at this point only for a few seconds without tension or until the eyes get tired. Pause at the slightest fatigue. If you feel any pain or tiredness in the eyes, close them, cover them with the palms, and relax the eye muscles.

52. Nasagra Drishti
(Nasal Gaze)

'Nasagra' means 'tip of the nose' and 'drishti', as mentioned earlier, means 'gaze' in Sanskrit. 'Nasagra Drishti' is achieved by lowering the eyelids and fixing the gaze steadily on the tip of the nose. Both the eyes must gaze at the tip of the nose with the same balance and lack of tension. The eyelids should be almost closed and only a slit of light should enter at the bottom. Hold this gaze as long as comfortable and avoid any strain on the eye muscles during the practice. Then open the eyes.

CAUTION

Learn the techniques of Nasagra and Brumadhya Drishti from a competent teacher since any wrong practice develops a squint in the eyes.

BENEFITS

Both Nasagra and Brumadhya Drishti will strengthen the eye muscles and help to preserve normal vision until a ripe old age.

53. Kapala Bhati
(The Cleansing Breath)

'Kapala' means 'skull' (and by implication, the brain) and 'Bhati' means 'shines' in Sanskrit. This practice cleanses the nasal passages in the skull and other passages of the respiratory system.

Exhalations and inhalations in quick succession without any pause, resembling the blowing of a blacksmith's bellows, constitute the practice of Kapala Bhati.

TECHNIQUE

- Sit firmly in a cross-legged posture with the spine, neck and head held erect.
- First, exhale completely and then take a few deep breaths. Relax the abdominal muscles. Inhale without taking a deep breath; make a short and forceful expulsion of the breath through both nostrils producing a hissing sound and, simultaneously, contract the lower abdomen by a rapid and vigorous thrust of the abdominal muscles. Release the

contraction of the abdominal muscles quickly and the lungs will automatically take in air. Follow at once by another forcible expulsion of your breath, contracting the abdomen in the same manner and letting it relax outward as the air is drawn in again. Repeat the exercise a number of times in quick succession, concentrating your mind on the region of the abdomen below the navel.

- After you complete a round and make the last exhalation, take in a deep and slow breath and then resume normal breathing to afford rest to the lungs.

- Increasing the number and speed gradually, try to do two expulsions a second (120 a minute) in each round which should be the maximum.

- Perform three rounds in each sitting, with sufficient pause between the rounds, when normal breathing should be done.

BENEFITS

Kapala Bhati flushes out stale residual air in the lungs and helps a fresh supply of air to reach them.

It lends elasticity to the diaphragm and increases the capacity of the lungs.

54. Sirshasana
(The Head-Stand)

'Sirsha' means 'head' in Sanskrit. The student is required to 'stand on his head' in this asana and hence the name.

SEQUENCE

- Spread a cloth or blanket folded several times on the carpet to serve as a cushion or pad for your head.

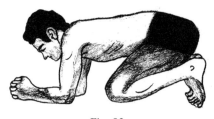

Fig. 92.

- Kneel down in front of the pad with only the toes and knees ouching the ground.
- Sit back between your heels.
- Stoop forward, raising the haunches

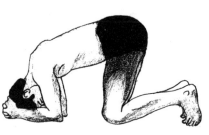

Fig. 93.

from the heels. While doing so, bend your arms and place your elbows, forearms and hands on the pad on either side of your head.

- Form a firm finger-lock to fit round the back of your head, palms facing inwards.

- Bring the elbows in towards each other and make a convenient angle in front of you with the forearms and elbows (Fig. 92).

- Bend the head down perpendicularly and place the hind part of the crown of your head on the pad with the interlocked fingers pressing the back of your head (Fig. 93).

- Raise your knees, hips and the lower part of your trunk and straighten out your legs. Bring the feet together (Fig. 94)

- Drag your feet slowly towards your face

Fig. 94.

Fig. 95.

Fig. 96.

and balance your feet on tiptoe. Knees should be close to the chest (Fig. 95).

- Pressing the toes, elbows, forearms and head against the floor, give a gentle kick and lift your feet together off the floor. The thighs should be upright, the legs horizontal and the trunk perpendicular to the ground. Keep the feet together and maintain balance (Fig. 96).

- Fold the legs back on the thighs.

- Raise the folded legs and thighs till the thighs come parallel to the floor. Straighten the back maintaining balance (Fig. 97).

- Straighten out the thighs fully in line with the trunk, with the legs still folded back on the thighs (Fig. 98).

- Open out your legs and stretch them up vertically. Bring the legs together and maintain balance. This is the final position (Fig. 99).

- Return to the starting position slowly in the reverse order.

- Lie down in Savasana and allow your muscles to relax.

Fig. 97.

Fig. 98.

Fig. 99.

BENEFITS

This asana directly stimulates the pineal and the pituitary glands in the brain whose healthy functioning is essential for proper metabolism.

A regular practise of Sirshasana benefits the nervous, circulatory, respiratory, digestive, excretory and endocrine systems. It also sharpens the sensitivity of the sense organs.

55. Uddiyana Bandha
(Abdominal Lock)

'Uddiyana' means 'flying up', and 'Bandha', as mentioned earlier, means 'lock' or 'tie' in Sanskrit. Uddiyana is the 'flying up' of the diaphragm in the thorax and the simultaneous pulling back of the abdominal viscera above and below the navel towards the spine.

TECHNIQUE

- Stand erect on the carpet. Place your feet about eighteen inches apart, in line with each other, and turned a little outward.
- Slightly bend your head and trunk forward from the waist and flex the legs in the knee-joints. Bend the arms and grasp the front of the thighs a little above the knees with the respective hands with all the fingers, including the thumb, pointing inward. Raise your head slowly. Leave the abdominal muscles loose.
- Exhale completely as fast as possible, breathing out the air from the lungs fully and forcefully, at the same time vigorously contracting the front muscles of the abdomen.

- Hold out your breath and do not allow the air to enter the lungs while the following abdominal movements are being performed:
- Pressing the palms mildly and evenly against the respective thighs, do vigorous 'mock inhalation' (false inhalation), without opening the glottis or allowing the air to rush into the lungs. While doing this, the thoracic cage will expand and the ribs will be lifted and as they do so, swiftly and completely relax the contracted front abdominal muscles. As soon as the ribs rise, the relaxed diaphragm will automatically rise up and, simultaneously, the front muscles of the abdomen, namely, the part of the abdomen above and below the navel (the abdomen including the navel), get sucked inward and upward towards the ribs automatically and fill the 'vacuum' in the thoracic cavity. The relaxed abdominal wall, in turn, undergoes a deep depression, extending from just below the ribs up to the pelvis and, as the abdomen thus hollows itself, it will take on a concave appearance. This is Uddiyana (Fig. 100).
- Holding the 'vacuum' in the lungs, maintain this position comfortably for five to ten seconds or until you can go without air without any discomfort. Concentrate your mind on the solar plexus.
- **Return:** When the breath can no longer be held out comfortably, start inhaling slowly and deeply. The deep hollow created in the abdomen will be effaced gradually, and the abdomen and the chest will assume their normal shape. Straighten your trunk and head, reduce the distance between the feet, and return slowly to the standing position. Exhale slowly and

breathe deeply a few times and then resume normal breathing. One round of Uddiyana is now complete. Take three rounds with sufficient periods of rest.

BENEFITS

Uddiyana is the sole exercise which helps to maintain abdominal fitness. It promotes the resilience of the abdominal muscles and improves the blood circulation in the abdominal cavity.

It provides a natural and powerful massage to the heart, stomach, liver, pancreas, spleen, kidneys, gall bladder, the transverse colon, and the upper part of the small intestine, all in one movement.

The participation of the abdomen in the respiratory processes and the increased mobility of the diaphragm make a deeper and fuller respiration possible.

Uddiyana restores the elasticity of the lungs and improves their capacity. The chest expands and the ribs are also exercised.

It tones up all the nerves which have their roots in the region of the solar plexus. The improved functioning of the somatic nerve helps the coordinated activity of the voluntary and involuntary nervous systems.

56. Finger-Lock

Bring your palms closer. Join tightly the fingers of the right hand and those of the left hand (except the thumbs) by interlacing the fingers of the two hands. When their roots are well-knit together, a fingerlock is formed.

UDDIYANA

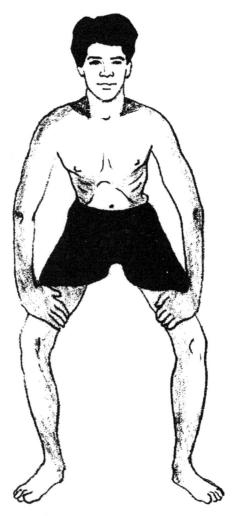

Fig. 100. Final position—Note the expansion
of the chest and the caved in abdomen.

MADHYAMA NAULI

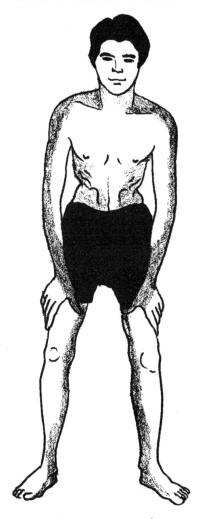

Fig. 101. Final position—Note the contracted
recti, standing out like a rope of muscle
in the middle of the abdomen.

57. Nauli

(Recti Isolation)

Nauli is a further development of Uddiyana in which the abdominal recti muscles are separated and exercised in a rotary movement.

TECHNIQUE

- Stand on a carpet and do Uddiyana. While holding out your breath and maintaining Uddiyana and while the abdomen assumes a concave appearance, stoop forward a little and concentrate your mind on the abdominal recti muscles rooted in the pit of the stomach, just above the pubic bone. First relax the muscles of the abdominal wall and then isolate the two recti muscles (Recus Abdomini) from the adjoining muscles of the abdominal wall and roll them from right to left and from left to right. This is Nauli (Fig. 101).
- Nauli consists of five continuous movements of the abdominal recti: a. its central isolation (Madhyama); b. its right isolation (Dakshina); c. its left isolation (Vama); d. its right and left isolation in rotation; and

e. its rolling manipulation in a circular rhythm, clockwise and anti-clockwise.

- The final stage of Nauli consists in rolling the recti from side to side several times without a break during exhalation. The recti should be manipulated from right to left, namely Dakshina, Madhyama and Vama, rhythmically and speedily, and then the opposite way, namely, Vama, Madhyama and Dakshina. In this continuous 'churning' action, the two recti are so manipulated as to maintain a rapid vertical wave across the abdomen from left to right and from right to left, and so on.

- Boys and girls in their pre-pubertal age should not practise Uddiyana and Nauli. Persons above fifty and those of advanced age who start this practice for the first time should do so only on the advice of a competent teacher.

- Women should not practise Uddiyana and Nauli during pregnancy.

BENEFITS

The lateral rolling of the muscles of the abdomen provides an excellent exercise for toning up the abdominal viscera and the gastro-intestinal system. The gonads, adrenals and the solar plexus also get stimulated.

Most diseases originate from the abdomen. The practice of Nauli makes the organs of the abdominal cavity strong. Digestive power improves and the elimination of waste matter gets regularized. For persons suffering from constipation, bowel movement will become regular after the practice.

8

Pranayama
(Preparation)

Before starting Pranayama, practise deep inhalations and exhalations through both nostrils, exhalation taking double the time of inhalation. Increase the timing gradually until the maximum possible slowness is reached. After a few weeks, practise inhaling and exhaling through alternate nostrils, using only one nostril at a time and keeping the same ratio for inhalation and exhalation. Control of inhalation and exhalation and the retention of the breath, which is Pranayama, should be introduced only after practising slow, deep and rhythmical breathing for at least two months.

1. Yoga Deep Breathing

- Sit erect in any comfortable cross-legged posture.
- Breathe normally a few times through both the nostrils and watch your breath.
- Expel by a deep exhalation as much of the used-up air as possible from the lungs, contracting the abdominal muscles.
- At the end of exhalation, inhale slowly, deeply and evenly without producing any sound and keeping the mouth closed. While you inhale, feel the air flowing down slowly and continuously into the lower, then the middle and then the upper part of the lungs.
- When you reach the peak of your inhalation, exhale again, feeling the reverse movement of breath by first emptying the lower part of the lungs, then the middle and finally the upper part.
- This completes one round. Practise up to twenty rounds at a time, depending upon your capacity and control, and then breathe freely a few times, relaxing the chest and abdomen.
- Both inhalation and exhalation should be silent and there is no need to half close the glottis.

- Concentrate your mind on the breath as it flows smoothly up and down through the nostrils.
- Though there appears to be three stages in this kind of breathing, each glides so naturally into the next that the whole process becomes one single, smooth, continuous, wavelike movement.

2. Alternate Nostril Breathing

Alternate breathing from the nostrils consists in breathing in and breathing out alternately through one nostril at a time. Take twice as long to exhale as to inhale. Do not produce any sound both during inhalation and exhalation.

- Sit comfortably in any cross-legged position.
- Exhale slowly and completely through the left nostril, the right one closed.
- Inhale slowly and deeply through the left nostril, the right one still closed.
- Close the left nostril and exhale slowly and completely through the right nostril.
- Keeping the left nostril closed, inhale slowly and deeply through the right nostril.
- Close the right nostril and exhale slowly and completely through the left nostril. This completes one round.

Measure: To start with, six rounds may be practised successively in one sitting, without any pause between the rounds and slowly work up to a cycle of twenty, adding two rounds per week.

The duration of each inhalation and exhalation may also be increased gradually in the ratio of 1:2 according to the capacity of your lungs.

3. Closing the Glottis

The glottis (epiglottis) is a thin leaf-like lamella of elastic fibro-cartilage which projects obliquely upwards at the root of the tongue and the body of the hyoid bone and in front of the entrance to the larynx. It is situated between the free margins of the vocal folds.

When the glottis is partially closed while inhaling and exhaling in some types of Pranayama, a soft sound is produced owing to the slight pressure created by its partial closure. This sound comes from the throat. It is different from the sound produced by the friction of the incoming or outgoing air with the nostrils during normal respiration when the glottis is open.

While practising Bhastrika and Ujjayi Pranayama, the sound produced by the partial closure of the glottis should be gentle and uniform which will ensure uniformity in the flow of air to and from the lungs.

4. Anuloma Viloma
(Alternate Nostril Breathing)

'Anuloma' means 'towards' and 'Viloma' means 'reverse' in Sanskrit. The order of using the nostrils for inhalation and exhalation is reversed every time in this Pranayama.

Sequence

- Sit comfortably in any cross-legged posture with the head, neck and the spine erect.
- Exhale completely through the left nostril, with the right one closed.
- Inhale through the left nostril, the right one still closed.
- Retain your breath according to your capacity, with both nostrils closed.
- Exhale through the right nostril, the left one closed.
- Inhale through the right nostril, the left one still closed.
- Retain your breath, according to your capacity, with both the nostrils closed.
- Exhale through the left nostril, the right one closed.

- Begin the entire process again by inhaling through the left nostril, and so on.

Retention of Breath: The duration of the holding of the breath varies in each individual case. Five seconds is a good measure for the average beginner to start with, which may be increased gradually and cautiously by units of five seconds up to twenty.

Ratio: With regard to the ratio of inhalation, retention and exhalation, the same ratio as in Ujjayi should be maintained, that is, 1:2:2 in the beginning which may be increased gradually to 1:3:2, and finally to 1:4:2, the ratio being kept the same. The numbers in the ratio could be taken as seconds.

- Elongation of the breath should be done gradually as the capacity increases.

Measure: Practise ten rounds at a time to start with, one after the other, without any pause after each round. The number of rounds may be increased each week by units of two up to twenty in one sitting, extending the count within the given ratio. You may practise in the morning and in the evening.

- After completing the practice, take a few normal breaths through both nostrils and relax completely in the sitting position.

BENEFITS

Anuloma Viloma Pranayma will purify the blood vessels and other channels (Nadis) in the body within three months of practise.

5. Ujjayi Pranayama

Ujjayi Pranayama is controlled inhalation and exhalation along with the retention of the breath.

TECHNIQUE

- Sit erect at ease on the carpet in Padmasana or Siddhasana.
- Breathe out the pent-up air in the lungs slowly and completely through both nostrils.
- Inhale slowly, deeply, steadily and evenly through both nostrils. While taking in air, partially close the glottis and produce gently a continuous frictional sound in the throat. The chest must expand naturally, and the abdomen must not bulge out. The abdominal muscles should be kept under control.
- As soon as inhalation is complete and your lungs are quite full, close your nostrils and the glottis and retain your breath according to your capacity.
- Exhale slowly, steadily and evenly through both nostrils, opening the glottis partially and producing a frictional sound gently and continuously, similar to

the one made during the inhalation. While exhaling, relax the chest in a natural way and the abdomen will retract simultaneously and naturally.

- After complete exhalation and after your lungs are quite empty, pause for a second before drawing in fresh breath and continuing the cycle.
- The ratio of the time of inhalation to exhalation is 1:2, namely, exhalation taking twice as long as inhalation.
- To begin with, practise only ten rounds continuously in one sitting. Increase the rounds gradually to one sitting of twenty rounds, adding two rounds every week from the start of the practice.

BENEFITS

Ujjayi Pranayama increases the capacity of the lungs and helps to establish the natural rhythm of the breath.

With long practise, large quantities of oxygen are assimilated in the blood.

Ujjayi Pranayama clears the nasal passages and helps to remove phlegm from the throat. It thus counteracts many diseases of the ear, nose and throat.

6. Bhastrika
(The Bellows Breath)

'Bhastrika' means 'bellows' in Sanskrit. Just as a blacksmith works his bellows, so are the abdominal muscles exercised during this practice in which air is forcefully drawn in and out.

Bhastrika Pranayama is a combination of Kapala Bhati and Ujjayi and the same technique should be followed in this.

TECHNIQUE

- Sit erect. Padmasana is the best asana to adopt.
- Practise Kapala Bhati vigorously, doing the required number of rapid expulsions of breath, say from thirty up to fifty, according to your lung's capacity. After the last rapid expulsion of breath in the series, empty the lungs completely and inhale as slowly and deeply as possible through both nostrils to the full capacity of the lungs, expanding the chest slowly and naturally and keeping the abdominal muscles controlled, as in Ujjayi. Inhalation should be gentle and complete

through the nose and throat. While inhaling, keep the glottis partially closed and produce the frictional sound of a low pitch in the throat.

- After complete inhalation through both nostrils, do Jalandhara Bandha (chin-lock); close both nostrils with the fingers of the right hand and hold the breath from ten to twenty seconds or as long as you are comfortable.

- When you can no longer hold your breath comfortably, remove the fingers from the nostrils, raise the head and exhale slowly, steadily and deeply through both the nostrils until the lungs are empty, producing the frictional sound again and at the same time relaxing the chest and contracting the abdomen slowly and naturally. Exhalation should take double the time of inhalation.

- The deep exhalation completes one round of Bhastrika. Place the right hand again on the knee. Take several breaths to recover and sit quiet for about a minute, breathing normally, before starting on the next round. Three rounds may be practised by a person with normal health.

- Practise this Pranayama regularly everyday. It may be practised both in the morning and in the evening.

BENEFITS

By practising this Pranayama, both the brain and the spinal regions and the roots of the nerves situated in these parts receive larger quantities of fresh blood.

The ribcage expands and the air which fills your lungs ventilates them completely.

9

Heart Disease

1. What is heart disease? 2. Angina Pectoris. 3. Heart Attack. 4. Arteriosclerosis. 5. Atheroma. 6. Atherosclerosis. 7. Thrombosis. 8. Coronary Artery Disease. 9. Rheumatic Heart Disease. 10. Peripheral Vascular Disease. 11. Cardiomyopathy. 12. Congenital Defects. 13. Arrhythmia. 14. Fibrillation. 15. Tachycardia. 16. Palpitation. 17. Heart Failure. 18. Pulmonary Embolism. 19. Stroke. 20. Preventive Measures.

1. WHAT IS HEART DISEASE?

1. Heart disease means a disease of the heart muscle, arteries, valves, the sac in which the heart is enclosed, or the heart's electrical system. It can result in breathlessness, severe chest pains, irregular heart beats, stroke, or heart attack.

2. Many people fear that any pain in the chest might be due to heart trouble, but many types of chest pain are not due to heart disease. Muscular and tissue

pains can also produce somewhat similar symptoms. Pain in the left chest is most unlikely to be a heart attack.

3. Most people who suffer a heart attack experience severe chest pain which is usually in the middle of the chest, in the front, spreading sideways towards the shoulders and sometimes into the arms.

4. Pain coming from the heart muscle is usually steady and may last for quite a long time, although its intensity may vary from a dull ache to a severe gripping pain.

5. Death is not inevitable in a heart attack even when it is massive since the heart has great reserves of power and a small affected area is not likely to affect its functioning very much.

2. ANGINA PECTORIS

1. Angina pectoris is the medical term for attacks of chest pain caused by a cry for more blood and oxygen by the heart muscle. 'Angina Pectoris' literally means the 'cry of the heart'.

2. The attacks are usually due to the narrowing of one or more of the coronary arteries caused by many factors. Important risk factors include high blood pressure, diabetes, obesity and reduced function of the thyroid glands. Forcible exertion, emotional stress or even exposure to cold are enough to provoke anginal pains.

3. The chest pains come on suddenly. You may experience a continuous tight feeling or oppression high up in the centre of the chest behind the breastbone. The pains may often radiate to the shoulders, neck, jaws,

arms, hand or back between the shoulder blades. They are of only a few seconds' duration and can range from mildly uncomfortable to severely disabling. They usually subside, if you rest, after two or three minutes. They do not permanently damage the heart muscles.

4. Angina Pectoris is not an illness in itself, but a warning sign of other cardio-vascular malfunctions. It is usually the precursor of a heart attack.

5. This disorder is much rarer in women than in men during middle age, but is equally common in both sexes in the older age groups.

Treatment

1. Regular practise of abdominal breathing and Savasana give real and lasting relief in this condition as well as in other heart ailments by dilating the obstructed coronary arteries and increasing the blood flow to the heart muscles. They also take the strain off the heart, which will then take care of itself.

2. An overweight person who develops angina must bring down his weight to normal levels since it is a significant risk factor in this disorder.

3. The elimination of obesity will reduce the load on the heart.

4. Moderate regular exercise is beneficial for victims of this disorder, but those who are limited by angina from doing so must practise only under regular medical supervision.

5. Limit your intake of animal fats and sugar in the diet.

6. Stay away from cigarettes.

7. Avoid tension and stress and enjoy regular periods of leisure and relaxation.

8. Making changes in your lifestyle plays an important role in the long-range treatment of this disorder.

3. HEART ATTACK

1. A heart attack (acute myocardial infarction) is a sudden, local blockage of the blood supply in one of the coronary arteries. It develops most frequently as a result of the sudden occlusion (obstruction) of a coronary artery, the function of which is to supply a certain area of the heart muscle (myocardium) with oxygen. Occlusive thrombosis over an atheromatous patch is the usual cause.
2. The imbalance between the demand for oxygen and the actual supply by the blood vessels is the main cause for heart attacks and Angina Pectoris.
3. Generally, males suffer from this devastating illness more than females.

A. Symptoms

The most common symptom is gripping or tight chest pain which is continuous for a few hours. The pain is usually most intense high up behind the breastbone. It may radiate from this position to the arms, neck, jaw and back. The victim may also experience restlessness and cold sweat.

B. Risk Factors

Heart attack, though it appears to be sudden, is the result of a long and complicated series of degenerative diseases. They can be prevented in the majority of cases by detecting and treating at an early stage the following primary risk factors which are metabolic as well as environmental. It should, however, be borne in mind that it is not a single risk factor, but an interplay of various risk factors that makes a person vulnerable to heart attacks. The following are a few: a. Atherosclerosis (hardening of the arteries; b. High blood pressure (Hypertension; c. High cholesterol level; d. Elevated uric acid in the blood (hyperuricemia; e. Overweight; f. Diabetes; g. Cigarette smoking; h. A sedentary occupation; i. Lack of regular exercise; j. Stress; k. Genetic disposition.

C. Value of Exercise

1. Graduated exercise and emotional relaxation greatly help to improve the total blood circulation and thus cut down the demand for oxygen and supply to the heart muscle. The dangers of acutely impaired blood circulation can be avoided by these measures. Regular and controlled exercise will also cause new blood pathways to develop.

2. Physical exercises help to lessen the myocardial work load by a decreased demand for oxygen. They also relieve stress and bring about relaxation, calmness and improved blood circulation in the heart.

3. A normal heart has great reserves of power, and this can be substantially increased by physical training.

4. During exercise, there is a greater venous return to the heart with consequent increase in diastolic filling and stretching of the muscle fibres.

5. Exercise helps control blood pressure by reducing the amount of fluids in the body and helping to lower weight. It also helps to normalize blood cholesterol levels.

6. Exercises which are continuous and rhythmic are the best for the cardiovascular system as the pulse rate increases and more oxygen is carried through the system.

7. Exercise keeps your muscles in trim, and this helps your recovery.
8. Taking regular controlled exercise is beneficial, but avoid strenuous and unaccustomed exercise as it can be harmful. Before beginning any exercise programme, talk it over with a doctor who knows yoga.
9. All exercises which involve forced breathing and competitive sports should be avoided.
10. Regular and brisk walking at a uniform pace for a mile or two a day helps most cardiac patients.
11. Climbing a few stairs will not hurt.
12. Yoga deep breathing is of immense benefit to ward off heart attacks.

Preventive Measures

1. Victims of heart disease should not overload their stomach and should avoid digestive upsets.
2. They should cut down substantially on all animal-fat food to reduce the deposit of cholesterol in the arteries. A low-salt diet is also beneficial.
3. Overweight and obese persons must reduce by a combination of diet and exercise.
4. Avoid excessive strain—physical, mental or emotional. Emotional tension increases the coagulation of the blood, upsets the body's equilibrium, and thus causes complications.
5. Rest quietly in Savasana as many times during the day as circumstances permit so as to reduce stress and tension and the propensity to heart disease.
6. A major change of lifestyle (not dramatically), including change of environment and giving up harmful personal habits, will be helpful.

7.   There is no convincing evidence that drugs reduce the frequency of heart attack. Most of the available evidence suggests that they have undesirable side-effects, particularly when taken in large amounts that may be necessary.

4. ARTERIOSCLEROSIS

(a) Arteries are tubes through which the heart propels blood to different parts of the body. Arteriosclerosis is the chronic clogging and consequent hardening and narrowing of the arterial walls, either local or general. This illness is often associated with high blood pressure and abnormal blood fats. It is the first step in the development of a heart attack.

(b) The complications which arise from narrowing, obstruction, clotting and embolism lead to serious forms of heart disease and stroke.

(c) The exact causes of this condition have not been determined, but it is mostly due to the silting up of fat (mainly cholesterol) and blood protein on the walls of the arteries over the years. Cigarette-smoking is a potent causative factor.

(d) This is a disease usually suffered by older people.

(e) A diet rich in fibre and low on fats and oils will help prevent this condition.

Aneurysm

Aneurysm is a local enlargement of the lumen of an artery. Alcohol, rheumatism and overexertion are the usual causes.

5. ATHEROMA

This disorder consists of fatty deposits, specially cholesterol, just under the inner lining of the arteries, narrowing them so that the blood flow is diminished, and clotting tends to occur. The arteries most often affected are aorta, and the coronary, cerebral and renal arteries, so that atheroma causes coronary thrombosis, strokes, and renal failure. Atheroma is the chief cause of ischemic heart disease.

Lack of exercise, overeating and smoking are the common causes of arterial diseases including Atheroma.

6. ATHEROSCLEROSIS

This is a form of arteriosclerosis characterized by the hardening and roughening of the inner walls of arteries with deposits of fatty material (such as cholesterol), cellular debris, and calcium. This raises the blood pressure, forcing the heart to work harder against the increased peripheral resistance, increasing the possibility of thrombosis. Its most frequent symptom is Angina Pectoris. If Atherosclerosis blocks the blood supply to the brain, a stroke occurs.

CHOLESTEROL

Cholesterol is a waxy, fatty substance which can be either absorbed directly from cholesterol-rich food, or it can be produced from fats by the liver and digestive tract. It continuously circulates in the bloodstream and forms part of every cell in the body.

Cholesterol is present in many food, such as egg yolks, cream, ghee, whole milk, fatty meat and fish. While only certain fats from animal food contain cholesterol, vegetable oils do not contain it.

Cholesterol in itself is not harmful; in fact, it forms the chemical skeleton upon which many of the body's hormones are constructed. It is only when there is too much of the wrong type that it becomes a problem; when it tends to leave the bloodstream and work its way gradually into the insides of the arteries, depositing the fatty streaks which become atheroma.

7. THROMBOSIS

Thrombus means a solid or semi-solid mass inside a blood vessel from the constituents of the blood. Thrombosis is the medical term for such clot formation. Most heart attacks result from a blood clot developing on or around a plaque of atheroma which blocks the coronary artery with a combination of plaque and blood clot.

8. CORONARY ARTERY DISEASE

Coronary artery disease results from a slow and progressive narrowing (Stenosis) and blocking of the coronary arteries which supply blood to the heart itself.

Though the basic process which causes this condition remains unknown, there are many known factors which make it worse including smoking, physical inactivity, diabetes, hypertension, obesity, abnormalities in fat metabolism and hereditary factors.

9. RHEUMATIC HEART DISEASE

Rheumatic heart disease is caused by an infection that scars heart valves. It makes the heart's valves grow increasingly thick, lose their flexibility, and leak and/or obstruct the flow of blood. The heart and the heart cavity also become inflamed in rheumatic heart disease.

10. PERIPHERAL VASCULAR DISEASE

Peripheral vascular disease is an illness that affects arteries and veins far from the heart including varicose veins, hardening of the arteries in the legs, and blood clot in the legs.

11. CARDIOMYOPATHY

Cardiomyopathy is a condition in which the heart muscle is damaged. It develops gradually and the heart grows larger and larger and the patient becomes more and more breathless during exertion. This is quite a common condition often resulting from the consumption of alcohol.

Avoid worry, muscular exertions beyond the normal, and overeating or drinking.

12. CONGENITAL DEFECTS

These arise if the heart has not been formed properly during its development in the womb. Many of these abnormalities can be easily treated in childhood.

13. ARRHYTHMIA

Arrhythmia (irregular heartbeat) is caused by injury to the heart muscle, usually by heart attack, by diseases of the heart valves or other areas of the heart, or by other ailments such as hyperthyroidism, and depletion of the blood's supply of electrolytes. This results in a weak quivering of the heart instead of regular, strong beats.

14. FIBRILLATION

Sometimes the heart sequence becomes disturbed, resulting in a rapid, chaotic and irregular rhythm in either the atria or ventricles. This is known as Fibrillation and can be rectified by the application of a direct-current electric shock to the chest with two large electrodes. This completely stops the heart's electrical activity and then a normal heart rhythm starts.

15. TACHYCARDIA
(Rapid Beating)

Normally, the pulse rate is about sixty to eighty beats per minute. If it is above hundred when in the resting position as a result of an electrical short-circuit within the conduction system it is said to represent Tachycardia. It is a symptom of abnormal heart function and not a disease and is easily detected on the E.C.G.

16. PALPITATION

Palpitation is a heightened awareness of the heart's rhythm. It is perfectly normal to be aware of one's heart rhythm and it should not be a cause for alarm. Brief episodes of palpitation usually do not require any treatment.

17. HEART FAILURE

Heart failure is caused by long-standing high blood pressure or a gradual loss of working heart muscle due to repeated heart attacks. The heart no longer pumps blood efficiently because of excess fluids in the legs, lungs, and sometimes the abdomen. (Ascitis.)

18. PULMONARY EMBOLISM

Embolus is a piece of blood clot floating free in the circulation which can cause damage by getting stuck in a small artery and blocking it off.

Pulmonary embolism occurs as a result of the dislodging of a clot from the deep veins, often of the legs, carried to the lungs. The accent must always be on prevention. Exercise promotes good blood flow in the deep veins, and this prevents blood from stagnating which is likely to clot and form emboli.

19. STROKE
(Cerebrovascular Accident)

When an artery that supplies blood to a part of the brain is blocked, or bursts due to very high pressure, a stroke occurs. There are three main causes: (a) Thrombosis or Occlusion; (b) Embolism; (c) Haemorrhage.

High blood pressure is the major cause of strokes. Abnormal blood fats and cigarette smoking are also important causes.

The likelihood of a first stroke can be minimized by reducing blood pressure and changing one's lifestyle.

A stroke is more common in men than women. It can vary in severity from a minor disturbance to a major attack, depending on the location, extent and permanence of the brain damage. Severe attacks may cause paralysis, speech impairment, unconsciousness and death.

Chances of stroke are remote if you adopt healthier eating habits, do regular exercise, give up smoking and normalize your weight, blood fat and blood sugar levels.

20. PREVENTIVE MEASURES

1. A heart patient should not bother about the fine distinctions in heart ailments as they interest only the medical profession. He should, instead, ascertain the factors that have caused the trouble and try to remove them. It is likely that many heart problems are merely different manifestations of the same causation which can

be removed by discontinuing the harmful practices or habits.

2. The prevention of heart and blood vessel diseases is preferable to the expensive and complicated medical treatment and surgical intervention and for human reasons. Effective prevention can only come about through a proper understanding of the underlying pathological processes both by the patient and the doctor.

3. Many forms of heart disease are preventable, particularly coronary artery disease, by eating wisely, avoiding obesity, giving up smoking, and performing yoga exercises regularly.

10

Yoga for Women

1. All women who keep normal health may practise asanas and Pranayama, taking into consideration their physique, age and physical activities at home. Regular practice will relieve stress, impart energy, improve the figure, and prevent many uterine and ovarian diseases and several disorders connected with menstruation and childbirth. Excess fat can be reduced and body developed symmetrically. They should, however, avoid difficult asanas such as Mayurasana, Poorna Matsyendrasana and so on.

2. Women should avoid yoga practice from the time the menses begins to flow until it stops; the normal period lasts from three to four days. It is better to rest during this time, for which Savasana will be specially helpful. Yoga practice may be resumed after the period is over. Practice during the period can cause increased bleeding, and inverted postures can disturb the menstrual flow.

3. After marriage and as a preparation for childbirth, asanas which loosen the muscles of the pelvic floor, stretch the hips, increase the flexibility of the spine, and strengthen the muscles of the abdomen and back should be given preference.

PRENATAL EXERCISES

1. Pregnant women, who have not done yoga asanas before, should not start practising them since the danger of miscarriage is greatest during the early months of pregnancy. Those who are regular practitioners may do so selectively, without too much bending, up to the fourth month, to keep the birth mechanism in good order and to ensure an easier time at childbirth.

2. Asanas, which tone up and relax those particular muscles that aid childbirth and the ones which increase the flexibility of the hips, may be practised up to the fourth month of pregnancy.

3. Sarvangasana may be practised as it stimulates the glands which secrete hormones, thus regulating the body's metabolism and protecting it against miscarriage.

4. Position 8 of Surya Namaskar may be practised from early on in pregnancy to exercise the shoulders, open and expand the chest, promote deep breathing, stretch the spine and legs, and work the feet.

5. Oordhwa Pada Hastasana strengthens the lower back for childbearing.

6. Low-back pain will be relieved by performing Ushtrasana.

7. The sideways position of the trunk in Trikonasana (variation) eases the weight of the baby on the pelvis.

8. Padmasana and Bhadrasana are recommended for women during pregnancy as they develop the pelvic floor. They also loosen up the muscles concerned during the second stage of labour, when the baby's head emerges.

9. Ardha Halasana, Akarshana Dhanurasana, Trikonasana and Oordhwa Pada Hastasana also loosen the pelvic girdle. Matsyasana, Supta Vajrasana and Baddha Konasana strengthen the pelvic structure.

10. The habitual use of Vajrasana will prove to be a good preparation for easy childbirth as the muscles of the pelvic floor become more elastic and the pelvic diameter is enlarged, allowing the baby to pass through safely during delivery. It will help to position the foetus correctly during early pregnancy. The practise of Mandukasana will also help.

11. Squatting postures like Utkatasana and Mandukasana promote elasticity of the vaginal muscles and the pelvis. They also help to widen the sub-pubic arch from under which the baby comes out at birth.

12. Squatting is a vital posture for pregnancy as it strengthens the pelvic floor muscles in preparation for childbirth. During labour, it opens up the birth canal, helping the delivery of the baby's head, and reducing the likelihood of tearing the perineum.

13. In the 'All Fours' position of Janu Vakshasana, the spine is held parallel to the floor and the abdomen is allowed to sag. This takes the weight of the uterus off the spine, pelvis and legs, and enables the internal organs to fall freely forward, consequently one gets relief from back pain as it stretches and counter-stretches the entire spine.

14. Gomukhasana and Bhadrasana help to make the muscles around the vulva more supple so that the enlargement of the birth canal is effected quickly and allows for easier delivery.

15. Perineal exercises keep the pelvic, anal and vaginal muscles strong and healthy. They stretch fully for the birth and return back quickly to normal, helping in an earlier birth and avoid postnatal problems like a prolapse or a leaky bladder.

16. Moola Bandha prevents the prolapse of the uterus, ovaries and/or rectum by exercising the perineum.

17. From conception until approximately the fourth month of pregnancy, the following asanas and breathing exercises may be practised by expectant mothers, taking into consideration their age, physical condition and circumstances: a. Surya Namaskar b. Naukasana (Supine) c. Aswini Mudra d. Moola Bandha e. Pavana Muktasana f. Janu Sirasasana g. Yoga Deep Breathing h. Ujjayi and i. Anuloma Viloma Pranayama. These asanas and breathing exercises are particularly beneficial to pregnant women as they eliminate constipation, release tension and improve the posture. Women should stay in these positions as long as they are comfortable so that they may have less difficulty in childbirth.

18. After the third month of pregnancy, all inverted, forward and backward bending postures—Halasana, Matsyasana, Supta Vajrasana, Shalabhasana, Dhanurasana, Ushtrasana, Pavana Muktasana, Ardha Matsyendrasana—and asanas which compress or stretch the abdomen should be avoided by those who are beginners in yoga and those whose health is below

par. Asanas which cause discomfort should be discontinued for the remainder of the pregnancy, particularly in later months as the abdomen enlarges.

19. From the start of the second trimester of the pregnancy up to the beginning of the fifth month, only Aswini Mudra, Ujjayi, Anuloma Viloma and Savasana should be practised. Regular practitioners of yoga may practise other asanas selectively under medical advice.

20. As the pregnancy progresses, from the beginning of the fifth month till the last month, all asanas should be discontinued except Savasana. However, those who are strong enough may consult their doctor and continue to practise postures which are particularly beneficial to them for relaxing and strengthening the pelvic floor muscles surrounding the urethral, vaginal and rectal openings.

Note

1. An understanding of the stages of labour and delivery helps to make childbirth easier and allows a woman a sense of greater participation.

2. Strolling in the open air is beneficial for all expectant mothers.

3. Abdominal breathing: Lie down flat on your back. Pull up your legs and rest the soles of your feet flat on the floor. Practise abdominal breathing for about twenty rounds at a time. This will promote a complete relaxation of the abdominal area and of the entire nervous system and help natural childbirth. This technique can also be used after childbirth for firming up the abdominal muscles.

4. Avoid drugs of all kind during pregnancy.
5. Relaxation in Savasana helps to relieve tension during pregnancy and labour.

Interventions During Birth

Any intervention during a delivery which disturbs a natural, normal, safe birth should be avoided as much as possible by medical practitioners in hospitals. This includes intrusive examinations, pain-killing drugs, forceps, episiotomy and an immediate cutting of the umbilical cord. Some of these procedures may be occasionally necessary for saving the life of the mother or child, but instances where they are really imperative are rare.

POSTNATAL EXERCISES

1. The first three months after the birth of a child should be devoted to a recovery from childbirth and what is needed is rest, sleep and relaxation rather than exercise.
2. After the third month of delivery when the body is back to normal, asanas, Pranayama and Surya Namaskar may be resumed as for a beginner, avoiding strain and fatigue, and subject to the consent of a doctor who knows yoga. Increase the time and intensity gradually till the seventh month after delivery.
3. All inverted postures like Sarvangasana and position 8 of Surya Namaskar are excellent for postnatal recovery as they counteract the effect of gravity on the internal organs during pregnancy and enables them to slide back to their original position. Sarvangasana helps to correct any enlargement of the uterus and ovary.
4. Assume the Viparita Karani posture and perform a cycling action by moving your legs slowly round and

round in the air as many times as possible. This will strengthen the abdominal muscles and help restore the displaced organs to their proper places.

5. Forward bends like Janusirasana and Paschimotanasana strengthen the abdomen, uterus and other internal organs after the birth of a child.

6. Utkatasana and Sasankasana are helpful in achieving a healthy involution of the uterus after delivery and in setting right minor prolapses of the pelvic viscera and relaxed vaginal and bladder muscles. They improve the tone of the vaginal urinary muscles by contracting them. Janusirasana helps to restore the womb to its original position after childbirth or prolapse.

7. Stooping forward and arching the back in Janu Vakshasana is useful in correcting retroversion (tipping backward) of the uterus besides strengthening the transverse back muscles which knit together the relaxed bones of the pelvis after childbirth.

8. Among the postnatal exercises for the contraction of the pelvic floor and retoning the muscles, Matsyasana, Bhadrasana, Yoga Mudra and Moola Bandha prove beneficial. If you have a cut or tear in the perineum, the pelvic floor exercises help the healing process since they stimulate blood circulation to the area.

9. Adequate periods of rest in Savasana help immensely in cases where the sacroiliac joints have become tender and painful due to the separation of the joints of the pelvis just before childbirth.

10. Uddiyana, Nauli and Ardha Halasana help to reduce the extended muscles and tighten the abdominal muscles which would have relaxed during pregnancy.

Regular practise of Aswini Mudra helps to keep the perineum supple, and firms up the muscles stretched during childbirth. Naukasana (Supine), Pavana Muktasana, Chakrasana (Supine) and abdominal breathing also recondition the abdominal muscles. These are difficult postures and must be done cautiously.

11. Parvatasana, which is easier to do, will help flatten the abdomen by pushing the abdominal organs firmly backward and upward against the spine. It will also prevent uterine prolapse.

12. The performance of Bhujangasana, Ardha Shalabhasana, Dhanurasana, Vajrasana, Supta Vajrasana, Ushtrasana, Ardha Matsyendrasana and Akarshana Dhanurasana help the body to get back to its normal size and shape. These asanas may be practised three months after the baby arrives.

13. The above asanas should be performed as slowly as possible since it is the slowness which puts the pelvic organs and supporting structures under tension and strengthens them.

14. Rest in Savasana after each asana, and at the end of the practice period.

15. The performance of the above post-partum exercises will enable the body to regain its shape and strength and help general mobility within a few weeks.

Caution

1. It is not necessary for expectant mothers to do all the asanas mentioned above. They should keep their physical condition in mind before doing any asana.

2. As soon as conception is suspected, women should not do anything that might adversely affect the position of the child. Sirshasana, Sarvangasana, Bhujangasana

and other asanas which require strenuous stretching of, or compressing the foetus, should not be attempted. Kapala Bhati and Bhastrika Pranayama should also be avoided.

3. Women who are pregnant should not do Uddiyana, Nauli and Paschimotanasana at any time during their pregnancy and up to four months after confinement.

4. Women should avoid Bhujangasana and full Halasana for three months after childbirth.

5. Women who have had a child recently and whose abdominal muscles and ligaments in the back are frail must particularly avoid Ardha Halasana. They must not sit up in bed with both legs kept straight.

Female Disorders

1. Most of the common problems affecting the uterus are not diseases but disorders affecting its functioning.
2. Menstrual disorders, whether it be pain, scantiness, profusion or irregularity, are not diseases in themselves but symptoms of other diseases. The treatment of these disorders should, therefore, aim at identifying the cause and correcting it and not just seeking the relief of symptoms.

Menstrual Disorders

The following are the common menstrual disorders:

a. Premenstrual tension. b. Amenorrhoea—physiological or pathological cessation of menstruation—may be primary or secondary. c. Menorrhagia—excessive and prolonged bleeding during the menstrual period, though the cycle remains unaltered. d. Dysmenorrhoea—difficult or painful menstruation. There are two types: primary or spasmodic; Pavana Muktasana and Savasana will be helpful for this condition. Leucorrhoea is a mucous discharge from the vagina.

Asanas Recommended

The following asanas will be helpful in correcting the disorders of the menstrual cycle and restoring the normal rhythmic pattern, but they should not be done during menstruation or in extreme cases of distress:

Specific: 1. Shalabhasana 2. Dhanurasana 3. Paschimotanasana 4. Ardha Matsyendrasana 5. Baddha Konasana 6. Yoga Mudra in Baddha Padmasana 7. Sasankasana 8. Janusirasana 9. Bhadrasana 10. Pavana Muktasana 11. Naukasana (Supine) 12. Bhujangasana. These asanas are especially helpful in normalizing the menstrual period.

General: Regular performance of the following asanas normalizes menstruation:

1.   Ushtrasana 2. Viparita Karani 3. Sarvangasana 4. Matsyasana 5. Halasana 6. Padahastasana 7. Supta Vajrasana 8. Uddiyana 9. Nauli 10. Moola Bandha 11. Trikonasana (variation) and 12. Utkatasana. 13. Relaxation in Savasana will reduce the tension of the body and the mind.

Special attention should be given to the asanas benefiting the female reproductive system.

Displacement of Uterus and Fallopian Tubes

The uterus may become loose and sag downwards and outwards (prolapse) due to the weakness of the pelvic and vaginal muscles, particularly after several deliveries.

Prolapse of the uterus is characterized by the protrusion of the vaginal walls of the uterus at the vaginal orifice due to straining. In severe cases, the cervix of the uterus may be pushed down to the level of the vulva. In extremely severe cases, the entire uterus may be extruded from the vagina.

Specific: All inverted postures like Sirshasana, Viparita Karani, Sarvangasana and Halasana will help the displaced internal organs to fall into their correct anatomical positions. Cycling movements in Viparita Karani will also help.

General: Other asanas which will be helpful are: 1. Matsyasana 2. Bhujangasana 3. Shalabhasana 4. Janusirasana 5. Paschimotanasana 6. Ushtrasana 7. Yoga Mudra 8. Aswini Mudra 9. Sasankasana 10. Naukasana 11. Baddha Konasana 12. Pavana Muktasana 13. Bhadrasana 14. Moola Bandha 15. Uddiyana 16. Nauli 17. Trikonasana.

12

Food for a Yogi

The yoga practitioner must take simple, nourishing and balanced food so as to keep his body fit. A regular practise of asanas and Pranayama will increase the appetite and hence the yogi should take sufficient and nutritive food. Otherwise, harmful consequences may follow.

You are the best judge of what to eat, when to eat, and when not to eat. The quality and quantity of food you take should be fixed by yourself, taking such factors into consideration as your age, size, weight, habits, taste, metabolism, season, climate, availability, resources, occupation, lifestyle, physical activity, cooking facilities and social custom. Even the type of food chosen by you should be changed suitably with advancing age and according to your medical history and circumstances.

HOW TO SELECT YOUR FOOD

Some broad principles for selecting the type of food are given below:

1. The intake of your daily food should be regulated with reference to time, quantity, quality, personal preferences and way of life.

2. The amount of food consumed should provide all the nutrients you need for vital functions, physical activities, replacement of tissues and should build up resistance against disease.

3. What matters is not the quantity of food you take, but how much you can digest and assimilate.

4. Your daily diet should contain all essential nutrients in proper amounts.

5. Prefer natural food to processed food.

6. Food items should be prepared simply and cooked lightly. They should be taken in a form that is as close to their natural state as your digestion permits.

7. Include natural fibres (roughage) in your diet which will counter any tendency to constipation. (Fibre is the indigestible part of food.)

8. Favour food which are nutritious, wholesome, energizing and body-building and yet simple. They should be non-stimulating and agreeable and of a high quality.

9. A balanced meal, which provides different kinds of proteins, carbohydrates, fats, vitamins, minerals, roughage and so-called trace elements in their proper proportion, should be selected from a wide variety of natural food. There is, however, no 'ideal diet'.

10. Lacto-vegetarian food is ideal for a yogi. A selection may be made from the following wide variety of food in the right proportion and combination for each meal: whole-grain cereals, pulses, legumes, wheat-germ,

gram-flour, oilseeds, vegetable oils, nuts, roots, tubers, green and fresh vegetables, fresh and dry fruits, honey, sugar, milk, ghee, butter, sweet buttermilk, sweet curd and germinated grams.

11. Steamed food taken with vegetables and buttermilk promote health.

12. Milk with honey makes a pleasant and nutritious combination. You may take this if it agrees with you.

13. Eat fresh fruit in season, particularly those which have ripened on the tree or plant. For drinks, unfermented fruit juice is the best.

14. Substitute fruit for chocolates or sweets.

MODERATION

1. Eating must not be governed by the clock, habit or palate but by natural hunger. Appetite is often unnatural. It is a mental condition, while hunger is a body process.

2. The food consumed should be adequate and must give you a feeling of fullness and psychological satisfaction, but do not take more food than what is required by your system. Practise moderation and eat only as much quantity of food as can be digested and the waste matter eliminated the next day.

3. Stop eating when you feel you have had enough and never eat to repletion.

4. A yogi must not eat his fill but have a little appetite left after finishing his meal.

5. Be careful to eat enough, but avoid overeating or taking very little food. Overeating does not necessarily mean consuming large quantities of food, but eating

more than your body needs. The need for food declines as age advances since growth ceases and metabolic requirements decline.

6. The stomach must not be heavily loaded. Fill about half of it with solid food, one-fourth with watery portion and leave one-fourth empty for air to circulate. Drink as much water as you please an hour or two after taking solid food.

REGULARITY

1. Form the habit of taking proper food in proper quantity at the proper time.

2. Be regular and punctual in your food habits and avoid eating too often and at irregular intervals. You should space out your meals over the day, but avoid very long intervals between meals as the stomach should not remain empty for too long.

3. Two main meals a day will be sufficient for most people. Avoid nibbling nuts, chocolates or snacks between the principal meals since the digestion process of the food already consumed will be under way and your appetite may be spoilt.

4. Avoid eating food late in the night or just before going to bed as there should be an interval of at least two hours between the last meal and sleep. You should always go off to sleep on a light stomach. Do not go to sleep on an empty stomach either.

DON'TS

1. Eschew food prepared and handled unhygienically.

2. Do not use aluminium utensils for cooking.

3. Avoid the use of refrigerators as much as possible.

4. Do not cook food too long since it will lose its nutritive value. Do not reheat it since it loses value with every heating.

5. Avoid unbalanced combinations of food in your menu.

6. Do not overindulge in your favourite food item, however good, as it will block the intake of other nutrients. Always prefer a varied diet, bearing in mind that no particular item of food is absolutely essential for life and there is always an alternative. .

7. Never eat anything which you dislike, thinking that it is good for you.

8. Avoid food which is hard to digest and that which does not suit your system.

9. Avoid concentrated and over-rich food which upset your digestion even if they are palatable. Do not eat food which only titillates the taste buds such as hot pickles, fancy desserts and condiments. Greasy and fried food are bad for the liver.

10. Avoid all kinds of refined, 'enriched', seasoned and adulterated food which upset your metabolic balance. Abstain from food which produce wind in the stomach and intestines and those which are thirst-promoting or tend to constipate.

11. Avoid as much as possible tinned, canned, bottled, frozen, fumigated and packaged food.

12. Steer clear of chemically preserved foodstuff as they poison the digestive system. Avoid chemical or inorganic additives as they cannot be assimilated by the body.

13. Abstain from food which is bitter, acidic, sour, saltish, pungent, or artificially coloured or flavoured. Avoid

dry, insipid, putrid, stale, decomposed, foul-smelling, discarded, instant, under-cooked and over-processed food.

14. Cut down the amount of fat and sugar in your diet and cut out chillies and synthetic food. Reduce salt to the minimum.

15. Avoid food that are not conducive to health such as candies, chocolates and carbonated drinks. Stay away from all fad diets.

CAUTION

1. Do not eat immediately before or after any vigorous exercise or hard physical work. Rest for a while and then eat.

2. Do not eat when you are under emotional tension or mental turmoil as they disturb gastric secretions.

3. Do not eat before the previous meal has been digested. A minimum of four hours should elapse after a full meal before taking any other solid food.

4. Eat heartily and leisurely and devote all your attention to eating while you are at the table. Make it a practice to eat in silence and do nothing else while eating. Do not read or chit-chat. Never eat while standing up or watching TV.

5. Relax for a while after food. Sit on a soft surface, if possible in Vajrasana, for about ten minutes immediately after lunch so that the body may concentrate its energies on assimilating the food. Strolling for a few minutes after supper will be beneficial to the system besides inducing sound sleep.

6. Do not lie down in bed or slump into an easy chair immediately after eating food as it will distend the abdomen.
7. After sitting down to eat, cultivate self-restraint and do not be a slave to any special food or drink.
8. Eating patterns are not easy to change. If and when you change them, do so cautiously. Do not do so suddenly as it may cause stomach upsets and psychological disturbances. Every change should begin with a short fast.

13

Benefits of Fasting

1. Fasting is not merely abstaining from food but is a means of conserving energy and eliminating waste matter accumulated in the body.
2. Fasting is not starving which begins only when the body has depleted its nutritional reserves.
3. When your digestive machine is not working properly and the appetite is dull, the bowels are clogged, the tongue coated and you do not feel like eating, forsake food and fast for the day or until hunger returns. Fast or be on a liquid diet when you are unwell or running a temperature.
4. Closing down the digestive process by skipping a meal or fasting for a day will not weaken a person since the body sustains itself on its energy reserves which are contained in food stocks in the cells and glycogen in the liver, protein in the blood and fat deposits stored in the tissues.

5. When a meal is missed and dinner time has passed, you will feel an unpleasant sensation, but you can soon get over it with some self-discipline; the appetite will disappear as the body begins to draw on its own reserves to nourish itself.

DURATION

1. The fast starts, not from the time the last meal was taken, but when a meal that is to be taken is skipped.
2. The duration of the fast should be fixed by you, taking into consideration your age, occupation and physical condition.
3. If you have never observed a fast, begin slowly with missing a meal and later on observe a partial fast and then a twenty-four-hour fast. Do not undertake a complete fast before you get accustomed to partial fasting.

HOW TO FAST

1. When you are fasting, you should not become obsessed with the thought of food. Your mind should not be upset by the fast and you must be happy about it.
2. You may drink a full glass of water as 'meal time' approaches which will help you to overcome the craving for food that occurs at the beginning of a fast.
3. If you are fasting completely for a day, abstain from food and drink of all kinds and take only plain water, either lukewarm or boiled and cooled to body temperature, avoiding ice. For a partial fast, you may

take milk, buttermilk, tender coconut water or fresh diluted fruit juice as substitutes for the regular meal, precisely at 'meal time', besides water in between. This will appease your appetite and help to eliminate waste matter.

4. Drink water frequently if you have a headache, foul breath, bad taste in the mouth or a tendency towards constipation. Drinking enough water will flush out the system and keep the body from becoming dehydrated.

5. Drink water if you are thirsty during the fast. Drink enough water even if you are not thirsty since it will help to dissolve and remove toxins from the body.

6. During the fast, keep yourself mildly active and occupied for the whole day with your normal routine. If possible, get absorbed in reading or do creative work which will make you forget the fast. Do not spend most of the fasting time resting in bed.

7. You may do light yoga exercises on days when you fast, avoiding strenuous ones. Avoid hard physical labour.

BREAKING THE FAST

1. Do not wait for hunger pangs to come back before breaking your fast since hunger will return only when you eat again.

2. Choose your first item of food with care after a fast.

3. Break your fast with liquids. You may sip half a glass of freshly squeezed fruit juice, such as the juice of lemon or orange, with water and a little honey at first, and follow with a full glass after an hour. Tender coconut water, fresh milk or thin buttermilk may also be taken for terminating a fast. After this, you may

take a light low-calorie cooked food an hour or two later if you have been fasting for a day.

4. Eat slowly and sparingly after a fast, without an overwhelming desire to eat. When you start eating, be careful both about quantity and speed.

5. At the end of the fast, start with only small amounts of food and very slowly build up to the normal intake. Do not eat a heavy meal or load the stomach with solid food immediately after a fast since your digestive system needs time to adjust after the absence of food and you may get severe intestinal pain. A bland diet in small quantities without salt is ideal for the initial intake.

CAUTION

1. Children, aged persons, pregnant women, nursing mothers and those who are extremely underweight or weak must not fast for extended periods of time. They may take fruit, fruit juice, milk or sweet buttermilk during the fasting period.

2. Persons suffering from diabetes, liver problems, poor kidney function, heart disease or duodenal ulcer should not fast.

3. Fasting for more than a day or two at a time is normally not necessary. Prolonged and complete fasting will lower vitality and resistance to disease and put your body out of gear. It should be attempted, if at all, only with the concurrence of your doctor.

4. Do not abstain totally from food when your vitality is very low.

5. Do not fast on a day when you have to undertake a lot of physical activity.

6. Do not fast if you are extremely tired.
7. Do not feast on the eve of the fast, thinking that you need extra energy to carry you through the fasting period. If you do, you will lose much of the benefit of the fast. Do not starve one day and overeat the next day to compensate for the previous day.
8. Fresh fruit and vegetables taken before commencing a fast will aid elimination. Do not worry if there is no bowel movement on the morning of the day after your fast and do not use laxatives.
9. Do not take tea, coffee, aspirin, alcohol, tranquilizers or drugs during a fast. Avoid smoking.

BENEFITS

The benefits of short-term fasting at regular intervals are many:
1. Fasting gives a holiday to the overworked stomach and gives rest to the organs of digestion. This, in turn, improves the power of digestion and assimilation, resulting in the rejuvenation of body tissues and cells.
2. As the basal metabolic rate, the pulse rate and blood pressure slow down progressively during the fast, there is less work for the bodily organs and repair work can be carried out.
3. Fasting for a day once a fortnight will initiate a cleansing process in the system and remove accumulated metabolic wastes and toxins in the digestive canal, from mouth to anus, without the use of purgatives.
4. The blood system is cleansed of all impurities.
5. Sticky mucus deposits in the lungs and other vital organs are eliminated.

6. Fasting for short periods reduces fatty deposits in a corpulent body and makes it brisk, nimble and agile. The body's weight becomes normalized, but do not fast merely to reduce weight, thinking that fasting is the fastest way to do so.

7. Fasting is a therapeutic tool which allows the body to build up its defence mechanism against disease.

8. It helps to cure arthritis and to bring down cholesterol levels. Indigestion, dysentery and stomach disorders can be corrected by fasting and drinking plain water when needed. The bowel movement also gets regulated.

9. Fasting helps you to know the real nutritional needs of your body and leads to better eating habits.

10. It relieves tension of both the body and mind.

11. Fasting sharpens the senses and quickens mental processes. It also controls wild passions, develops will power, and aids concentration and meditation.

14

Yoga Hygiene

1. Usha Panam. 2. Call of Nature. 3. Bath. 4. Water. 5. Sleep. 6. Regular Habits. 7. Vices. 8. Moderation. 9. Conserve Energy.

To completely eliminate physical, mental and emotional tension and to acquire physical fitness and mental poise through yoga as a way of life, it is essential to have a disciplined life and a preparatory training of both the body and mind. The methods and practices involved in this are hygienic and scientific and can be adopted by anyone without much effort. A few are dealt with below:

1. USHA PANAM

1. After waking up in the morning, cleaning the teeth and washing the face, drink a glass of warm water. It is beneficial to add two teaspoonful of pure honey. A few drops of lime juice may be added if it does not cause any irritation to the throat. This is known as Usha Panam.

2. Usha Panam may be taken without any harmful effects since lime and honey are natural food, and drinking water will not do any harm.

3. Usha Panam taken early in the morning increases peristalsis and facilitates the movement of the bowels. It will eliminate constipation in the long run.

2. CALL OF NATURE

1. Before starting your yoga exercises in the morning, attend to the call of nature and make it a habit.

2. Practising asanas after evacuation from the bowel and the bladder is always the best. Those who are constipated may practise asanas before the evacuation from the bowel and with time, constipation will be relieved.

3. BATH

1. The body must be clean before performing the yoga exercises, and bathing is the best method.

2. Bathing keeps the skin healthy, removes sweat, reduces excessive heat, stimulates the circulation, invigorates the nerves, induces hunger, promotes digestion and reduces physical and mental tensions. By bathing regularly, the body rids itself of toxins through the skin. The chances of catching a cold are also less.

3. Bathe at least once a day in all seasons of the year. Do so in the morning, preferably before sunrise. Bathing again in the evening will induce sound sleep at night. In summer, you may bathe twice daily.

4. The water used for bathing must not be too cold or too hot compared to the normal body temperature (36^0-37^0C). Cold water is always the best as it stimulates the blood circulation.

5. Avoid taking too hot or too cold a bath so that the normal temperature of the body is not violently altered by it. Extremes in the temperature of water will sap the energy in your system.

6. Bathing in bearably cold water (normal temperature) is invigorating, and you may get accustomed to it. A prolonged hot bath is injurious to health by diverting blood from the brain.

7. In summer, bathing in cold water is refreshing. When the climate is very cold, the water may be slightly warmed to take off the chill.

8. Those who are not accustomed to bathing in cold water in all seasons of the year, may start it in summer and continue it uninterruptedly throughout the year. It is not advisable for them to start this in winter.

9. Persons who are weak and are accustomed to bathing only in hot water may reduce the temperature of the water gradually and finally get accustomed to bathing in cold water.

10. Take a bath only when the skin is dry, and never when it is damp.

11. Never take a cold bath when your body is cold. Take it after you warm up a little by doing some exercise and cool off.

12. Never pour hot water on your head since it is bad for hair, eyes and brain.

13. Before taking a plunge bath, wet the head first and then the hands, feet, legs, arms, abdomen, chest and back.

14. You may begin practising yoga right after a head bath, preferably in cold water. Head bath means bathing including the top of the head and not the head

alone. Besides being refreshing, a head bath has a beneficial effect on the mind.

15. A head bath before starting yoga exercises promotes blood circulation uniformly throughout the body. The diversion of richer blood supply to a particular part which needs it also becomes easier.

16. If you cannot have a head bath before doing yoga asanas for some reason or the other, have a good wash or a friction bath as follows: dip a rough towel in cold water, wring it out partially, and give your body a vigorous rubbing, Rinse the towel and go over your body a second time. If you feel cold, do it part by part. After the rub-down, dry the body with a rough dry towel.

17. If it is not possible to take even a friction bath before doing yoga asanas due to cold weather, at least wash your hands, feet and face.

18. If one wants to bathe after finishing yoga practices, one should do so after fifteen minutes so that perspiration subsides, the body cools down, and the temperature comes down to normal. A bath after practising the asanas will definitely give you a feeling of well-being. If an oil bath is preferred occasionally, it should also be taken not less than fifteen minutes after the practices.

4. WATER

1. Many diseases such as constipation and indigestion can be cured by drinking just plain water. Water cleanses the system and also acts as a laxative.

2. Drinking water filtered, boiled and cooled and kept in an earthen pot is the best.

3. Avoid drinking iced water since it will impair your digestion.

4. Drink enough water during the day in between meals when there is little food in the stomach. The quantity of water to be taken should be increased or decreased according to the season and individual requirements.

5. Small quantities of water taken two hours after meals and thereafter at intervals of every three or four hours has been found to be beneficial for most people.

6. Drinking too much water during or soon after meals will not be advantageous since it dilutes the digestive juices.

7. Solid food should not be washed down with liquid of any kind.

5. SLEEP

1. Deep and undisturbed sleep provides rest to the organs and tissues and recharges the energy batteries in the body. It refreshes both the body and mind and is also a great help in healing diseases.

2. The body's demand for oxygen is lowered during sleep.

3. Many bodily functions slow down during sleep including muscular activity, heart rate, metabolic rate, blood pressure and body temperature. The body repairs itself during sleep.

4. Work hard during the day so that you can sleep soundly at night like a child. Rest provided by sleep must be preceded by work, but do not work right up to the last minute.

5. If your body is tired enough, sleep comes right away within a few minutes of resting your head on the pillow

without turning and tossing restlessly in bed trying to get to sleep.

6. Sleep can be easily induced by those who breathe correctly, do Pranayama, practise meditation, and relax completely in Savasana.

7. Sleep will be sound if the body does not remain tense and the mind active, while going to bed.

8. The amount of sleep which a person needs to function at his best is a highly individual matter as sleep cycles vary according to age, vocation, habits and way of life. Persons over sixty rarely need as much sleep as youngsters and they can manage quite well with five to six hours of restful sleep at night. For youngsters and middle-aged persons, about eight hours of sleep a day is generally enough, according to their age and occupation so that both their body and mind are rested. Even in the same individual, sleep requirements change with age, with the hours of sleep getting shorter as age advances.

9. In sleep, it is the depth and relaxation that count and not the duration. Yoga practices improve the quality of sleep and curb the necessity for too much sleep which brings on lethargy.

10. Maintain your sleep rhythm and manage to get as many hours of sound sleep as you can between ten in the night and four in the morning. The best hours of sleep are in the early part of the night, before midnight. The first few hours of sleep are the most refreshing and restful.

11. Do not linger in bed after waking up in the morning. Also, do not jump out of bed when you wake up. Stretch your body a little before getting out of bed.

How to Overcome Sleeping Problems

1. Since sleep is influenced by the daily circadian rhythms, get off to sleep at a fixed time in the night, and wake up at a fixed time in the day and make it a habit. Getting into a routine will help to regulate your sleep and establish a pattern. Untimely or excessive sleep is harmful.

2. Get up at the same time every morning, irrespective of how much sleep you got in the night so that you may acquire a consistent sleep rhythm.

3. Do not keep irregular or late hours for sleep since you will not feel refreshed when you get up in the morning.

4. Try to sleep in relatively quiet surroundings. Sleep in a dark room as it is more restful to the eyes and nerves and is most conducive to sleep. The room should be well-ventilated and reasonably warm.

5. Use a moderately firm bed in order to support the normal curves of your back. Your bed must not be too soft and the pillows too high as the spine may get too curved during sleep. A bed which is too soft will sag in the middle under your weight and some muscles may tense up. Try to manage with one thin pillow as more than that will twist the neck and spine and stretch the nerves and ligaments in the back.

6. Your bedclothes must not be too heavy or too light. Wear only the minimum loose-fitting clothes.

7. Cover the body lightly, and do not cover the face.

8. Do not have a large meal too close to bedtime since it will disturb your slumber. Avoid late hours for supper and your stomach must be near-empty before going to bed so that you get sound sleep. If possible,

walk for some time after supper. Eating and drinking far into the night will make it difficult for you to fall asleep and to sleep soundly.

9. Avoid spicy food and stimulating drinks before going to bed.

10. A drug-induced sleep is a dangerous habit and is never as restful as the one that comes naturally. Tranquilizers and pills act as depressants, bring on toxic side-effects, create addictions and an acute withdrawal syndrome.

11. Washing your feet in cold water and wiping them clean as the last thing at night is a good idea. This will improve your ability to sleep, both readily and soundly.

12. Reduce emotional and physical tension before you retire for the night, and drift off to sleep as relaxed in your body and mind as possible. Relax every muscle and organ in the body and get rid of tension before you go to sleep. Sleep will not oblige you unless you are relaxed. The secret of sleep can be learnt from the technique of voluntary and conscious relaxation in Savasana.

13. Compose yourself for at least ten minutes before you get into bed and go to sleep. Free your mind from the anxieties of the day and do not carry the worries of your waking life. Do not read or listen to anything which excites or makes you tense and disturbs your sleep. If sleep still eludes you, do not lie half-awake and half-asleep, allowing your mind to revolve around the day's events or the problems of the next day. As you feel yourself dozing off, just 'let go' your body and allow yourself to sink into peaceful slumber. You will then get a good night's sleep and experience a

sense of well-being when you wake up. By using these techniques, you can train yourself to sleep under all conditions.

14. Any difficulty in getting off to sleep at bedtime and staying asleep can be overcome by a daily regimen of exercise and taking a long walk at a fast pace in the evenings which will induce normal fatigue and help to send you to sleep. Taking a warm bath about fifteen minutes before bedtime will also be conducive to a quicker onset of sleep. Deep breathing for a few minutes in the evening followed by Bhastrika Pranayama or Anuloma Viloma (on an empty stomach) will be helpful in getting back to a normal sleep rhythm.

15. Do not have a long noonday nap even if you are tired since you may wake up in the middle of the night. Practise a relaxation technique instead for about twenty minutes. If sleep overpowers you during the day, you may doze off in a reclining or horizontal position for about an hour or take a catnap at the same time everyday, but daylight dozing will not give you sufficient rest. Too much sleep during the day is a common cause of insomnia at night.

6. REGULAR HABITS

1. Develop hygienic habits from early childhood. Habits once developed are difficult to overcome as you advance in years when they would have become second nature. Therefore, build up good habits and avoid the bad ones early in life. Also, rectify irregular habits.

2. Habits are easy to form but difficult to change.

3. Habits are formed through repetition. Hence, while establishing a new habit, persevere in it until it becomes second nature.

4. Every day, get up early and go to bed at a particular time and make it a habit. Bathe, eat food, and exercise at fixed hours.

5. Wake up with the birds so that you get enough time to perform your morning ablutions and exercise with a relaxed mind and body.

6. It is always a healthy practice to go to the privy once or twice at a particular time. Whenever there is an urge for defecation, it must be promptly attended to.

7. The bowels should move easily and normally in the morning as it will give you a sense of relief. So, cultivate this habit.

8. Clean your teeth. Rinse out your mouth with fresh water several times. Massage the gums and the soft palate at the top of the mouth with your forefinger and the soft side of the thumb. Gargle your throat. Wash your face with plenty of cold water and rub vigorously. Splash cold water gently on your half-closed eyes. Clear the nostrils one by one by blowing them a few times and clean them with a wet towel or handkerchief. Wash your feet. Without going through this cleansing routine, do not start your yoga practice. You should make it a regular part of your daily agenda of personal hygiene.

9. If one nostril remains slightly blocked when you wake up, it will clear up during the exercises. If it is chronic, a few rounds of Anuloma Viloma Pranayama may be done after finishing your toilet.

10. Rinse out your mouth before and after every meal.

11. It is a good idea to wash your hands and feet and clean your teeth before retiring to bed at night.

7. VICES

1. Yoga greatly minimizes, if not completely halts, the tendency to indulge in vice.
2. Vices shorten the lifespan by lowering the efficiency of the body organs. If you are plagued by any vice, give it up gradually by modifying your way of life so that you may derive maximum benefit from your yoga exercises. After getting away from vice, do not drift back to your old habits.
3. Stay away from stimulants as whatever stimulates must react. Stimulants increase blood pressure and the pulse rate. Give up intoxicant drinks since they dull the senses and mind.
4. Tobacco in any form is taboo as it constricts the smaller blood vessels, raises the blood pressure, and increases the workload of the heart.
5. Give up smoking as it may cause lung cancer, coronary heart disease and other serious diseases. Make a firm decision to stop completely. Once you have managed to give up smoking, by sheer will power, never light up another cigarette as you are likely to relapse into smoking.
6. Drink tea and coffee as little as possible, and have weak concoctions of them. Tannin, caffeine and theophylline in tea and caffeine in coffee are stimulants and acid-forming, besides being toxic. Food and drink containing caffeine stimulate the liver to release stored sugar.

    If you have become addicted to tea and coffee, get over it gradually by trying alternatives since indulgence in stimulants will weaken your system. Too much and very strong tea or coffee will cause constipation, nervous tension, stomach disorders and high blood pressure. They produce unpleasant side-effects such as nausea, restlessness, palpitation and depression besides increasing temperature and heart-beat and causing frequent urination and sleeplessness. They also dull the appetite and interfere with the body rhythm.

7. Give up the habit of coffee-drinking. If you can't, it should at least be kept to a minimum. Do not drink it on an empty stomach as it weakens the nerves. Drink a little warm water before drinking coffee in the morning. If you drink coffee later in the day, have it just after taking some food. Avoid strong coffee.

8. Do not drink coffee or tea before retiring to bed as you may have to get up at night to urinate.

8. MODERATION

1. A practitioner of yoga must avoid doing anything in excess, be it eating, drinking, talking, working, sleeping or indulging in pleasures of the flesh. He must apply moderation in everything and lead a regulated life.

2. A practitioner of asanas and Pranayama must avoid taking too many medicines to keep fit.

9. CONSERVE ENERGY

A student of yoga must always try to conserve his energy and not squander it on fruitless physical and mental exertion and indulgence.

15

Yoga Therapy

1. Yoga was never intended to combat disease but to keep the body fit and the mind quiet for spiritual upliftment. Yet yoga works silently upon the system with accuracy and helps to set it in order in case ailments occur, whether psychic or somatic.
2. Yoga therapy is directed at the body as a whole, the processes occurring within being interrelated and interacting.
3. Yoga performed as therapy is not a panacea for all ills. It is useful only as a therapeutic aid. It is not a substitute but only an adjunct to medication, psychotherapy and surgical procedures.
4. Since yoga limbers up the body from head to toe, many minor illnesses can be prevented or stopped from getting worse if they occur; in some cases, the symptoms subside and the chances of relapse are eliminated altogether. In severe cases, however, relief may not be immediate and yoga alone may not help.

5. Some common and chronic disorders which can be prevented or corrected by yoga are given in the text ahead. The results are not guaranteed, but relief from symptoms can be obtained for most of them. Yoga is also effective in rehabilitation after illness.

6. Patients suffering from the diseases listed in the following pages are advised to take treatment under the personal guidance and supervision of a skilled yoga therapist who is able to adapt the exercises to individual needs. They should bear in mind that no disease can be cured by the mere performance of asanas and that they are only of partial help since yogic practices are primarily preventive and only secondarily curative.

7. As there is no specific exercise to cure a particular disease, the results in the treatment of any disease should be considered as only cumulative. As the relative merit of each technique and the precise mechanism involved in its practise cannot be proved scientifically, the effectiveness of the various techniques used should be judged on the whole.

8. If you find the asanas for each ailment too demanding, select those which are the most beneficial and the least strenuous. Practise regularly, according to your age and ability. If your system is weak, practise only the simple asanas.

1. Cure of Constipation by Yoga

1. Any food residue and other waste matter should not remain in the colon for more than twenty-four hours if normal health is to be maintained. It is the function of the intestines to propel the waste matter towards the rectum at the other end of the alimentary canal and to discharge it from the body. If the bowels are not able to perform this function properly, the faecal matter gets hard and stagnates too long at different centres of the colon. This condition is called constipation, resulting in irregular, difficult and incomplete bowel action.
2. Constipation is not defined by the frequency of bowel action, but by the type of motion passed. The rate and amount of pressure exerted and the area of bowel distended also count.

CAUSES

1. The causes of constipation can be traced mostly to wrong diet, overeating, too little eating, irregular eating habits, internal medication, lack of regular exercise and poor toilet facilities.

2. The root causes of constipation, however, are mainly two: a. poor muscle tone of the abdomen and colon; b. degeneration or absence of the normal nervous and muscular control of the colon wall.

EFFECTS

The lack of natural, regular and easy bowel action produces toxins in the body. The toxins habitually absorbed from the colon, particularly the cecum, result in headache, backache, lethargy, restlessness, irritability, loss of appetite, coated tongue, bad breath, acidity, flatulence, dyspepsia, insomnia, nervous exhaustion, peristaltic irregularities, distension of the abdomen, colitis, diverticulosis, hernia and piles, malformation of the lower abdomen and obesity in rare cases.

SUPERFICIAL REMEDIES

1. Purgatives and laxatives are not the answer to constipation; they irritate the stomach and intestines and weaken them by frequent purging. At best, they can only provide relief at the risk of becoming habitual.
2. The enema cleanses only the lower bowel and is useful only in acute conditions. The constant use of this appliance will distend the gut and weaken it besides becoming a habit.
3. Suppositories and enemas given over prolonged periods also tend to ruin the natural reflex which is nature's call to empty the bowel.
4. Muscular exercises, massage and regulation of diet to aid bowel movement offer only temporary relief and will not solve the problem permanently.

5. Visiting the toilet with clockwork precision will not eradicate the disease if it is chronic.

REAL REMEDY

1. The best method for eliminating constipation and restoring the normal rhythm of bowel activity is to regenerate the nervous and muscular control of the colon and stimulate the sluggish peristaltic action by the yogic practices of Uddiyana and Nauli. These exercises tone up almost every muscle of the abdomen and pelvis and are effective in increasing intra-abdominal pressure and building up the muscular strength of the colon walls.

    By prolonged practise, the colon gets toned up, abdominal tonicity is increased and the expulsive power of the colon and the rectum is improved. These two yogic postures not only help to fight back constipation arising from the weakness of the abdominal muscles but also activate the pelvic floor and the diaphragm and correct displacements of the bowels, if any. Since the bowels are triggered to move more freely and regularly, a normal cycle of elimination can be re-established by these practices.

2. Persons may practise Uddiyana in the morning, first thing on rising, so as to overcome the recalcitrance of their bowels and to induce them to move easily.

POSTURES

The following postures also help in the battle against constipation as they strengthen the abdominal and pelvic muscles, increase intra-abdominal pressure, reduce abdominal fat, stimulate peristalsis and help to send out the colon contents by means of natural stimulation.

Specific

1. Bhujangasana; 2. Shalabhasana; 3. Dhanurasana (Rocking); 4. Ardha Halasana; 5. Paschimotanasana; 6. Padahastasana; 7. Janu Sirasana; 8. Pavanamuktasana.

General

1. Naukasana; 2. Trikonasana; 3. Sasankasana; 4. Yoga Mudra; 5. Sarvangasana.
2. Of these, perform initially, the asanas which come to you easily and add on the rest one by one every week. All inverted postures tone the bowels and ensure the daily evacuation of normal stool.
3. Perform Ardha Halasana and Pavanamuktasana after rising in the morning and cleaning your teeth. After the exercise, you may drink two to three glasses of warm water. These two exercises can also be performed in bed.
4. Cycling movements in Viparita Karani daily will induce the bowels to move naturally.

HELPFUL HINTS

1. To combat constipation and regulate your bowels, sip a glass of warm water on rising in the morning and cleaning the teeth and before visiting the privy. One or two teaspoonful of pure honey and a few drops of lime or lemon juice added to it will stimulate peristalsis and prepare the bowels for easy movement even in stubborn cases of constipation.
2. Drinking enough water (not iced) during the day in between meals will help to keep the colon clean. Increase your intake of fresh fruit juice and non-carbonated soft drinks.

3. Avoid irregular bowel habits. Visit the toilet at a fixed time every day, preferably before sunrise, with a will to evacuate even if no bowel action results. This way, the bowels can be trained and you can set a regular pattern of bowel function.

4. Half an hour or even more assigned to the toilet at the same time of the day for about a month will often bring relief from constipation.

5. Avoid straining to pass stool.

6. Answer the call to defecate at once whenever you feel the urge so that constipation may be avoided.

7. A brisk walk in the morning for about ten minutes just before going to the toilet will help to overcome the difficulty in starting a motion.

8. Perform a few Surya Namaskars at sunrise. Special exercises which involve the abdominal muscles are also in order.

9. Yoga breathing exercises stimulate bowel action and keep constipation at bay.

10. Choose a balanced diet comprising enough raw food, ripe fruit, whole grain cereals, minerals and roughage. Increase the bulk of food with green leafy vegetables and reduce the intake of fats and acid-forming food. High-residue food with adequate fibre will be beneficial.

11. Have regular meals and eat nothing between meals. Avoid snacks.

12. Eat your food two or three hours before going to sleep. Avoid taking food late at night.

13. Fast occasionally, say, once in a fortnight. Take sufficient quantity of water during the fasting period.

CAUTION

1. Drinking tea or coffee and smoking to induce free motion is a harmful habit. They should be gradually withdrawn when the bowel movement has become regular.
2. Missing an occasional bowel movement should not cause worry.

2. Overweight and Obesity

A. OVERWEIGHT

1. Since weight depends on height, build, physical activity, basal metabolic rate, age and sex, it is not possible to arrive at the 'ideal' weight of men and women of different heights and skeletal size. The control and normalization of weight is, therefore, an individual problem and must be tackled accordingly. However, some basic methods applicable to all overweight persons are given below.
2. The major causes of overweight are lack of exercise and overeating. Improper elimination or endocrine disorders also cause overweight, though to a lesser extent. These factors, individually or collectively, cause overweight. The problem of correcting overweight should, therefore, be tackled by suitable action in these four directions, though success can be achieved only in the long run.
3. Treatment for overweight should consist of two phases: reduction and maintenance.

POSTURES

1. The functioning of the thyroid gland determines to a great extent the formation and distribution of fat in the body and its weight. Sarvangasana and Halasana stimulate the activity of this gland and hence the regular practise of these asanas will stabilize the weight of the body.

2. To regulate, normalize and maintain your body weight, Sarvangasana is the best because of its effect on the thyroid gland. If you are overweight, it will bring it down, and if you are underweight, it will help to put on weight. Increase the maintenance period of this asana up to five minutes. Halasana also helps to reduce excess weight due to its effect on the thyroid gland.

3. The following yoga exercises are useful specifically for breaking up or distributing deposits of fat and slimming the body besides firming up and strengthening the flabby areas. They prevent the accumulation of fat either generally or in specific areas of the body and thus help to reduce and rebalance your weight. a. Ushtrasana b. Sirshasana c. Bhujangasana d. Shalabhasana e. Dhanurasana f. Chakrasana (Supine) g. Naukasana h. Ardha Matsyendrasana i. Paschimotanasana j. Padahastasana k. Janusirasana l. Akarshana Dhanurasana m. Supta Vajrasana n. Yoga Mudra o. Sasankasana p. Utkatasana q. Uddiyana. Hold these postures as long as possible without strain.

These postures work on the glands, improve circulation, strengthen the weak areas of the body and induce deep breathing which help to reduce excess fat and bring down weight to the optimal levels.

4. Skipping without a rope, walking long distances, swimming or performing Surya Namaskars also help an individual to lose any excess weight.

DIET

1. The intake of food must be commensurate with the energy you expend.
2. Eat moderately and avoid overeating.
3. Do not nibble anything between meals, specially sweets, biscuits and nuts.
4. A sensible adjustment in your diet which is rich in vitamins and minerals and without too much sugar, fats and salt is essential to maintain the desired weight loss.
5. Avoid too much starch in your diet as the extra carbohydrate will be converted into fat and you will become overweight.
6. Switch over to milk, buttermilk, fresh fruit, vegetables and cooked dal (legume). Replace animal fats by vegetable oils. Substitute honey for sugar, buttermilk for curd, and fruit for sweets.
7. Avoid fried food.

OTHER MEASURES

1. Complete Yoga Breathing and Bhastrika Pranayama twice a day will help those who are overweight to become slim without risk.
2. As the majority of overweight persons suffer from chronic constipation, they should avoid it by taking laxative food and practising asanas that will tone up their sluggish bowels.
3. Fasting once a fortnight will help to reduce weight significantly, but do not undertake frequent fasts merely to lose weight.

CAUTION

1. In your battle against the bulge, bestow more attention to fat loss or weight loss since being overweight is mostly a result of excess fat. Also, pay more attention to weight control than to weight loss.
2. Reduce weight gradually and cautiously over several months and keep it down at a fairly constant level.
3. Massively overweight persons should not embark upon any crash dietary programme or exercise to lose weight dramatically since they go against nature and the excess weight taken off will creep back again. Weight loss should occur naturally.
4. Any severe calorie reduction will lead to malnutrition and the depletion of energy reserves.
5. Do not dose yourself with drugs since they will have serious systemic side-effects. Reducing weight this way is risky and can be even more dangerous than overweight itself.

B. OBESITY

1. Obesity is a chronic metabolic disorder characterized by a surplus of fat in the storage areas of the body. It is not a matter of weight but of body fat.
2. Although genetic factors play an important part, obesity is mainly due to overeating and a lack of exercise. Hence, diet and exercise are the principal means to combat corpulence.
3. In their daily yoga practices, obese persons should pay more attention to the exercises for the chest, abdomen, waist, hips, buttocks, thighs and back of the upper arms since it is here that superfluous fat usually shows up.

However, specific exercises for a given region, though they are good for toning up the muscles in that area, do nothing special to reduce the fat.

A. Abdomen

1. The movements of Uddiyana and Nauli are unrivalled in strengthening, firming and toning up the muscles of a weak and flabby abdomen and reducing the excess fat in the abdominal region.
2. Assume the Viparita Karani posture. Breathing in and out rhythmically, perform slow cycling action as many times as possible. Pedal the legs in as large a circle as you can, exactly as if you were riding a stationary bike. Bring your kneecaps as far down towards the forehead as possible so that your legs have a full stretch. Repeat the exercise in the opposite direction also by rotating the legs backwards, like back-pedalling. Continue circling in a smooth rhythm, clockwise and anti-clockwise. The pedalling action of the feet will exercise the thighs and abdominal muscles and helps to reduce a sagging tummy. Do this exercise on an empty stomach.
3. Perform gentle rocking movements in Dhanurasana, forward and backward and from side to side.
4. The following asanas will help to reduce a bulging belly. You may select those that suit you the best: a. Pavana Muktasana b. Bhujangasana c. Ardha Shalabhasana d. Shalabhasana (Full) e. Akarshana Dhanurasana f. Dhanurasana g. Ardha Halasana h. Halasana i. Paschimotanasana (also Variation) j. Janu Sirasana k. Yoga Mudra l. Ardha Mastyendrasana m. Sirshasana n. Pada Hastasana o. Viparita Karani

p. Sarvangasana q. Matsysana r. Ushtrasana s. Naukasana t. Makarasana u. Chakrasana (Supine).
5. Perform Kapala Bhati regularly.

B. Waistline

The following asanas will help trim the waistline: a. Ardha Halasana b. Bhujangasana c. Shalabhasana d. Dhanurasana e. Akarshana Dhanurasana f. Paschimotanasana g. Ardha Matsyendrasana h. Yoga Mudra i. Ushtrasana j. Padahastasana k. Trikonasana l. Chakrasana (in Standing).

OTHER MEASURES

The following measures will help to keep obesity at bay:
1. Always sit, stand and walk erect and set right faulty habits of the posture.
2. Persons with a sedentary lifestyle must be physically more active.
3. Take regular and moderate all-round exercise every day, whether yogic or conventional, which will tone up your muscles and help to burn up some of the excess fat. Systematic exercise will help to lose both weight and fat.
4. Take a brisk walk in the fresh air daily for at least half an hour.
5. Avoid excess sleep as it may lead to obesity. Avoid sleeping during the day.
6. Minimize the consumption of animal fat and dairy products and use vegetable fats as alternatives.
7. The inclusion of adequate fibre in the diet will be helpful in the management of obesity.

Note

Since obesity is usually accompanied by hypertension, the practise of Savasana will be greatly beneficial for patients suffering from both complaints.

3. Asthma

Bronchial asthma is a respiratory disorder characterized by recurrent bouts of cough, shortness of breath and wheezing due to narrowing of the bronchial airways and increase in airways resistance. The narrowing can be due to excess production of mucus in the tubes leading to the lungs, to swelling of the bronchial mucosa, or to spasm of the thin muscles in the walls of the airways or to a combination of these factors. Genetic factors also determine vulnerability to asthma, though it is not wholly predictable.

Asthma is caused mostly by allergy which may be dietetic, catarrhal, psychosomatic or emotional. (Allergy is an enhanced sensitivity, an unusual reactivity.) Attacks of asthma may also be triggered off by acute or chronic infection of the respiratory organs.

TREATMENT

The following exercises help to relieve the symptoms, improve pulmonary ventilation, reduce drug intake, frequency of attacks, and correct the immune system:

1. Regulate your breathing habits by doing Kapala Bhati (morning and evening), abdominal breathing, Yoga

Deep Breathing, Alternate Nostril Breathing, Bhastrika and Ujjayi—all without Kumbhaka (retention of breath). Kumbhaka should be introduced gradually and cautiously on the advice of a doctor who knows yoga. While practising these breathing exercises, aim at increasing the use of the diaphragm and the abdominal muscles. These help to remove congestion and accumulated secretions, cleanse the respiratory passages, restore the elasticity of the tissues, and regularize breathing.

2. Try to avoid pollen, dust, fumes, smoke and chemical irritants from entering the nostrils as they can spark off allergic reactions. Avoid colds and exposure to cold air and fog and air pollution which may cause obstruction to the air flow through the airways of the lungs. A change of environment may bring about some relief.

3. Do not sleep under a fan if you can avoid it.

4. Avoid smoking.

5. Lying with the head lower than the chest (postural drainage) twice a day will help clear air passages of accumulated mucus.

6. Correct faulty postures by doing asanas.

7. Maintain a nutritionally sound diet.

8. Avoid canned food and all foodstuff to which you are allergic.

9. All artificially flavoured and coloured food and drinks should be given up. Avoid sweets, cold drinks and iced products.

10. Fresh fruit and fruit juice diluted with water, to which some honey has been added, may be taken.

11. Dinner should be light and should be taken two to three hours before going to bed. Heavy meals at bedtime may provoke an attack at night.

12. Never overload the stomach.

13. Fast once a week or at least once a fortnight. Fasting during an acute attack will help to remove mucus from the lungs and to breathe freely.

14. A short fast for a few days (on water or only on fruit juice), followed by a diet with a low starch content, plenty of fresh salads, and the avoidance of sugar will be immensely helpful.

15. Cut down on the use of drugs and eliminate them gradually as they have potentially dangerous side-effects and produce withdrawal symptoms. Tobacco also is taboo.

16. Drinking plenty of water helps to thin out and loosen the mucus in the airways. Water is the best and most natural expectorant in the world.

17. Live a lifestyle that does not allow stress to accumulate.

18. Avoid emotional upsets, positive or negative, as they may precipitate an attack or aggravate the difficulty in breathing.

YOGA PRACTICE

Victims of asthma may perform the following asanas and yoga exercises every day under the supervision of an expert. These asanas promote the capillary, lymphatic and venous circulation and prevent congestion to build up or remain in the alveolae. A regular and graded practice will help an asthmatic person to reduce the frequency, severity and duration of the attack and ward off anticipated ones.

A. General

1. Mild exercises, which require constant, steady deep breathing such as slow cycling and easy swimming, will bring about significant physical and emotional benefits, but do not exhaust yourself.
2. Walking at a steady pace in the open air will help, but avoid running.
3. Cultivate the habit of deep relaxation in Savasana.

B. Specific

1. Abdominal breathing is beneficial to an asthmatic person as it employs the diaphragm while breathing in and out and thereby ensures the proper ventilation of the lower areas of the lungs.
2. Deep breathing in Mastyasana helps to remove the spasm from the bronchial tubes and aborts the attack or at least mitigates it when it comes. The overstretched air sacs also regain their elasticity and the oxygen content of the blood increases sufficiently.
3. Yoga Mudra in Vajrasana will help to release the air trapped in the upper lobes of the lungs.
4. Practise Sasankasana when the asthma attack seems imminent so that you can breathe more easily when the attack occurs.
5. Supta Vajrasana will ease breathing with regular practise.
6. Jala Neti and Kapala Bhati will clear the nasal passages and facilitate breathing. They also help develop the accessory muscles of respiration.
7. All backward bending asanas help to open the clogged airways and relieve respiratory distress.
8. Other yoga exercises which are helpful in the management of this disability are: a. Sirshasana;

b. Viparita Karani; c. Sarvangasana d. Halasana
e. Bhujangasana f. Dhanurasana g. aschimotanasana
h. Padahastasana i. Ushtrasana j. Supta Vajrasana
k. Uddiyana l. Nauli m. Makarasana n. Pavana
Muktasana o. Surya Namaskar p. Ardha Shalabhasana
q. Naukasana (Prone-lying) r. Chakrasana (Supine)
and s) Savasana.

CAUTION

1. A regular and moderate exercise is not harmful to
   the asthmatic. The exercises should not, however, be
   attempted during an attack but only after recovering
   from the paroxysm.
2. Breathing exercises should be done only during the
   interval between attacks.
3. If breathing difficulties develop during an exercise,
   whether yogic or non-yogic, rest in Savasana until
   the symptoms subside and then resume the activity.

Note

1. Wheeziness is not asthma, but only a symptom.
2. For patients with predominant emphysema,
   physiotherapy and breathing exercises will be helpful.

4. Blood Pressure

1. The pressure exerted upon the walls of the arteries by the blood when it flows through them is termed as Blood Pressure. It is a guide to the tension in the muscular elastic walls of the arteries.

2. Systolic blood pressure is the highest pressure reached at each heart beat, and diastolic pressure is the lowest pressure offered by the resistance of the arterial walls. In other words, systolic pressure is the pressure at the point at which the heart contracts, and diastolic pressure is the continous pressure which keeps the blood flowing even when the heart is relaxed.

3. Blood pressure varies with age, sex, diet, body-build, occupation and the lifestyle of the patient. Instrumental error, if any, must also be taken into consideration.

4. Normally, the blood pressure of a healthy young man or woman at rest should range between systolic 100 to 140 mm. Hg. and diastolic 60 to 90 mm. Hg. in the mercury manometer. (Hg. is the chemical symbol of mercury.)

5. When the blood pressure is constantly above normal, it is termed as high blood pressure or hypertension.

When the pressure is constantly below 100 mm. Hg. during systole and 60 mm. Hg. during diastole, it is termed as low blood pressure or hypotension.

6. Hypertension is not a disease but a chronic disorder, and there are no specific symptoms. The most common cause is the constriction of the muscular wall of the blood vessels which forces the heart to work harder to push blood through the system.

7. Hypertension may be severe, moderate or mild. Constantly raised blood pressure leads to kidney damage and increases the risk of a heart attack. It may also damage the brain, causing a stroke. It is a prime and silent 'killer' and 'crippler' of man today, but proper treatment can bring down the pressure and prevent heart and brain complications.

HIGH BLOOD PRESSURE

1. Make rising early a part of your life and follow a well-balanced programme of activity and rest during the day which will help to reduce arterial pressure and maintain it within normal limits.

2. Get enough sleep.

3. Avoid coffee, tea and tobacco.

4. Substitute vegetable oils for animal fats and cut down sustantially on your intake of cholesterol-rich food, particularly coconut oil. A tablespoonful of honey may be included in the diet. Reduce salt in the diet to the minimum as excessive dietary sodium leads to drug resistance resulting from an over-expansion of the plasma and extra-cellular fluid volumes.

5. Avoid stress, worry, overwork and emotional outbursts since they affect the autonomic nervous system and

elevate the blood pressure. Change your reaction to stress by understanding its cause and effect and adopting yoga as a way of life.

6.   A change of environment and pattern of living and slowing down the pace of life will have a wholesome effect in most cases.

7.   As overweight and blood pressure often go hand-in-hand, reduce weight to normal levels for which regular exercise, dietetic discipline, physiotherapy and fasting once a fortnight are always helpful.

8.   With yoga exercises, drugs may be stopped gradually as they merely mask the symptoms without modifying the causes, besides producing undesirable side-effects.

9.   Do not take tranquilizers and sedatives which will cause unpleasant side-effects unless warranted by an emergency. Savasana can be a good substitute for tranquilizers.

10.   Hypertensives should avoid strenuous physical labour which involves lifting and carrying heavy loads. They should avoid exercises demanding sudden exertion or sustained effort including all sports involving pressure-breathing, which raise the blood pressure.

YOGIC EXERCISES

1.   Persons with hypertension may do regular and moderate yogic exercises without experiencing fatigue, but they should avoid inverted postures or bending downward from the waist which will bring extra blood to the head. If the blood pressure is constantly high, discontinue all asanas and do only Savasana until it is controlled and stabilized.

2.   The following asanas and breathing exercises will help to gradually bring the elevated blood pressure

back to normal: a. Makarasana b. Matsyasana
c. Vajrasana d. Padmasana or Ardha Padmasana
e. Yoga Deep Breathing f. Abdominal Breathing
g. Anuloma Viloma Pranayama (without retention
of breath) h. Ujjayi (without retention of breath).

3. The practise of Savasana daily will be immensely
rewarding by lowering both blood glucose and serum
fat (lipid) levels, providing adequate rest and release
of tension.

4. Sit in Vajrasana for ten minutes after each meal. Avoid
large meals.

5. High blood pressure of unknown cause (Essential
Hypertension) will respond favourably to a daily
practise of diaphragmatic breathing. Heredity is a
major factor in this type of hypertension.

LOW BLOOD PRESSURE

1. Low blood pressure, when not accompanied by
symptoms of acute disease, is not generally harmful.

2. Add more protein to your diet.

3. The following asanas and breathing practices will
help to keep the blood pressure up: a. Surya
Namaskar b. Sarvangsana c. Viparita Karani d.
Halasana e. Bhujangasana f. Pavana Muktasana g.
Paschimotanasana h. Yoga Mudra i. Ujjayi
Pranayama.

5. Cold

When the mucous membrane in the nose cavity becomes infected, the condition is called common cold (*Acute Coryza*). It starts with the inflammation of the mucous membrane of the nose and pharynx, the swelling of the entrances to the sinus cavities, the accumulation of crusts of mucus in the nose, the clogging of the air passages, sneezing, nasal catarrh, uneasiness and slight fever.

A common cold with fever has to run its course. To ward off or ameliorate the condition, observe the following precautions:

1. Take care of a cold at the earliest stages of its development by keeping your body well protected from cold winds and draughts but without too much clothing.

2. Avoid exposure to too much cold or heat or getting drenched in rain. In acute conditions, avoid a head-bath.

3. Avoid inhaling air contaminated with dust, fumes or chemicals.

4. Should the first sign of a cold appear, take complete rest in bed and sleep well. Observe partial fasting for the day or go on a liquid diet.

5. Practise Jala Neti (nasal wash) several times during the day if you feel a cold coming on. In cases of severe cold, steam inhalation helps to loosen the mucus in the air passages and relieve sore throat and a blocked nose.

6. Frequent gargles with lukewarm water, with a little salt added, gives relief if you are suffering from sore throat.

7. Regular practise of Kapala Bhati and Bhastika clears the congested nasal passages and sinuses and eradicates the susceptibility to cold and catarrh.

8. Yogic breathing exercises increase the resistance to viral infection.

9. Persons afflicted with cold will benefit by practising the following asanas which will increase their resistance to the condition: a. Sirshasana b. Sarvangasana c. Bhujangasana d. Shalabhasama e. Matsyasana f. Dhanurasana g. Chakrasana (Supine). Do not practise these asanas if you have fever along with a cold or a running nose.

10. Medication is not a long-term solution for this disorder. Avoid drugs totally as they do not treat the condition, though they may temporarily soothe the symptoms.

6. Backache

1. Most back problems are due to herniated interverte-bral disc, degenerative joint changes, incorrect movement, faulty posture, weak abdominal muscles or obesity.

2. Every back pain is unique and there are many reasons why back pain occurs. The most common cause of backache, however, is the lack of regular exercise for the muscles of the back and abdomen, leading to muscular weakness and inadequate flexibility of the muscles and tendons.

3. Patients with slipped vertebral disc will benefit immensely by all backward bending postures as they exert traction on the area, loosen and strengthen the muscles, release muscle spasm and free the nerves which have been pressed. They should not do forward bending postures.

4. People suffering from back troubles must avoid emotional tension.

5. Avoid sleeping on a very soft bed.

YOGA PRACTICE

The following asanas will increase the mobility of the spine and its range of motion which will prevent or ameliorate this disabling disorder. They should be practised without straining the back and only after the acute symptoms have abated.

A. Specific

1. Bhujangasana 2. Shalabhasana 3. Dhanurasana 4. Halasana 5. Ushtrasana 6. Paschimotanasana 7. Yoga Mudra 8. Trikonasana 9. Gomukhasana 10. Matsyasana 11. Supta Vajrasana 12. Ardha Matsyendrasana 13. Janu Sirasana 14. Makarasana 15. Chakrasana (Supine) 16. Padmasana 17. Pavana Muktasana 18. Parvatasana 19. Padahastasana helps to relieve arthritis of the lower back.

B. General

1. Viparita Karani 2. Sarvangasana 3. Naukasana (Prone-lying) 4. Savasana.

Radiculitis or inflammation of the spinal nerve roots, most often in the lumbar region (lower back), will respond easily to physiotherapy or medicines when the first onset of pain occurs.

Note

Most cases of back pain get better spontaneously.

7. Diabetes Mellitus

1. Diabetes Mellitus is a chronic metabolic disorder in which the ability of the body to utilize carbohydrates is more or less completely lost due to the absolute or relative deficiency of a hormone called insulin which is secreted by the pancreas.

2. Glucose (mainly), fructose and galactose (sugar), which are the normal end-products of carbohydrate metabolism, are metabolized with the help of insulin secreted by the body's pancreatic cells to give energy, and the unspent sugar is converted into glycogen and stored in the liver and muscles. Whenever there is a lack of insulin, the glucose metabolism is not complete. The level of sugar in the blood increases beyond the normal fasting range of 80 mg% to 120 mg% and post-prandial range of 120mg% to 180mg% and sugar starts escaping in the urine. These are the main features in Diabetes Mellitus.

3. Diabetes creeps up without warning and if not properly controlled, is a progressive disease. Heredity also plays a prominent role in it.

4. It is difficult to find out by the usual routine urine examination whether a person is diabetic or not as it is possible even for normal persons to have sugar in the urine as a temporary phenomenon due to stress, after an accident, an operation or a serious illness. Sugar may also appear in the urine due to hormonal disorders or as a result of taking certain drugs.

5. Diabetes may be mild, moderately severe, or severe according to the blood sugar level of the patient. There are many kinds of diabetes caused by different factors.

6. Though the exact cause or causes of this complicated disease are many, once a person is a diabetic, he requires lifelong treatment. As there is no effective cure, diabetics should learn to live with the malady, though control and reversal of symptoms are possible in many cases, enabling the patient to live a near-normal life without complications.

7. The disease is characterized by the persistent rise of blood glucose level (hyperglycemia) and passing of glucose in urine (glycosuria).

8. The disease is marked by one or more of the following symptoms: frequent urination, excessive thirst, dryness of mouth, nagging hunger, undue fatigue, loss of weight, itching of the skin and genitals and general weakness of the body. Even simple wounds heal slowly. Possible complications include impaired vision, kidney disease, heart conditions, coma, carbuncles and gangrene.

PRECAUTIONS

In the management of diabetes, the following precautions may be taken:

1. Establish the precipitating cause in the patient.
2. It is vital to give comprehensive attention to diet, exercise and medicine to control diabetes.
3. Have regular and uniform meals with a variety of permissible dishes. Avoid overeating and be always on guard against eating the wrong food.
4. If the diabetic stops overeating and eats less sugar and starch, many symptoms of diabetes will disappear.
5. Choose a well-balanced diet without excess of fat and carbohydrates but rich in vitamins and minerals. Lacto-vegetarian diet is best. Fresh vegetables (except root vegetables and tubers) and food items which have a low sugar content, may be taken. Milk and bread can also be taken in moderation. Increase the intake of unrefined cereals and such food that are high in fibre content. Garlic may be included in the diet. Reduce salt to the minimum. Cut out sugar completely and stay away from fried food.
6. Reduce obesity and overweight gradually by physical activities and dietetic adjustments.
7. Guard against any sudden gain in weight as it will cause the symptoms to reappear.
8. Avoid sedentary habits.
9. Regular and moderate physical exercise is essential for diabetics (except in acute conditions), as it reduces the sugar in urine and blood by improving the burning up of sugar in the muscles. Exercise thus lessens the requirement for insulin. It also prevents cardiovascular complications. Brisk walking and swimming, without getting exhausted, help.
10. Avoid emotional upsets and mental tension.
11. Any drug, if abused, will produce side-effects.

12. Insulin therapy is not curative but only substitutive because in those patients who require insulin, this therapy is given as a substitute when their pancreas is not capable of secreting insulin for carbohydrate metabolism.

13. Insulin therapy is the only method of treatment in juvenile diabetics whose pancreas is totally incapable of secreting natural insulin.

YOGA PRACTICES

The following yoga practices improve blood circulation, enhance the activity of the pancreas, stimulate insulin secretion and promote digestion which greatly help to bring the disease under control. Start with the simplest asanas and perform regularly according to your capacity:

A. Specific

1. All inverted postures help the stimulation of the pancreas. However, patients with high blood pressure should avoid all inverted postures.

2. Viparita Karani, Sarvangasana, Janusirasana and rocking in Dhanurasana are highly beneficial for the pancreas.

3. Nauli will have a salutary effect on the disease as it rotates the abdominal muscles and tones them up.

4. Sitting in Vajrasana for ten minutes after meals will have a positive effect on the digestive processes.

5. Regular practise of Kapala Bhati will significantly bring down the blood sugar level.

6. Other exercises which bring significant improvement in the condition are: a. Surya Namaskar b. Matsyasana c. Halasana d. Bhujangasana e. Shalabhasana f. Ardha

Matsyendrasana g. Paschimotanasana h. Pavana Muktasana i. Sasankasana j. Uddiyana k. Savasana l. Bhastrika Pranayama m. Ujjayi Pranayama.

B. General

1. Naukasana 2. Pada Hastasana 3. Yoga Mudra (as a replacing exercise) 4. Ushtrasana 5. Vajrasana.

The yoga practices which have been cited are only an adjunct to medical treatment.

8. Arthritis

1. Arthritis is the inflammation of a joint or joints characterized by fever, pain and general systemic disturbances. About fifty types of arthritis are known.
2. Osteoarthritis is a wear-and-tear degenerative disorder of the joints, particularly the weight-bearing ones like the spine, hips and the knees, and commonly affects middle-aged and elderly persons. It originates from the loss of elasticity in the cartilage around the joint. If this disorder does not bother you with real symptoms of pain and limitation of motion, do nothing about it.
3. Rheumatoid Arthritis is a chronic inflammatory condition of the joints and the tissues around them and women are more prone to this.
4. Gout is a chronic metabolic disease. It is characterized by an excess of uric acid content in the blood which causes an accumulation of tiny salt crystals in the joints and in the discs of the spinal column. This leads to inflammation and pain in the joints and damages the articular cartilages.
5. Exercising the body once a day is a must for persons suffering from any of these problems. Limbering and

progressive resistance exercises of the joints and limbs will help to correct the condition. Swimming and walking are highly beneficial.

6. Yogic exercises are of indirect benefit in these conditions by reducing obesity, correcting faulty posture habits and improving the mobility of joints. They strengthen the supporting musculature and protect diseased joints from further damage. These exercises should be done only when the acute symptoms subside.

7. Avoid emotional upsets as some forms of arthritis are psychosomatic.

9. Varicose Veins

Varicose vein is a dilated and twisted vein, occurring particularly in the back of the legs and often painful. Elderly people often get this.

1. Inverted postures like Sarvangasana and Sirshasana alleviate varicose conditions, as inverting the body reverses the effect of gravity, resting the valves and vein walls. The elevated position of the legs helps to drain the stagnant and pooled blood from the lower extremities back to the heart and reduces pressure on the veins. These postures help to relax the muscles and joints, increase valvular competence, and allow the blood to flow freely to the legs and feet.

2. When the lower leg begins to swell, it is beneficial to keep the legs elevated by raising the feet at night so that the legs are higher than the heart. This may be done intermittently during the day also.

3. Padmasana slows down the blood circulation in the legs and relieves the pressure of blood.

4. Surya Namaskar, Talasana, Padahastasana, Paschimotanasana and cycling in Viparita Karani will

help to stretch the veins and develop the 'muscle pump'.

5. Regular practise of the following asanas help to relieve the condition or prevent it from becoming worse after it has once started:

(a) Janusirasana (b) Gomukhasana (c) Vajrasana (d) Supta Vajrasana (e) Sasankasana (f) Trikonasana (g) Shalabhasana (h) Utkatasana.

6. A brisk walk and swimming will reduce swelling in the veins and speed up the circulation of the blood.

7. Avoid prolonged sitting and standing.

10. Hernia

Hernia is the sliding out of an organ or part of an organ through the wall of the cavity which contains it. Hernia occurs where the cavity wall or musculature is weak or when there is an increased pressure within the cavity. A common form of hernia is the protrusion of part of the intestine through any weakened part of the abdominal wall.

The following asanas will help in preventing hernia or rectifying the disorder in its early stages. They also strengthen the abdominal muscles and may eliminate the need of an operation:

1. Baddha Konasana, Uddiyana, Halasana, Sirshasana, Sarvangasana, Pavana Muktasana and Yoga Mudra (as a replacing exercise).
2. Persons with hernia should avoid all asanas which involve any form of straining or exertion that increases pressure in the abdominal cavity.
3. Persons who have undergone an operation for hernia should not practise the following asanas for a few months: a. Bhujangasana b. Shalabhasana

c. Dhanurasana d. Yoga Mudra e. Paschimotanasana f. Padahastasana g. Naukasana and h. Uddiyana. Any asana which requires bending forward at the waist should be avoided.

11. Sciatica

Sciatica is the pain felt along the back of the thigh and legs along the course of the sciatic nerve which starts in the lower spine and runs down the back of each leg.

1. Pavana Muktasana (with alternate legs) will be of benefit in this painful affliction.
2. Paschimotanasana will alleviate pain caused by the pressure of the vertebral discs on the sciatic nerve by stretching the vertebral column and freeing the nerve.
3. Sciatica will also respond favourably to the following asanas: a. Shalabhasana b. Janu Sirasana c. Gomukhasana d. Bhadrasana e. Vajrasana f. Utkatasana g. Padmasana h. Akarshana Dhanurasana i. Halasana.

Note

The asanas which have been cited may be done regularly, but never during bouts of acute pain.

12. Bronchitis

Bronchus is one of the two branches into which the windpipe (***Trachea***) bifurcates in the chest. Bronchitis is the inflammation of the mucous membrane of the trachea and bronchi caused by virus or bacterial infection, smoking, dust, air pollution or cold weather. It is often accompanied by persistent cough, excessive production of sputum, difficulty in breathing, slight fever, cold, sore throat and muscular pain in the back. It may be acute or chronic.

The following yoga exercises will minimize breathing difficulties and increase resistance to the disease: a. Padahastasana b. Ushtrasana c. Yoga Mudra d. Sasankasana e. Bhujangasana f. Shalabhasana g. Chakrasana (Supine) h. Viparita Karani i. Sarvangasana j. Matsyasana k. Halasana.

Kapala Bhati, Ujjayi, Anuloma Viloma and Yoga Deep Breathing are particularly beneficial as they enhance and develop the respiratory capacity and resistance.

Jala Neti (Nasal Wash) can be practised daily. Steam inhalations will also give relief.

The intake of honey will be beneficial.

13. Angina Pectoris

Angina Pectoris is the medical term for attacks of chest pain caused by an increased demand for blood by the heart muscle. The attacks are usually due to narrowing of coronary arteries brought on by many factors. Not only forcible exertion but also emotional stress can cause anginal pain. The attacks are of short duration, usually relieved by rest.

Angina Pectoris is not an illness in itself, but a symptom of other cardio-vascular malfunctions.

Abdominal breathing and Savasana will give lasting relief in this condition by dilating the coronary arteries and increasing blood flow to the heart muscle. They also take the strain off the heart.

14. Piles

1. Piles (haemorrhoids) is the swelling or enlargement of the veins occurring in the wall of the rectum or within and around the anus. It is often characterized by bleeding through the anus. Piles may be external or internal or a combination of both. Internal piles are located higher up in the anal canal than external piles.

2. Constipation leading to the difficult passage of faeces and straining at stools is the principal cause of piles.

3. Aswini Mudra has a direct effect on the area concerned with piles and will help prevent it from progressing. The patient may practise it also in Viparita karani after complete exhalation.

4. All inverted postures like Sarvangasana and Sirshasana help to drain stagnant blood from the anus and may reduce or eliminate the symptoms of this disease, if detected early.

5. Other postures which are recommended are:
   a. Gomukhasana b. Janusirasana c. Bhadrasana

d. Paschimotanasana (variation) e. Pavana Muktasana
f. Sasankasana g. Ardha Halasana h. Padmasana
i. Shalabhasana j. Matsyasana k. Moola Bandha
l. Uddiyana and m. Nauli.

15. Flatulence

Flatulence is the distension of the stomach or colon with gas. Excess production of gas or loss of its absorption in the gastro-intestinal tract may cause expulsion of the gas through the mouth or the anus.

Many cases of flatulence respond well to the following asanas:

Specific

1. Bhujangsana 2. Shalabhasana 3. Dhanurasana 4. Pavana Muktasana.

General

1. Ushtrasana 2. Padahastasana 3. Janusirasana 4. Naukasana 5. Position No. 8 of Surya Namaskar 6. Viparita Karani (for gas in the colon) 7. Moola Bandha 8. Makarasana 9. Sasankasana 10. Ardha Halsana 11. Kapala Bhati 12. Nauli 13. Vajrasana. (Sit for ten minutes in this posture after meals.)

Note

1. Avoid fried and fermentable food and carbonated drinks.
2. Constipation, if present, must be eliminated.

16. Dyspepsia (Indigestion)

This disorder is characterized by a lack of appetite and the slowing of the process of digestion.

1. Sitting in Vajrasana for at least ten minutes after meals will be highly rewarding.
2. Do cycling movements in Viparita Karani.
3. The intake of acid-forming food and animal fats should be reduced, and the intake of alkaline-forming food increased.
4. To reduce hyperacidity of the stomach, drink plain water between meals, which will neutralize the excess acid in the stomach.
5. Avoid worries and emotional upsets as they deplete nervous energy, weaken the power of digestion and assimilation of food, and cause over-acidity of the stomach.
6. The following yoga asanas will ameliorate the condition: a. Paschimotanasana b. Pada Hastasana c. Sasankasana d. Ardha Halasana e. Pavana Muktasana f. Uddiyana g. Nauli.

17. Some Common Diseases

Some alarmingly common ailments which can be prevented by practising yoga regularly are given below:

Adenoids: an overgrowth of the glandular tissue between the back of the nose and throat, disturbing respiration.

Adiposity: excess of fat deposit in the subcutaneous tissue.

Anaemia: deficiency in quality or quantity of the red blood cells and haemoglobin percentage in the blood. It may be primary or secondary.

Arteriosclerosis: arteries are tubes through which the heart propels blood to different parts of the body. Arteriosclerosis is the chronic inflammation and consequent hardening of the arterial walls, either local or general, due to the deposition of fat and protein. This condition is often characterized by high blood pressure. It particularly occurs in old age.

Atheroma: in this disorder, deposits of fatty material just under the inner lining of arteries break up, leaving rough areas where blood clots can form.

Atherosclerosis: hardening and roughening of the inner lining of arteries due to fatty deposits.

Cerebral Haemorrhage: stroke.

Colitis: inflammation of the colon or the first part of the large intestine.

Congested Throat.

Coronary Thrombosis: a partial or total blockage of one of the arteries supplying blood to the heart by a blood clot, commonly known as a heart attack.

Cough.

Debility (General): physical weakness.

Embolism: blockage of a blood vessel by a blood clot or air bubble.

Emphysema: excessive dilation of the air sacs (alveolae) of the lungs, where oxygen exchanges occur.

Enteroptosis: downward displacement of the intestines.

Epilepsy: a disorder of the cerebral function which recurs periodically and is characterized by convulsions or fits.

Fistula: long pipeline ulcer with a narrow mouth/abnormal or surgically made passage in the body.

Gastritis: inflammation of the walls of the stomach which may be acute or chronic. Malnutrition associated with dietetic errors is the main cause of this syndrome.

Goitre: enlargement of the thyroid gland.

Gout: arthritic condition caused by excess of uric acid in the blood.

Headache: chronic or functional.

Hemiplegia: paralysis of one side of the body.

Hyperacidity: excess acid in the stomach.

Impotence: lack of sexual power.

Insomnia: inability to sleep soundly.

Ischaemia: reduced blood supply to an organ. For example, ischaemic heart disease is caused by a reduced blood supply to the heart muscle.

Kidney Damage: the main function of the kidneys is to filter waste products and to keep the body's fluid and chemical balance in check. Kidney damage is one of the most devastating complications of both diabetes and high blood pressure. Nephritis, formerly called Bright's disease, is the inflammation of the kidneys.

Liver and Spleen Disorders.

Lumbago: acute rheumatism of the muscles and joints in or around the lumbar region of the spine.

Migraine: characterized by periodic headaches which are usually on one side and often associated with visual disturbance and nausea.

Myalgia: pain in the muscles or muscular rheumatism.

Neurasthenia: weak nerves causing fatigue, dizziness and nausea.

Neuritis: inflammation of the nerves. Pain follows the nerve channels.

Oedema: dropsical swelling due to an abnormal accumulation of fluid in the subcutaneous tissues of the body, such as in the legs, ankles or face. The excess fluid leaks out of blood vessels into the internal organs or under the skin.

Ovarian Disorders.

Peptic Ulcer.

Pharyngitis: throat infection.

Pleurisy: inflammation of the pleura, a delicate serous membrane that covers the lungs and lines the inner surface of the ribs.

Prostate Gland Enlargement: this occurs in males, usually in old age.

Ptosis: prolapse or drooping of any organ.

Rectal Prolapse.

Rheumatism: a disease affecting the bones and joints, characterized by pain, fever and involvement of the heart in the later stages. Muscular rheumatism is pain in the muscles.

Sclerosis: hardening of the tissues.

Seminal Weakness.

Sinusitis: inflammation of the air sinuses with systemic upset characterized by fever, headache, pain or discomfort in the face and localized tenderness in the maxillary and formal sinuses.

Slipped Disc: an intervertebral disc that has been forced or squeezed out of position, producing damage to nerve roots with symptoms of pain in the back and the lower limbs.

Spermatorrhea: involuntary seminal discharge.

Spinal Deformities: (early stages.)

Spondylitis (Cervical): inflammation of the cervical (neck) vertebrae. Its degenerative variety is called Spondylosis.

Sterility: inability to conceive. May be physiological or pathological.

Stomach Disorders.

Tonsillitis: inflammation of the tonsils which are situated one on each side at the entrance of the throat. It may be acute or chronic.

Trauma: morbid condition of the body produced by a wound or external violence.

Tuberculosis: (early stages.)

Underweight.

Visceroptosis: sagging forward of the abdominal organs. Due to the weakness of the abdominal muscles and the constipation which results, the abdominal viscera tends to droop into the pelvic region.

Wheezing: noisy and difficult breathing, usually due to bronchial asthma.

1 6

Vital Role of Glands

The endocrine glands in the body, which are closely inter-related, secrete energizing juices called hormones which directly flow into the blood stream. These substances not only regulate some of the most important biological activities in the body, but also profoundly affect both the mind and the personality. They control growth, energy, weight, size, sexual power, metabolism, pregnancy and birth and coordinate many of the body's systems. Deficiency or excess of secretion of hormones may lead to many disorders. Yoga postures and breathing exercises correct such imbalances and promote the harmony of these glands which will ensure the health of the whole body.

1. THE PITUITARY

This gland is nestled almost exactly in the centre of the head at the base of the skull and just behind the root of the nose. It controls the secretions of other endocrine glands and helps, directly or indirectly, the hormonic regulation of the whole body. It is the 'master gland of the endocrine orchestra'. It is responsible for the proper growth of the body by maintaining the efficiency of its various parts and by preventing excessive accumulation of fat. This gland controls metabolism, menstruation, pregnancy, birth, lactation and water balance through its influence on the kidneys. It influences the pressure in the blood vessels and the functioning of the reproductive system. It promotes the ability to resist disease by mobilizing the white blood cells and antibodies.

Sarvangasana, Viparita Karani, Matsyasana and Aswini Mudra will stimulate the activity of this gland. Sirshasana is the most beneficial in this respect.

2. THE PINEAL

This pea-sized gland is situated in the roof plate of the forebrain below the pituitary gland and behind the centre of the eyebrows. The precise function of this small gland is still not known, though its secretions are stated to play a profound role in the development of the reproductive system and bodily growth in general.

Sirshasana, Viparita Karani, Sarvangasana, Matsyasana and Aswini Mudra stimulate this gland.

3. THE THYROID

This gland is located in front of the neck on either side of the larynx (voice box). Its secretion regulates oxidation or the use of the oxygen by the tissue cells and keeps the nerves and tissues healthy. It is thus the 'pacemaker', governing metabolism. If too much is produced by this gland, loss of weight, rapid heart action, profuse sweating and a highly strung nervous temperament result. If too little is produced, metabolism slows down, fat settles in the tissues and the activity of the nervous system is reduced. The parathyroid glands, which are either enveloped in the thyroid gland or are close beside it, maintain the metabolic equilibrium of the body by regulating the distribution and activity of calcium and phosphate in the blood, which are necessary for the development of strong and healthy bones.

Halasana, Ushtrasana, Bhujangasana, Matsyasana and Jalandhara Bandha activate these glands. Sarvangasana is the most beneficial asana to tone up this gland.

4. THE THYMUS

This gland is situated in the lower part of the neck and the upper part of the chest, just above the heart and betweeen the two lungs. It is present only in children up to the puberty period and atrophies during late adolescence. It is associated with the immune system in the body and plays a major role in fighting infection. During the early years, this gland prevents premature mineralization and hardening of the bones so that growth and development take place normally.

5. THE ADRENALS (Suprarenals)

These are two tiny triangular glands, about two inches in length, lying on top of the kidneys, one on each side. They consist of two layers. They secrete three groups of hormones having influence over the glucose and mineral metabolism and also over the sex glands. These hormones are essential for maintaining normal blood pressure and for the body's equilibrium. They also prepare the body and mind for emergencies.

Ardha Matsyendrasana, Ushtrasana, Dhanurasana, Bhujangasana, Halasana and Uddiyana will keep these glands in good condition.

6. THE PANCREAS

This gland, situated below the stomach, regulates the body's capacity to store and utilize sugar for energy. It secretes insulin which maintains the blood glucose level and also glucagon which has an influence over the blood glucose level. If too much insulin is produced, it will result in low blood sugar. If too little insulin is produced or if the insulin is defective, it will result in high blood sugar, a condition known as Diabetes Mellitus.

Halasana, Yoga Mudra, Paschimotanasana and Uddiyana will keep this gland healthy.

7. THE GONADS

These are the reproductive glands, namely the testes contained in the scrotum in the male, and the ovaries which are set low down on each side of the pelvic area in the female. These regulate the development of the sex organs and reproduction. The hormone secreted by the ovaries regulates the menstrual cycle, pregnancy and female physical appearance and sexuality.

Ardha Matsyendrasana, Ushtrasana, Uddiyana, Paschimotanasana, Aswini Mudra and Sarvangasana will stimulate and keep these glands healthy.

8. PROSTATE

A sex gland shaped like a chestnut, it is situated around the neck of the bladder in men and surrounds that part of the urethra lying within the pelvis. Its purpose is to supply fluid to carry sperm.